THE APHRODYSIAL OR SEA-FEAST

THE MALONE SOCIETY
REPRINTS, VOL. 189
2022

PUBLISHED FOR THE MALONE SOCIETY
BY MANCHESTER UNIVERSITY PRESS

Altrincham Street, Manchester M1 7JA, UK
www.manchesteruniversitypress.co.uk

British Library Cataloguing-in-Publication Data
A catalogue record for this book is available from the British Library

Library of Congress Cataloging-in-Publication Data applied for

ISBN 978–1–5261–6951–8

Typeset by New Leaf Design, Malton, North Yorkshire

Printed in the UK by Henry Ling Limited, at the Dorset Press, Dorchester, DT1 1HD

This edition of *The Aphrodysial or Sea-Feast* has been prepared by Maria Shmygol and checked by Siobhan Keenan. Initial work on the edition was facilitated by a Malone Society research grant, for which the editor expresses her thanks. The editor also wishes to thank Steven Tabor and Martin Wiggins for their generous assistance and advice, as well as Christopher Hunwick and Andrew Jack at the Alnwick Castle Library for help with reference enquiries.

The Malone Society is grateful to the Huntington Library for permission to reproduce the play, preserved in Huntington Library MS HM4, and six images from the original manuscript (Plates 1–6).

March 2022   SIOBHAN KEENAN

© The Malone Society 2022

CONTENTS

LIST OF PLATES	ix
INTRODUCTION	xi
PROVENANCE	xii
PHYSICAL DESCRIPTION	xv
PAPER AND WATERMARKS	xv
HAND	xix
AUTHORIAL REVISIONS	xx
PENCIL ANNOTATIONS	xxiv
DATE	xxiv
AUTHORSHIP	xxv
WILLIAM PERCY	xxvi
AUDIENCE, READERSHIP, AND PERFORMANCE	xxx
EDITORIAL CONVENTIONS	xxxvi
PLATES	1
THE TEXT	7
APPENDICES	
APPENDIX 1: PENCIL ANNOTATIONS AND MARKS IN HUNTINGTON MS HM4 COPY OF *THE APHRODHYSIAL*	111
APPENDIX 2: VARIANTS BETWEEN HUNTINGTON MS HM4 AND ALNWICK MS 509 COPIES OF *THE APHRODHYSIAL*	113

LIST OF PLATES

1: Huntington MS HM4, fol. 120r
2: Huntington MS HM4, detail of fol. 120v
3: Huntington MS HM4, fol. 131r
4: Huntington MS HM4, detail of fol. 137v
5: Huntington MS HM4, fol. 138r
6: Huntington MS HM4, detail of fol. 146v

INTRODUCTION

The Aphrodysial is one of six plays written by William Percy, brother of the ninth Earl of Northumberland. The plays were originally composed between 1601 and 1603, but they are extant in three holograph copies prepared by the author in the mid-1640s: Alnwick Castle MSS 508 (1644, incomplete) and 509 (1646), and Huntington Library MS HM4 (1647).[1] This semi-diplomatic Malone Society edition reproduces the play from Huntington Library MS HM4, which appears to have been prepared as a fair copy by Percy. The play is identified as a 'Marinall' (fol. 120ʳ) set at the underwater court of Oceanus, which is visited by Cytheræa on the occasion of her festival, or 'Aphrodysial', and she is given charge of presiding over the court for the day.[2] There are several distinct plots revolving around amorous pursuits, including an imaginative adaptation of the Hero and Leander myth, and Vulcan's attempts to commit infidelity by wooing the nymphs Arida and Humida. The play likewise follows the attempts of Jupiter and Neptune, disguised as Arion and Talus, to find Thetis's lost magic ceston in order to win her hand. A substantial portion of the play also focuses on piscatory pursuits, most notably the attempts of some fishermen, under Proteus's command, to capture a talking whale who speaks oracles. The play's conclusion sees the capture and dissection of the whale, whereby it is revealed that an apprentice boy was couched inside the creature along with Thetis's ceston, which bestowed prophetic and linguistic abilities onto the boy. Following this revelation, various amorous tangles and pursuits are resolved, and Cytheræa departs the court, relinquishing her temporary power back to Oceanus.

Aside from the publication of Percy's *Sonnets to the Fairest Coelia*, printed by Adam Islip for William Ponsonby in 1594, and a commendatory madrigal for Barnabe Barnes's *Four Bookes of Offices* (1606) none of Percy's other writing appears to have been published.[3] Percy's plays were first mentioned in print in an auction catalogue in 1796, referencing the author only by his initials as given in the manuscript, not by his full name. Joseph Haslewood, a previous owner of Huntington MS HM4, was the first to identify William Percy as the author of the plays in this manuscript in an introduction to the 1824 Roxburghe Club volume, which reproduced two of Percy's plays in print (see 'Provenance'). Following this publication, Percy's plays received occasional mention in studies of early modern drama, beginning with John

---

[1] For a description of the contents of each of the three copies see pp. xii–xiii, and Matthew Dimmock, ed., *Mahomet and His Heaven* (Aldershot, 2006), 46–9.

[2] References to Huntington Library MS HM4 will be cited in the text and will refer to the foliation added by a later hand to the manuscript (see 'Pencil Annotations').

[3] In the preface to *Sonnets to the Fairest Coelia*, Percy writes 'I will impart vnto the world another Poeme which shall be both more fruitfull and ponderous' (sigs. A2ʳ–A2ᵛ), but there is no evidence that he ever published such a poem. His laudatory madrigal appears on sig. A3ʳ of Barnes's *Four Bookes of Offices* (London, 1606).

Payne Collier's *The History of English Dramatic Poetry* in 1831.[4] More pronounced scholarly interest in Percy's writing emerged at the turn of the twentieth century, with some debate about what Percy's dramatic oeuvre might have to reveal about Elizabethan staging practices.[5] In the 1930s and 1940s Madeline Hope Dodds published a series of articles based on her examination of the Alnwick MSS, including several that provided useful summaries of some plays, *The Aphrodysial* among them.[6] In the second half of the twentieth century Percy's plays began to receive further attention in a number of thesis editions, and *The Aphrodysial* is currently available in two such editions, one in old spelling, the other in modern spelling, both prepared from Huntington MS HM4.[7] The only published edition of a Percy play thus far is Matthew Dimmock's edition of *Mahomet and His Heaven* (prepared from Alnwick MS 508, under the play's earlier title, which is changed to *Arabia Sitiens* in HM4).[8]

PROVENANCE

This Malone Society edition reproduces the version of *The Aphrodysial* found in Huntington MS HM4, which is a holograph manuscript containing the plays and poems of William Percy. HM4 was copied by Percy

---

[4] John Payne Collier, *The History of English Dramatic Poetry and Annals of the Stage to the Restoration*, 3 vols. (London, 1831), vol. 2, 351–2; vol. 3, 357–8, 377n.

[5] For example, Carl Grabau, 'Zur englischen Bühne um 1600', *Shakespeare Jahrbuch*, 38 (1902), 230–6; Victor Albright, 'Two of Percy's Plays as Proof of the Elizabethan Stage', *Modern Philology*, 11.2 (1913), 237–46; George F. Reynolds, 'William Percy and his Plays, with a Summary of the Customs of Elizabethan Staging', *Modern Philology*, 12.4 (1914), 241–60.

[6] Madeleine Hope Dodds, 'William Percy's *Aphrodysial*', *Notes and Queries*, 161.14 (3 October 1931), 237–40 and 161.15 (10 October 1931), 257–61; 'A Dreame of a Drye Yeare', *Journal of English and Germanic Philology*, 32 (1933), 172–95; 'A Forrest Tragaedye in Vacuum', *Modern Language Review*, 40.4 (1945), 246–58.

[7] Caroline E. Jameson, 'An Edition of *A Forrest Tragedye in Vacuum*', unpublished MA thesis, University of Birmingham (1972); Clayton Joseph Burns, 'William Percy's *Arabia Sitiens*', unpublished PhD thesis, University of New Brunswick (1984); Robert Denzel Fenn, 'William Percy's *Faery Pastorall*: An Old Spelling Edition', unpublished PhD thesis, University of British Columbia (1998); Patrick Kincaid, 'A Critical Edition of William Percy's *The Cuckqueans and Cuckolds Errants*', unpublished PhD thesis, University of Birmingham (1999). Robert Denzel Fenn, 'William Percy's *Aphrodysial*: An Old-Spelling Edition', unpublished MA thesis, University of Saskatchewan (1990); Caroline Carpenter, 'Through a Masque Darkly: William Percy's *Necromantes* and the Gunpowder Plot of 1605', unpublished PhD thesis, Claremont Graduate University (2015). The latter is an edition of both *Necromantes* and *The Aphrodysial*. A typescript of *The Aphrodysial* was also prepared when Huntington MS HM4 was in the Duke of Devonshire's collections, and was consulted by George F. Reynolds in preparation for his article on Percy and the Elizabethan stage. See Reynolds, 'William Percy and His Plays', 391, n. 1.

[8] Dimmock, ed., *Mahomet and His Heaven*. Misha Teramura has also prepared a modernized edition, with gloss and collation, of Act 4 Scene 1 from this play, published in 'William Percy's Logical Song', *Medieval and Renaissance Drama in England*, vol. 32 (2019), 163–202, pp. 180–93.

from his more 'experimental' draft of the material preserved in the Duke of Northumberland's Papers at Alnwick Castle Library as MS 509 (dated 1646 on its title page). Another, earlier and incomplete, copy of the plays is extant in Alnwick MS 508 (dated 1644 by internal evidence), but this copy does not contain *The Aphrodysial*.[9] All three holograph copies were prepared by William Percy in Oxford during the final years of his life. Since Percy died a bachelor in 1648, it is very likely that upon his death ownership of all three manuscripts went to Percy's nephew, Algernon Percy, tenth Earl of Northumberland, who was 'granted administration of his estate'.[10] Each of the holographs bears a volume number, which were probably attached to them when they entered the Earl's collection, or possibly later: Huntington MS HM4 is labelled as 'vol: 1st:' on its first leaf; Alnwick MS 508 is labelled 'vol: 2nd:' and 509 is labelled 'vol: 3rd:'. In the case of the Alnwick manuscripts, the volume numbers also appear on the spines of the binding, and this seems to have been the case with Huntington MS HM4 before the volume was rebound in the nineteenth century (see 'Paper and Watermarks').

MSS 508 and 509 have probably resided at Alnwick Castle since the seventeenth century (except for a temporary period on loan to Armstrong College, Newcastle-upon-Tyne in the early 1930s). Huntington MS HM4 was separated from the other two holographs in the eighteenth century, and was, for some time, in the possession of Sir William Burrell (1732–96). In May 1796 the manuscript was listed in an auction catalogue of Burrell's library; it was purchased for the Duke of Roxburgh, and was later bought by Joseph Haslewood, who allowed two of the plays contained in the volume to be published as a Roxburghe Club volume in 1824, prefaced with his introduction. The manuscript was later acquired by the Duke of Devonshire (see 'Paper and Watermarks') and was then sold to Henry E. Huntington when the Duke's collection was put on sale.[11] It has resided at the Huntington Library in California ever since.

Some additional light is shed on Huntington MS HM4's provenance by a handwritten account entitled 'What I know of the following M: S:',

---

[9] Alnwick MS 508 lacks a title page, but contains Sir Philip Sidney's song, 'Chaunge is no Roberye or The Bearing down of the Inne' (an earlier version of the title for *Cuckolds and Cuck-queanes Errants*), 'Mahomet and his Heauen, or Epimenide graund Empress of the deserts of Arabia or a Dreame of a drye summer or the weather-woman' (an earlier version of *Arabia Sitiens*), 'The Faerye Chace or a Forrest of Elues' (an earlier version of *The Faery Pastorall*), and 'A Forrest Tragaedye in Vacuinum or Loues Sacrifice', which is incomplete and breaks off at the beginning of Act 5. Also present in Alnwick MS 508 are the two 'Oxford Libels' (collected poems from other sources), which are not in Huntington MS HM4 but present in Alnwick MS 509. A letter in Act 1 of 'The Faerye Chace' in Alnwick MS 508 is dated 1644 (this date changes in the other manuscripts to reflect the year in which they were initially copied out, so it can be taken with some degree of certainty as the year in which this volume was copied).

[10] Mark Nicholls, 'Lavatory Humour: Two Epigrams Addressed to Sir John Harrington', *Notes and Queries*, 51.3 (September 2004), 303–4, p. 303. See also Dimmock, ed. *Mahomet and His Heaven*, 53.

[11] Dodds was the first to provide a published account of the provenance in 'A Dreame of a Drye Yeare', 172.

written by Joseph Haslewood in 1825, which accompanied MS HM4 into the Huntington Library's collections.[12] The four-page document includes pasted cuttings from the auction catalogue of Burrell's library, including one that describes what was sold at the auction as Lot 302:

> *Comœdyes* and *Pastoralls* with their Songs, as also one Booke of *Epigrammes*, by W. P. Esq. *MSS.* containing the following:
>
> 1. The *Cuck-Queanes* and *Cuckolds Errants*, a *Comœdye*—1601
> 2. *Arabia Siticus* [*sic*]; or a *Dreame* of a *drye Yeare*, a Tragy-Comœdye—1601
> 3. The *Faery Pastorall*, or *Forrest* of *Elves*
> 4. A *Country Tragœdye in Vacuniam*, or Cupids Sacrifice—1602
> 5. The *Aphrodysia* [*sic*], or *Sea-Feast*—1602
> 6. *Necromantes*, or the *two supposed Heds*, a comical Invention
>
> With various Alterations, additional Songs, &c. to be occasionally used, or omitted; accompanied with Directions to the Actors, throughout the several Pieces.
>
> They appear to have been written for the *Children* of the *Revels*.
>
> After which follows, *One singular Booke* of *Epigrammes* (in Number 357) concluding:
>
> 'To shewe what you be, now gentle Sir Lun,
> 'You may uncase you, for my Playe is done.'
>
> Finis, 1610. W. P. Esq.[13]

Haslewood reports that the manuscript is recorded as having been sold for £5 in another copy of the auction catalogue that came into his possession, and speculates, 'we may surely with tolerable confidence assume that it was then purchased for the literary & late Duke of Roxburghe'. The volume then apparently 'rested in quiet seclusion' in Haslewood's possession until an application was made to have material from it prepared for publication by the Roxburghe Club at the expense of John Arthur Lloyd. A transcription of *Cuck-Queans and Cuckolds Errants* and *The Faery Pastorall* was prepared 'with much precision by Mr. William Thompson of Leadenhall Street, the Illuminator' and publication proceeded in the summer of 1824.[14] Haslewood notes that William Percy's authorship of the manuscript was 'strongly evidenced by the letter from D^r [Philip] Bliss of the Bodleian Library here given', which implies that Bliss's letter originally accompanied

---

[12] The two folio leaves are not paginated, with only a grey pencil Huntington Library shelf mark, 'HM4', appearing in the top left corner of the second leaf's verso. I am very grateful to Steven Tabor at the Huntington Library for generously sharing images of this document with me.

[13] *A Catalogue of the Town-Library of the late Sir William Burrell … which will be Sold by Auction, at the Turf Gallery, opposite the Chapel, in Conduit Streete, Hanover Square, on Monday, May 2, 1796* ([London], 1796), sigs. D3^r–D3^v.

[14] Hillebrand speculates that only about a dozen copies were printed, and adds 'the editorial work is very inaccurate, so that the text bristles with errors' ('An Elizabethan Amateur', 402). Fenn notes that thirty-one copies were printed ('William Percy's *Faery Pastorall*', 18).

Haslewood's note when HM4 left his possession, although it is now lost.[15] Haslewood then speculates about the possible means by which the manuscript might have come into the possession of Sir William Burrell, and here he draws attention to another item in the auction catalogue: Lot 467, 'Percy, Henry Algernon, fifth Earl of Northumberland, the Regulations and Establishments of his Houshold at his Castles at *Wresill* and *Lekinfield* in *Yorkshire*, begun A.D. 1512 ... a matchless *Collectanea*, the elaborate Work of the late Sir William Burrell'.[16] On the basis of Burrell's evident interest in the Percy family, Haslewood supposes that he must have borrowed and subsequently failed to return the manuscript. At the time of writing this note in 1825, the manuscript was almost certainly still in its original binding, since Haslewood reports that 'This volume the binder announces as "Vol. I"', which confirms that it was indeed numbered as part of a three part 'set' together with Alnwick MSS 508 and 509 (see p. xiii).

PHYSICAL DESCRIPTION

Paper and Watermarks

Huntington MS HM4 is bound in a standard brown Devonshire calf, measuring 305mm by 207mm. The spine has eight horizontal bands embossed in gold, which create seven panels; the topmost panel bears the text 'PLAYS / VOL. 16.', and the bottom panel features the Duke of Devonshire's monogram, an upper-case italic '*D*' with a crown above it. Both these panels are inlaid on dark green leather, with gold embossed text and tooling. The volume has marbled endpapers, the one on the inside of the front cover bearing a bookplate with a crowned garter inscribed with 'Honi soit qui mal y pense', with the Duke of Devonshire's armorial crest (a serpent knotted above a torse) at the centre, and ornamentation around and below the garter. Four leaves of wove paper (added when the volume was rebound) are present at the beginning of the volume, and two are present at the end.

Huntington MS HM4 contains 219 leaves, numbered in pencil by a later hand in the top right corner of the recto of each leaf. *The Aphrodysial* occupies fols. 120^r–151^v, but it totals thirty-three leaves rather than thirty-two, on account of some duplication in the numbering: the hand responsible for the pencil pagination must have made an error and skipped a page in the count, whereby two separate leaves are numbered 142. To differentiate between these, the letters *a* and *b* have been added, also in pencil, paginating the leaves as fols. 142a and 142b, respectively. This problem also arises earlier in the volume, on fols. 20a and 20b, and fols. 44a and 44b. The three instances of mis-pagination mean that although the page number given on

---

[15] Haslewood quotes from Bliss's letter in his introduction to the Roxburghe Club volume; see n. 39.
[16] *A Catalogue*, sigs. F1^r–F1^v.

the last folio is 216, 219 folio pages are actually present in the volume. The final leaf of *The Aphrodysial* (fol. 151) has been replaced; it is written in different ink on different paper stock and glued in with pasted strips of paper at the seam (one joining the inserted leaf to fol. 150^v, the other joining it to fol. 152^r).[17] The state of the equivalent leaf in Alnwick MS 509 reveals that copious revisions were made to the last page of the play. It would appear that after copying the 'final' revised state into Huntington MS HM4, Percy then added further revisions to both copies and must have thought it best to simply copy the final state of the emended text onto a fresh leaf and paste it into HM4, rather than to patch it with smaller pasted slips (see 'Authorial Revisions').

The manuscript begins with a leaf bearing 'vol: 1st:', added in a later italic hand when all three of Percy's holographs were numbered. The leaf itself is original, since it carries some ink transfer from text on the recto of the following leaf, written in Percy's hand. The watermark on the initial leaf also appears to be the same as the pair found on the paper used for the rest of the manuscript. The contents of Huntington MS HM4 are as follows: an epigraph (fol. 3^r); a song by Philip Sidney intended for inclusion in *The Faery Pastorall* (fol. 4^r); a general title page (fol. 5^r); the 'Prologue Generall' (fol. 6^r); *The Cuck-queanes And Cuckolds Errants or the Bearing down the Inne A Comædye* (fols. 7^r–31^v); *Arabia Sitiens or A Dreame of a Drye yeare A TragæComadye* (fols. 32^r–61^r); *The Faery Pastorall or Forrest of Elues* (fols. 62^r–91^r); *A Forrest Tragædye in Vacunium. or Cupids Sacrifice* (fols. 92^r–119^v); *The Aphrodysial or Sea-Feast 1602. A Marinall.* (fols. 120^r–151^v); *Necromantes or the Two Supposed Heds. A Comicall Inuention* (fols. 152^r–191^r), a 'Note to the Master of children of Powles' (fol. 191^r); a collection of 'Songs That be vacant in the foresayd Pastoralls and Comædyes. All of them made Anno 1636' (fols. 192^r–193^v). Fol. 194 is a stub of approximately 45mm, the rest of the page having been torn out. It contains partial text, likely from an additional song or songs.[18] The remainder of the manuscript is occupied by 'One Singular Booke Of Epigrammes' (fols. 195^r–216^r). There are no blank leaves at the end of the manuscript, but it is possible that any original blank leaves were removed when the volume was rebound.

Huntington MS HM4 is written on paper, with leaves measuring approximately 295mm by 185mm. No stitching is visible on account of the tightness of the binding, and it is difficult to work out the quiring with absolute certainly, but it appears that the volume is made up of gatherings of twelve folio leaves (i.e. six sheets folded once vertically), with some instances of ten leaves to a gathering. It appears that in some gatherings of twelve leaves one or two leaves might be missing. Based on the paper evidence, it is possible to discern that the contents of MS HM4 were written

---

[17] Fols. 190, 191, 193, and 194 (which is a stub, as most of the leaf has been torn out) are also cancels written in darker ink on what appears to be different paper stock.

[18] It appears that the verso of the stub contains parts of an alternative version of *The Aphrodysial*'s seventh song. A version of this alternative song is preserved in Alnwick MS 509, fol. 221^v, where it has been marked for deletion with a large cross.

on the same paper stock, although several leaves were replaced by the author with different paper stock. The paper is marked by vertical chain lines that are approximately between 21mm and 25mm apart. The paper stock carries a pair of pot watermarks, one in each of the two moulds used for making the paper. In the section of HM4 occupied by *The Aphrodysial*, watermarks appear on fols. 124, 125 (upside-down), 126, 127, 129 (upside-down), 130, 133, 134, 138, 139 (upside-down), 141 (upside-down), 142a, 142b, 143, and 144 (upside-down). One of the watermarks measures approximately 95mm by 44mm; its twin measures 98mm by 50mm. The design consists, bottom to top, of a base with a bottom border and a fleur-de-lys; a vase-like jug with an 'S' shaped handle on the left side, a semi-circular lid with five lobes, each bearing a trefoil, with the middle lobe bearing a quatrefoil and a 'wet' crescent moon (i.e. with the points facing upwards). The main body of the jug is divided into four sections horizontally; the top section is blank, the following one has a 'wet' crescent moon (smaller in size than the one that sits atop the jug), the next section the initial 'P', and the bottom section the initials 'L M'.[19] A third watermark from a different paper stock is present on fols. 190 and 193: it is also a pot, albeit of a different design, and measures approximately 75mm by 28mm.[20] The paper in HM4 shows signs of discolouration and staining, mainly around the outer edges of the leaves and on leaves that bear pasted slips, where the glue has leeched into the paper and caused stains that often show through or stain the surrounding folios. The leaves of HM4 were folded to make four columns, with the column on the extreme left of the page serving as a margin of between approximately 35mm and 50mm. Speech prefixes and marginal stage directions are written in the left margin, as are some corrections, and the word 'dilue', which Percy uses to indicate deletions.[21] Shared lines of verse are written on the same line, with speech prefixes given in parentheses to separate them from the dialogue. There are occasions where speech prefixes that would normally be expected to appear in the left margin are indented right and separated from the text that follows by means of a closing bracket. Such indentations usually occur because those speech prefixes are preceded by marginal stage direction text that extends into the space where the speech prefix would usually be written; this suggests that in the process of transcribing the play from Alnwick MS 509 the marginal text pertaining to a line was written

---

[19] The design of the watermark is similar to no. 80 in Edward Heawood, 'Papers used in England after 1600', *The Library*, 4th series, 11.3 (1930), 263–99 (299). See also similar designs in Gravell Online: POT.003.1 (Gravell No. FOL 0012); POT.128.1 (Gravell No. FOL 0537); POT.401.1 (Gravell No. FOL 1961). On watermarks in Alnwick MSS 508 and 509, see Dodds, 'A Dreame of a Drye Yeare', 173; Kincaid, 'A Critical Edition of … *Cuckqueans and Cuckolds*', 93–5.

[20] The other cancels (fols. 151 and 191) do not have watermarks (fol. 194 is also a cancel, but most of the leaf has been torn out, so it is unclear whether it contained a watermark).

[21] The meaning of the word 'dilue' can most likely be traced to the Latin singular imperative 'dilue' (wash away) or French 'diluer' (to dilute).

out first, followed by the main text of the line(s) in question.²² There is no set right margin, since Percy tends to write to almost the edge of the page; sometimes prose text or long verse lines stretch to the end of the right-hand edge of the page and words are broken up and carried over to the next line. The average number of lines per full page of text (including deleted lines, inserted lines, and stage directions given in the main body of the text) in *The Aphrodysial* is forty-seven, with the maximum and minimum number of lines per full page being forty-two and fifty-two, respectively. The exceptions to this count are fols. 120ᵛ and 151ᵛ, which leave half the page blank. Pasted slips are used throughout the play to cover up previous text with revised text; they appear on the following folios: 126ʳ, 126ᵛ, 127ʳ, 130ʳ, 132ʳ, 134ʳ, 134ᵛ, 137ᵛ, 139ʳ, 139ᵛ, 140ʳ, 141ʳ, 145ᵛ, 146ʳ, 146ᵛ, 147ʳ, 148ʳ, 148ᵛ, 149ʳ, 150ʳ, and 150ᵛ.

The Aphrodysial, like the other plays in the volume, begins with a title page (fol. 120ʳ, see Plate 1) consisting of an epigraph and the list of persons, which continues onto the verso and is followed by a description of the 'Properties' (fol. 120ᵛ, see Plate 2). The following page (fol. 121ʳ) once more gives the title of the play and is followed by a prologue and the play proper. The play is divided into acts and scenes, and follows the author's convention of using classical scene divisions, whereby a new scene begins each time a new speaker enters. Massed headers are used in each scene to list the speakers. Exits are not marked. At the end of the first four acts, a musical interlude is called for, with a stage direction announcing 'Here they knockt vp the consort' (ll. 560, 1118, 1980, 2545). The play is written mostly in English, but also contains phrases or whole lines in other languages, namely: Latin (ll. 6–11, 13, 69–70, 141, 314, 357, 361–2, 363, 365, 479, 517, 539, 542, 682, 734–5, 814, 842–3, 876–8, 912, 1226, 1230, 1237, 1322, 1423, 1524–5, 1528, 1547–9, 1609–12, 1619–20, 1630–1, 1660, 1667, 1672, 1720, 1726, 1731, 1838, 1951, 2028–9, 2240, 2266–7, 2292, 2318, 2332, 2358, 2372, 2582, 2590 SD, 2687–9, 2699–700, 2771, 2784, 2841, 2844, 3034, 3056, 3062–3, 3075), Greek (l. 776), French (ll. 808, 811, 862, 866), Welsh (l. 800), and nonsensical speech (ll. 785–6).²³

---

²² Speech prefixes that have been indented on account of marginal SD text and separated from the main text with a closing bracket appear on ll. 266, 390, 619, 949, 1094–5, 1208, 1681, 1695–6, 1901–3, 1906–7, 1912, 1929, 2243, 2353, 2936, and 2968. Some speech prefixes are partially indented and have not been separated with a bracket (e.g. see ll. 1678–80, 1683, 1685, 1689, and 1691); their position has been regularized in this edition, but their original placement is shown in Plate 5. An indented speech prefix which is abbreviated to only the first letter of the speaker's name is interlined at l. 2352.

²³ The Latin phrase 'Nulla Desunt' is also used in the play to indicate that no text is missing from blank space introduced into the text on pasted slips (see ll. 1825, 2619, 2665). On the origin of 'dilue' see n. 21.

Hand

Huntington MS HM4 is a holograph manuscript, written by Percy in a legible but somewhat idiosyncratic, informal italic hand.[24] Percy's hand is characterized by the tendency to form letters separately rather than in cursive, saving for a few ligatures such as *in*, *im*, *to,* and occasionally *sh* and *ch*. There are multiple forms of particular letters, such as long *s* and short *s*, and *e*, which is usually formed with two strokes, sometimes joined, but usually with a break; it is not uncommon to find *e* formed with only one stroke (i.e. only the mainstroke is present, without a lobe). Another form of *e* that is less frequent in the play is what looks like an attempt at a Greek *e*, which is formed from three strokes; this form of *e* is likely the result of either a *currente calamo* or later alteration of imperfect two-stroke *e* that resembles a *v*. Other examples of letters that are likely altered *currente calamo* are *h* and *w*, whereby *h* sometimes receives a long downward stroke on the base of the limb, which gives the letter an exaggerated descender, and *w* sometimes has an additional vertical stroke in the middle of the letter to give it more definition. See Plates 2 and 4 for examples of these letter forms.

Some aspects of Percy's italic hand are inconsistent, and there is a tendency to form certain letters imperfectly. It is often difficult to distinguish between miniscule and majuscule forms of *c*, *k*, *o*, *s*, *v*, *w*, and *y*. Majuscule *C* sometimes has an additional stroke added to form a serif at the top; other times it is distinguishable from miniscule *c* only by its size relative to the letters that follow. The mainstrokes of majuscule letters that have a cross-stroke, such as *A* and *H*, are often not fully joined by the cross-stroke. Miniscule *t* is often formed without a headstroke, which is also frequently the case for miniscule *f*. Miniscule *a* and *o* tend to have an open bowl, meaning that *o* is often similar in appearance to *v*, and *a* is similar in appearance to *u*. Sometimes *a* and *o* are tightly formed, meaning that they essentially look like heavily inked points. Sometimes miniscule *i* lacks a point. The textual notes to this edition do not provide an exhaustive account of imperfectly formed letters; they are generally only noted where they potentially introduce ambiguity in terms of spelling or sense.

The size of the hand is largely consistent throughout the main text. A larger hand is used for speech prefixes, headings, act and scene divisions, names in massed headers at the beginnings of scenes, and musical directions throughout. First words of speeches that begin the prologue, epilogue, and the beginning of an act are written in a larger size, as is reported text on locality boards and other inscriptions, such as the words on Oceanus's brooch (ll. 1094 and 2050) and the signature of Vulcan's name on his letters

---

[24] Dimmock describes Percy's hand as 'careful' (*Mahomet and His Heaven*, 12) but also applies Kincaid's description of it as a 'shaky italic' (Kincaid, 'A Critical Edition of ... *Cuckqueans and Cuckolds*, 95). Hillebrand mistakenly describes it as a 'reasonably good secretary hand' ('Elizabethan Amateur', 400). John Payne Collier described it as 'peculiar handwriting' (*English Dramatic Poetry*, vol. 2, 352).

to Humida and Arida (ll. 969 and 988).²⁵ The names of the characters in the list of persons are likewise in a larger hand (see Plate 1). Some scenes feature long stage directions given in the main body of the text under the heading 'The Direction', but shorter stage directions that represent action intended to occur simultaneously with the dialogue are given in the left margin, usually in a noticeably smaller hand. An asterisk at the end of a given line of main text indicates which part of the dialogue the marginal direction is intended to accompany. The phrase 'Nulla Desunt' (Latin to indicate that no material is missing) is added in a significantly larger hand to fill blank space left on larger pasted slips on fols. 139ᵛ, 146ᵛ, and 147ʳ (see Plate 6 for one such example).

In terms of punctuation, Percy's writing is characterized by a frequent use of commas. Another form of punctuation that appears regularly in the play is a symbol that looks halfway between a question mark and a right-leaning exclamation mark, which is represented in this edition by ?, although in the manuscript this mark is used interchangeably for both interrogatives and exclamations (see Plate 5 for numerous instances of this mark, showing examples of the variation in the curvature of the mark's mainstroke). A double dash (=) is frequently used in place of a hyphen when a word is divided between two lines, and there are instances of long dashes used in the text to indicate an interruption, as in ll. 820, 822, 1320, 2090, and 2728. Parentheses are mostly used to enclose speech prefixes on shared lines, to separate text of hanging lines, and offset indented speech prefixes. There are also some instances of parentheses used in the main text. Colons and semi-colons are used sparingly. A series of marks that resemble *H*s is used to fill up blank space at the end of line 904. It is likely that Percy paused his transcription from Alnwick 509 at this point, and instead of continuing the line when he resumed copying, he began on a new line and then backfilled the empty space.

AUTHORIAL REVISIONS

Huntington MS HM4 appears to have been prepared by Percy as a fair copy of material found in his earlier manuscript, Alnwick MS 509, which is a far more experimental text that does not demonstrate the same preoccupation with tidiness as does the later copy.²⁶ A comparison of the two extant copies of the play demonstrates that in copying out *The Aphrodysial* from MS 509, Percy implemented the emendations that he had initially made in the earlier

---

²⁵ Examples of larger script for first words of speeches that begin the prologue, epilogue, and opening speeches of new acts, can be found on ll. 77, 122, 569, 1123, 1986, 2555, and 3064. For reported text on scene boards see Plate 2.

²⁶ Jameson describes Alnwick MS 509 as 'experimental' ('An Edition of *A Forrest Tragedye*', xix). On revisions in Alnwick MSS 508 and 509, see Dimmock, ed., *Mahomet and His Heaven*, 49–52; Kincaid, 'A Critical Edition of … Cuckqueans and Cuckolds', 99–104; Jameson, 'An Edition of *A Forrest Tragedye*', xvi–xix.

copy (but see Appendix 2 for a list of variants). It is generally accepted that the material as found in Huntington MS HM4 represents a 'final authoritative text'.[27] It is possible that HM4 was intended as a presentation copy, although it does not appear to have been given away, since it was kept with the earlier holographs, Alnwick MSS 508 and 509, as demonstrated by the somewhat later numbering of the three volumes.

Although care has been taken to prepare Huntington MS HM4 as a fair copy, *The Aphrodysial*, like the other plays in the volume, contains various types of authorial emendations, and appears to be the most heavily revised play of the lot. There are a number of minor corrections of errors caused by false starts or errors caused by eye-skip which are corrected *currente calamo*, but it is also evident that further, more substantial, layers of emendation were carried out by the author after the transcription was completed in 1647. These revisions take different forms, including deleted letters, words, or phrases, interlined insertions of letters, words, or phrases, and additions of replacement text in the margins. Small and large pasted slips are also used throughout the play to add replacement text in the left margins and in the main text.[28]

The types of revisions that were made *currente calamo* generally correct errors arising from false starts or errors in transcription, where an incorrect letter or beginning of a word is marked for deletion using a vertical stroke or several vertical strokes. For instance, in line 1393, the word 'sel[f]ues' is initially falsely written as 'self', but the *f* is then marked for deletion and the rest of the letters follow to make up the correct word 'selues'. Another example is 'say[d]st' in line 2292, where the past tense of the word was initially written, but then corrected to the present tense.[29] In some instances the correct letter(s) or word is formed from the false start or incorrect letters. An example of this can be found in line 100, where the word 'vs' has been written over the word 'our', with the *o* marked for deletion with a vertical stroke.[30] Some of these types of minor alterations were also made after the copy was finished, as in line 954, where 'Curst' has the *u* written in darker ink over another character.

Other types of errors that are corrected are accidental omissions of letters, words, or phrases. For instance, there are several times where a letter that was omitted in the process of copying is supplied above the space that it ought to have occupied (see e.g. ll. 26, 50, 60, 438, and 590). Interlineations of whole lines are rare in *The Aphrodysial* (ll. 50, 146, 1719, 2096, 2521,

---

[27] Kincaid, 'A Critical Edition of … *Cuckqueans and Cuckolds*', 104.

[28] See Plate 6 for an example of pasted slips. There is only one instance where a small slip bearing a single word is pasted into the main text in its actual position rather than in the left margin; see note on l. 2769.

[29] Other examples of minor deletions of this type can be found in ll. 108, 112, 142, 372, 525, 806, 1319 SD.1, 1338, 1444, 1620, 2222, 2296, 2470, 2567, 2749, and 2973.

[30] For a selection of similar examples of this type of alteration, see notes on ll. 129, 159, 212, 285, 405, 596, 702, 790, 1107, 1145, 1318, 1455, 1601, 1645, 1800, 1968, 2179, 2312, 2318, 2320, 2358, 2600, 2628, 2664, 2723, 2937, 2941, and 3011.

and 2702), but single words or phrases are added as interlineations quite frequently in the text (see e.g. ll. 77, 94, 96, 144, 211, 278, 406, 496, 581, and 634).

Sometimes, interlined corrections remedy oversights in transcription from the earlier copy of the play (see e.g. ll. 94, 96, 144, 210, 211, 278, 581, 634, 768, 863, 885, 966, 1089, 1145, 1240, 1334, 1444, 1453, and 1683). In other instances, interlined additions in Huntington MS HM4 are also found interlined in Alnwick MS 509, which suggests that they belong to a separate layer of revision undertaken after or during the copying process. Some examples of such additions can be found in, for example, ll. 406, 799, 851, 928, 955, 1455, and 1495. Normally, Percy uses a caret below the line to mark the place of the intended insertion; sometimes the carets are bracketed by a point below each side of the caret (˷), other times a single point is used below the left or right side of the caret, or not at all. There are a number of instances where a word is missing from the very beginning or end of a line, in which case that word is added not via interlineation but simply placed to the immediate left or right of the line in question (see e.g. ll. 81, 756, 982, 1740, 1917, 2080, and 2455).

While vertical strokes are used to mark single letters or short words for deletion, whole-word deletions are underlined and usually marked by an elevated point before the beginning of the word. The word 'dilue' is added in the left margin to indicate that the underlined material is intended for deletion.[31] Words intended to be replaced are likewise underlined and usually preceded by an elevated point, and replacement text is supplied in the left margin. In some instances, the replacement text has also been cancelled and replaced with an alternative, which is added on a small pasted slip on top of the no longer visible cancelled reading. This type of alteration demonstrates that the Huntington MS HM4 copy of *The Aphrodysial* underwent at least two layers of revision after the play was copied out in its entirety. An example that supports this assessment can be found in Percy's revision of the term used to describe Thetis's enchanted piece of jewellery, which features prominently in the play in three versions: the original, an imitation forged by Vulcan, and as a 'dream' obtained from Proteus. In Huntington MS HM4 the original term used throughout the play is 'Louerolle', which is then underlined for deletion, and the term 'Ceston' added in the left margin, usually on a small pasted slip, meaning that the slip obscures a cancelled alternative term.[32] An examination of Alnwick MS 509 reveals that the cancelled alternative is most likely 'Bracelet', since in that copy of the play 'Loue-rolle' is underlined for deletion, 'Bracelet' is added in the left margin and then struck out, and 'Ceston' added. There are several instances in the HM4 copy of *The Aphrodysial* where 'Loue-rolle' and 'Bracelet' are left uncorrected in the main text when referring specifically to the original

---

[31] On 'dilue', see n. 21.
[32] Where an instance of this type of correction occurs on a larger pasted slip, the word 'Ceston' is added in the left margin of that slip rather than on a smaller slip.

object, which is otherwise always referred to as a 'Ceston' (see ll. 1820, 2847, and 2851), which might be an oversight or inconsistency on Percy's part. 'Bracelet' or 'Bracelets' are used in the text to refer to the forged copies (in l. 2519 'Bracelets' replaces 'wrest-rolles'; in l. 2813 it replaces 'Rolles'; see also emendation at ll. 2847–9). It would appear that Percy generally reserves the emended term 'Ceston' for instances where the original enchanted object is meant.

There are numerous instances where larger pasted slips are used to replace whole lines in the main body of the text. This method of introducing revisions into the text supports the general scholarly consensus that Huntington MS HM4 was intended as a fair copy. The corrections that are found on pasted slips in Huntington MS HM4 were added as interlineations or marginal annotation in Alnwick MS 509, although there are also instances of pasted slips in the earlier manuscript.[33] Normally, the slips are pasted singly, but, in some cases, there is a layering of slips; Plate 6 reproduces the most extreme example of pasted slips not only in *The Aphrodysial*, but in the volume as a whole. The layering of the slips on fol. 146^v, and the fact that some text has been written in darker ink, indicates that two layers of revision have been made to this part of the text. A third stage of revision might be evident in the additional minor correction in the spelling of 'Ioc[o]\u/lus' on the layered slips containing lines 2594–600. It appears that some revisions were carried out simultaneously on both copies of *The Aphrodysial*. This is suggested by the fact that the same type of lighter, browner ink that is used throughout Huntington MS HM4 is also present in some revisions made to Alnwick MS 509, which is generally written in a much darker ink, and initially revised in darker ink too.[34] A substantially larger revision than those found on the pasted slips pertains to the ending of the play on fol. 151^{r-v} in the Huntington copy. This leaf replaces an excised leaf, and the text on it is written in darker ink. A comparison of the equivalent section of the play in Alnwick 509 reveals that this part of the play was heavily revised in several stages. Those revisions must have been adopted onto the original leaf in the Huntington copy as well, but the extent of subsequent additional revisions undoubtedly made the page too unsightly for a fair copy. This might have led Percy to decide in favour of copying out the final accepted version of the play's ending onto a fresh leaf, which he then added in place of the original fol. 151.

---

[33] Revisions on pasted slips appear in the Alnwick MS 509 copy of the play on fols. 134^v, 136^r, 138^r, 143^r, 143^v, 146^r, 152^r, 152^v, 153^r, and 156^v.

[34] For a similar observation about the concurrent revision of the two manuscripts, see Kincaid, 'A Critical Edition of … *Cuckqueanes and Cuckolds*', 101–4, and Jameson, 'An Edition of *A Forrest Tragedye*', xix, xviii–xxiii.

PENCIL ANNOTATIONS

Pagination in Huntington MS HM4 was added in grey pencil by a later hand, possibly after the manuscript was acquired by the Huntington Library, but perhaps earlier. A number of other pencil annotations in grey pencil, likely by a different hand, appear in *The Aphrodysial* and elsewhere in the volume, although this play has the highest concentration of such marks. These annotations mostly take the form of crosses (*x*) of varying size, although there are also some instances of straight vertical and horizontal lines that run in the margins of the text, next to the text, or that partially box off marginal text. The original pencil marks have caused transfer onto the facing folio pages; in most instances, however, it is possible to distinguish the original marks from the transferred ones. The marks might possibly have been added when the manuscript was examined and partially transcribed for the Roxburghe Club publication in 1824, but this seems somewhat unlikely given that the two plays that were published for the Club do not bear extensive marks. It seems more plausible that the markings were added when the manuscript was in William Burrell's possession while he worked on his '*Collectanea*' of the Percy family, which he completed in 1770 (see p. xv). The latter possibility is supported by the fact that the annotations seem to mark out locations: for example, 'Wolues Hill. A Man= / nour howse in Sus= / sex so called' (line 69 SD.1–3) and 'Iron Milles in Sussex' (line 372). The nature and position of these pencil annotations is described in Appendix 1.

DATE

The title page of Huntington MS HM4 (fol. 5^r) indicates that the 'Comædyes and Pastoralls / with their Songs, As / Also one Booke / of Epigrammes / By W. P. Esquier' were written out or transcribed ('Exscriptum') in 1647. The original dates of composition for the plays, songs, and epigrams are also given in the manuscript, which indicate that the material was composed much earlier. The first five plays were composed between 1601 and 1603: *The Cuck-queanes And Cuckolds Errants* in 1601 (as noted in the *explicit* at the conclusion of the play); *Arabia Sitiens* in 1601 (*explicit*); *The Faery Pastorall* in 1603 (*explicit*); *A Forrest Traædye* in 1602 (*explicit*); and *The Aphrodysial* in 1602 (noted on the play's title page and in the *explicit*). The final play, *Necromantes*, was written some decades later in 1632 (*explicit*). The 'Songs That be vacant' were 'All of them made Anno 1636' (fol. 192^r), while the epigrams are dated 1610 in their *explicit* (fol. 216^r).

E. K. Chambers questioned the dates supplied by Percy and suggested that the plays were possibly written prior to 1590, and were perhaps revised by the author after 1599, but the scholarly consensus largely sides with the dates as Percy gives them in his manuscripts.[35] The original dates of composition as given in the manuscript are supported by the dates supplied in

---

[35] E. K. Chambers, *The Elizabethan Stage*, 4 vols. (Oxford, 1923, repr. 1961), vol. 3, 464–5.

Alnwick MS 509. The dates as noted in the extant manuscripts and the contents of several plays also coincide with important familial occasions for which they might have been written. For instance, Dodds proposes that *The Aphrodysial* was probably written to celebrate the christening of Henry Percy's son and heir, Algernon, which took place at Essex House on 14 October 1602.³⁶ Dodds also suggests that *The Faery Pastorall* was written for the occasion of James VI and I's visit to Henry Percy's estate at Syon House on 8 June 1603.³⁷ Likewise, the date of *Necromantes* suggests that it was likely written in response to Algernon Percy's accession to the Earldom in 1632 in a possible bid to secure favour and ensure a continuation of the annuity that Percy received from Algernon's father before his death.³⁸

The Aphrodysial is dated 1602 both on its title page (fol. 120ʳ) and on its terminal page (fol. 151ᵛ). The state of the play in Huntington MS HM4 incorporates amendments and corrections carried out by the author nearly forty-five years after the play's composition, when he copied the play from a no longer extant draft into Alnwick MS 509 in 1646 and revised it before transcribing the material into Huntington MS HM4 in 1647. Yet more revisions were carried out on both copies of the play in 1647 or 1648. Thus, the copy of *The Aphrodysial* in Huntington MS HM4 can be dated to 1647, with some revisions possibly dating from 1648. The overall dating of the play itself is further complicated by the fact that this mid-seventeenth-century manuscript in large part reproduces the text of a '1602' play that might also have been revised in the 1630s.

Authorship

William Percy's authorship of Huntington MS HM4 has been accepted by critics since the publication of two of his plays in the 1824 Roxburghe Club volume. Percy's candidature as the author is most obviously confirmed in the manuscript by 'W. P. Esquier', which appears on the general title page, and which is repeated elsewhere in the volume. Joseph Haslewood, who was in possession of the manuscript when the Roxburghe volume was published, asserted in his introduction to that volume that William Percy was the author, citing as his initial evidence an epigram from the manuscript which is addressed to Charles Fitzgeoffrey and accompanied by an annotation: 'Vpon his printed Epi=/gramme to mee euer / my name written in

---

³⁶ Dodds, 'Aphrodysial', 237. For John Chamberlain's account of who was present at the christening, see Norman Egbert McClure, *The Letters of John Chamberlain*, 2 vols. (Philadelphia, 1939; repr. 1962), vol. 1, 167.

³⁷ Madeline Hope Dodds, 'William Percy and James I', *Notes and Queries*, 161.1 (4 July 1931), 13–14 (13). See also Fenn, 'William Percy's *Faery Pastorall*', 23–36.

³⁸ On Percy's numerous financial troubles and familial income, see Madeline Hope Dodds, 'The Financial Affairs of a Jacobean Gentleman', *Archeologica Aeliana*, 32 (1944), 91–109; and Mark Nicholls, '"As Happy a Fortune as I Desire": The Pursuit of Financial Security by the Younger Brothers of Henry Percy, Ninth Earl of Northumberland', *Historical Research*, 65 (1992), 269–314.

/ golden Magicall letters / in forme and Nature' (Epigram 350, fol. 216ᵛ). With the aid of Philip Bliss, custodian of the Bodleian Library, Haslewood was able to ascertain that the identity of 'W. P.' was indeed William Percy, since Fitzgeoffrey's *Caroli Fitzgeofridi Affaniae: sive Epigrammatvm Libri tres* (Oxford, 1601) contains only one poem addressed to someone with those initials ('Ad Gvliemvm Percivm', sigs. D2ᵛ–D3ʳ).³⁹ The handwriting used throughout Huntington MS HM4 matches that of Percy's extant letters, so there is little plausible grounds for questioning his authorship of the volume.⁴⁰

WILLIAM PERCY

William Percy was the third but second surviving son of Henry Percy, eighth Earl of Northumberland. He was born into an important family whose turbulent politics and Catholic sympathies landed many of their members in trouble during the reigns of both Elizabeth I and James VI and I.⁴¹ The exact year of William's birth has been the source of some disagreement, but it is most likely that he was born in 1570 in the North of England.⁴² Although not much is known about his childhood, it is likely that he was sent to Paris with a younger brother in 1583 to join their older brother, Henry, who was being educated there. The two younger sons were called back not long thereafter, but Percy was sent back to Paris in 1595 to deliver news of their father's death to Henry, who returned to England with his brother the

---

³⁹ Haslewood's introduction to the 1824 Roxburghe Club volume quotes a letter sent to him by Bliss, who checked the Bodleian copy of *Fitzgeofridi Affaniae*: 'There can be no question, I think, that the author of your MS. was the above William Percy, for this is the only name throughout Fitzgeffry's rare volume answering to the initials you have given me; and from the above lines [i.e. Fitzgeoffrey's poem, quoted] it is evident he was a poet' (*The Cuck-queanes and Cuckolds Errants or The Bearing Down the Inne … The Faery Pastorall or Forrest of Elues* (London, 1824), sig. b1ʳ).

⁴⁰ Alnwick MS Letters and Papers, vol. 16, fol. 91; Syon House MSS Q.I.60–2. For a discussion of the letters, see Nicholls, 'As Happy a Fortune', 300. Transcriptions of the Syon House MSS (held at Alnwick Castle) were published by Dodds in 'Financial Affairs', 101–2, 104–6.

⁴¹ For a history of the Percy family, see Gerald Brenan, *A History of the House of Percy from the Earliest Times down to the Present Century* (London, 1902), and Edward Barrington de Fonblanque, *Annals of the House of Percy from the Conquest to the Opening of the Nineteenth Century*, 2 vols. (London, 1887), vol. 2.

⁴² Reavley Gair states that Percy was born in 1574 in Tynemouth ('William Percy', *Oxford Dictionary of National Biography*, online edition, https://doi.org/10.1093/ref:odnb/21962). This estimate is based on Percy's Oxford matriculation record, which notes that he was fifteen on 13 June 1589. See Joseph Foster, *Alumni Oxonienses: The Members of the University of Oxford, 1500–1714* (Oxford, 1891), vol. 3, 1147. Nicholls proposes 1570, Beamish, as the year and place of birth, based on Bishop Thomas Percy's genealogical research carried out in the eighteenth century ('As happy a fortune', 298, n. 12, citing British Library Add. MS 32327 fol. 42 as evidence). See also Hillebrand ('Elizabethan Amateur', 391), who gives 1575 as the birth year, and notes that 1573 is given as the birth year in a manuscript note attached to the Bodleian copy of Anthony Wood's *Athenae Oxonienses*, ed. by Philip Bliss (London, 1913–20).

following year and became the ninth Earl of Northumberland. The eighth Earl died under suspicious circumstances in the Tower of London following his implication in the Throckmorton conspiracy; his body was discovered on 20 June 1595, with suicide ruled as the cause of death, but this provoked much suspicion in Catholic circles both in England and abroad. There is some speculation about the role that William and Henry might have played in a possible coup planned with the Duke of Guise following their father's death, but there is no firm evidence to support this.[43]

William Percy matriculated at Gloucester Hall, Oxford, in 1589, which was associated with recusancy, although his own religious inclinations remain uncertain.[44] He never took a degree, but, while at Oxford, Percy was part of a literary coterie that included Barnabe Barnes, Charles Fitzgeoffrey, and Thomas Campion (even though the latter did not attend Oxford).[45] Barnes dedicated his collection of sonnets, *Parthenophil and Parthenope* (1593) to Percy; the title page dedication announces Percy as 'his deerest friend'. Percy included a sonnet in response to Barnes's sequence, appended to his own *Sonnets to the Fairest Coelia*, which was published the following year (sig. D1ʳ). While Barnes's prominent and flattering dedication to Percy might have been motivated by a bid for favour or patronage as well as friendship, Percy's poetical abilities are also noted in William Covell's *Polimanteia* (1595), which includes his name in a list of Oxford gentlemen who can 'sing sweetly'.[46] A complimentary poem to Percy was also included in Charles Fitzgeoffrey's *Caroli Fitzgeofridi Affaniae* (1601), as mentioned previously.

Percy relocated to London in 1593 or earlier, where he seems to have resided until at least 1598, but probably later.[47] In 1602–3 he was living in Sussex.[48] During his years in London he undoubtedly attended theatre

---

[43] Percy's early life and familial fortunes are discussed in more detail by Hillebrand, 'Elizabethan Amateur', 391–400, and Nicholls 'As Happy a Fortune', 298–301.

[44] See also Foster, *Alumni Oxonienses*, vol. 3, 1147. For an account of Gloucester Hall's reputation as a hotbed of Catholicism, see Hillebrand ('Elizabethan Amateur', 393). Dodds discusses Percy's possible views on Catholicism and Protestantism in relation to his epigrams in 'William Percy's Epigrams', *Notes and Queries*, 161.4 (25 July 1931), 57–60 (58).

[45] For a more extensive discussion of this coterie and its members, see Hillebrand, 'Elizabethan Amateur', 394–5.

[46] *Polimanteia, or, The meanes lawfull and vnlawfull, to iudge of the fall of a common-wealth … Whereunto is added, a letter from England to her three daughters, Cambridge, Oxford, Innes of Court* (London, 1595), sig. Q3ᵛ notes in the margin 'Britton. / Percie. / Willobie. / Fraunce. / Lodge. / Master Da- / uis of L. I. / Drayton. / Learned M. / Plat'.

[47] A record of a loan places Percy in London in 1593; see Dimmock, ed., *Mahomet and His Heaven*, 14 and Nicholls, 'As Happy a Fortune', 298–9. In 1596 he fought a duel and perhaps spent some time in the Tower, before being deemed innocent of his opponent's death, which occurred several weeks after the duel was fought. He was imprisoned once more, probably for debt, in 1598. On this period of Percy's life, see Hillebrand, 'Elizabethan Amateur', 396–7, and Dodds, 'Financial Affairs', 96–7.

[48] A note in *The Aphrodysial*, which is dated 1602, states that the play was written at 'Wolues Hill. A Man= / nour howse in Sus= / sex so calld' (ll. 69 SD.1–3). The *explicit* at the end of *The Faery Pastorall* reads 'Finis 1603 Wolues Hill my Parnassus' (fol. 90ʳ). On Percy's ownership of property in Sussex, see Dodds, 'Financial Affairs', 94.

performances.⁴⁹ In the early years of the seventeenth century Percy turned his attention to playwriting, perhaps in part inspired by his experiences of theatre-going in London and in part prompted to put his poetical abilities to use in the service of his elder brother's political ambitions. Henry Percy keenly advocated for James VI's accession to the English throne, and it is entirely plausible that some or all of William Percy's plays were composed for familial occasions at which politically important visitors were entertained. James VI and I's visit to Syon House in 1603 marked an important moment for the Percy family, and although direct evidence is lacking, it is highly probable, as Madeline Dodds suggested in the 1930s, that *The Faery Pastorall* was performed before the monarch. If some or all of the plays composed between 1601 and 1603 were indeed performed privately, then this might have led Percy to seek out a larger audience for his plays on the professional stage (see pp. xxx–xxxvi). However, the family fortunes of the Percys were left shattered by their implication in the Gunpowder Plot in 1605; one of the conspirators was Thomas Percy, and suspicion also fell on the ninth Earl, who was imprisoned in the Tower and ordered to pay a fine of £30,000. He remained in the Tower until his release in 1621.

William Percy likely returned to Oxford after the events of 1605, perhaps wishing to distance himself from further intrigue. He can be located in Oxford with certainty in 1612–13, and 1617–18 when he was imprisoned for debt in Oxford Castle, which served as the city's prison.⁵⁰ Perhaps it was the return to Oxford that prompted Percy to finish his collection of epigrams, many of which deal with aspects of Oxford life during his time as a student there in the early 1590s. According to both Alnwick MS 509 and Huntington MS HM4, the epigrams were completed in 1610. Percy was still writing poetry in the opening years of the seventeenth century, as evidenced by his laudatory poem for Barnabe Barnes's *Four Books of Offices* (see p. ix). It is impossible to know what entirely new material Percy might have written beyond what survives in his extant holographs. He wrote *Necromantes* in 1632, and supplementary songs for his other plays in 1636, before copying out the plays of his youth together with the newer material into three copies, one of which is partially incomplete (Alnwick MS 508). Percy began copying his plays in 1644, while Royalist forces were besieged in Oxford, and his motivations for doing so remain unclear; perhaps it was a wistful remembrance of happier times, an outlet for a creative process that had not quite come to its ultimate conclusion, an attempt to create presentation copies to win favour (with Royalist exiles in Oxford or else with the tenth Earl of Northumberland), or a means of settling debts.⁵¹ A 1638 letter describes Percy as living 'obscurely in Oxford, [where he] drinks nothing but ale', and

---

⁴⁹ Some of Percy's epigrams demonstrate his familiarity with the work of professional dramatists. See Matteo A. Pangallo, *Playwriting Playgoers in Shakespeare's Theater* (Philadelphia, 2017), 130.

⁵⁰ On Percy's return to Oxford and financial troubles there, see Dodds, 'Financial Affairs', 94–5; Nicholls, 'As Happy a Fortune', 299.

⁵¹ On the last point see Dimmock, ed., *Mahomet and His Heaven*, 48, n. 194.

the sense of withdrawal from society is likewise echoed in Anthony Woods's account of Percy dying 'an aged Bachelour in Pennyfarthing Streete, after he had lived a melancholy & retired life many yeares'.[52] Percy was buried in the Cathedral of Christ Church on 28 May 1648.

Percy's dramatic oeuvre reveals a wide range of literary allusions, sources, and influences. In *The Aphrodysial* Percy weaves together, adapts, and innovates upon a wide array of source material, including Ovid's *Amores* (seen in his adaptation of the Hero and Leander story, likely also influenced by Marlowe's poem on the same subject); Ovid's *Metamorphoses* (for various strands of the plot, including Talus's story of his demise, Proteus's prophecy about Thetis having a son greater than the gods, and various echoes of Glaucus's pursuit of Scylla that can be found in Percy's play).[53] Percy quotes repeatedly from Virgil's *Aeneid* and *Eclogues* in various epigraphs throughout the volume, so it is no surprise that some of the mythological and mythographic material in *The Aphrodysial* draws on Virgil as well as Ovid. Percy is likewise influenced by the plays of Plautus, particularly in the fishermen subplot, where he takes names such as 'Rudens' and 'Gripus' from Plautus's play *Rudens* (Latin for 'Rope'), the second act of which focuses on the fortunes of a group of fishermen. The name of 'Harpax' is similarly taken from another of Plautus's plays, *Pseudolus*, where the character (an enslaved Macedonian soldier) is, like Percy's Harpax, tasked with carrying letters. Percy also incorporates material from more contemporary writers, such as Guillaume de Saluste, Sieur du Bartas, part of whose poem *Le Sepmaine* Percy offers in what seems to be his own original translation when he has Jupiter, disguised as Arion, recount his kidnapping and escape from pirates: 'Arion his Speech is translated, / worde for worde, out of the first weeke and fifth / day of Seigneur du Bartas' (ll. 116–18).[54] Undoubtedly, the catalogue of fishes in Bartas's retelling of Arion's narrative served as an inspiration for Percy's various lists of fishes in the dialogue of the fishermen, in some of the Songs, and in the angling 'competition' held by the Graces and the Nymphs. Percy's focus on the denizens of the underwater world is supplemented by his knowledge of Pliny's *Historia Naturalis*, which he references directly in a stage direction (ll. 1547–50). Martin Wiggins also identifies additional sources for *The Aphrodysial*, such as Plautus's *Cistellaria*, Terence's *Andria* and *Eunuchus*, Horace's *Ars Poetica*, and the Book of Matthew.[55]

---

[52] Reverend G. Garrard and Anthony Wood quoted in Hillebrand, 'Elizabethan Amateur', 399–400.

[53] On Percy's borrowings from Ovid's *Metamorphoses*, see Maria Shmygol, 'Protean Objects in William Percy's *The Aphrodysial or Sea-Feast*', in *Dynamic Matter: Transforming Renaissance Objects*, ed. Jennifer Linhart Wood (Pittsburgh, 2022), 207–30.

[54] Percy does not clarify whether he translates from the French or Latin versions of the poem; the poem was first published in French as *Le Sepmaine, ou creation du monde* (Paris, 1578), but a Latin translation was subsequently published in London in 1595 under the title *Guilielmi Salustii Bartassii Hebdomas a Gabriele Lermæo latinitate donata*.

[55] Martin Wiggins, in association with Catherine Richardson, *British Drama 1533–1642: A Catalogue* (Oxford, 2012–19), vol. 4 (2014): no. 1357, 419.

There are likewise several elements of the play that echo material from Shakespeare. Percy incorporates action that clearly calls to mind *The Merry Wives of Windsor*, which was first published in early 1602; namely, there are strong echoes of Falstaff's unsuccessful amorous exploits in Vulcan's plan to send identical love letters to Humida and Arida, his donning of attire that makes him appear 'bigger in the body then he was before' (l. 1606), the comic failure of his love plot, his subsequent disguise as 'Madame Reuenge' (l. 1969), and his ultimate humiliation.[56] Similarly, the competition between Glauce and Hero over Leander loosely recalls that of Hermia and Helena in *A Midsummer Night's Dream* (first published in 1600), particularly Percy's insistence on Glauce being taller than her rival and having darker skin (see ll. 30–1), which echoes the slights about skin colour and height applied to Hermia and Helena in Shakespeare's play.

Audience, Readership, and Performance

Although there is no evidence that Percy's plays were ever performed (either by amateurs or professional players), they have long been a source of critical interest and speculation in terms of the likelihood of their professional performance.[57] Percy clearly must have hoped for, or at least envisaged, such a possibility, since his plays contain copious stage directions aimed at facilitating performance by both child and adult actors (except for *Necromantes*, which was originally written in 1632 and is intended 'For Actors onely', fol. 190ʳ). The stage directions that envisage professional performance were likely added to the play at some relatively early stage following its composition, since the Children of Paul's are thought to have ceased their theatrical activities sometime between mid-1606 and 1608.[58] Although there is no direct evidence, it is possible that *The Aphrodysial* was written for private performance at the christening celebrations of Algernon Percy on 14 October 1602 at Essex House in London. In first proposing this possibility, Dodds noted that the play's emphasis on Proteus's prophecy about Thetis bearing a son

---

[56] Dodds discusses the similarities with *Merry Wives* in 'Aphrodysial', 237.

[57] See n. 5, also Patrick Kincaid, 'John Marston's *The Dutch Courtesan* and William Percy's *The Cuckqueanes and Cuckolds Errants*', *Notes and Queries*, vol. 48: no. 3 (2001), 309–11. Kincaid suggests the possibility that this play might have been passed on to, and perhaps served as an influence for, John Marston, who played 'an important role in the opening and modification of St. Paul's in 1599' and seems to have served as a 'de facto theatre manager' there until 1603 (p. 311).

[58] The Children of Paul's last performance at court was in July 1606 and Roze Hentschell suggests that their theatrical performances 'seem to have ceased shortly after' (*St Paul's Cathedral Precinct in Early Modern Literature and Culture* (Oxford, 2020), 181, n. 87). Reavley Gair suggests that some theatrical activities continued, and that the company's demise likely came as late as 1608 (*The Children of Paul's: The Story of a Theatre Company, 1553–1608* (Cambridge, 1982), 165). See also Michael Shapiro, 'Boy Companies and Private Theatres', in *A New Companion to Renaissance Theatre*, eds. Arthur F. Kinney and Thomas Warren Hopper (New Jersey, 2017), 268–81, p. 273, where the termination of the Children of Paul's theatrical activities is dated to '1607 or 1608'.

who would be greater than the gods would have been a fitting compliment to the infant heir, and the marine theme of the play would likewise have been appropriate as a tribute to Charles Howard, the Lord High Admiral, who was present at the christening as one of Algernon's godfathers.[59]

If *The Aphrodysial* was originally indeed written for private performance in 1602, Percy might have been writing under the assumption of performance by amateur actors or hired professional actors. If composed with the latter possibility in mind, then some of the directions 'for Actors' might reflect elements of the play's presentation as he originally envisaged it in 1602. If Dodds's suggestion about performance at Essex House is correct, then it might be the case that Percy was keen to recommend his drama to Charles Howard, who was the patron of the Admiral's Men, and might have thereafter revised his directions to include more explicit instructions fitting for a professional theatre (such as the use of 'chambers'). The imagined audience of *The Aphrodysial* is 'Gentlemen', who are addressed in the prologue (ll. 77, 97, 103), and 'Gallants' and 'sirs' in the epilogue (ll. 3064, 3074). The fourth song is likewise sung by Hero for 'the gentlemen' (l. 2101 SD.3).[60] This repeated emphasis on a male audience sits awkwardly with the kind of mixed audience that one would expect at a private, court, or professional performance. Hillebrand raises and ultimately rejects the possibly of university performance at Oxford or at the Inns of Court, since the dates do not work for the former possibility, and there appears to be a lack of a firm connection between Percy and the Inns of Court.[61]

The stage directions in Percy's plays demonstrate that he must also have held some ambition for their being performed by a children's company.[62] The general title page in Huntington MS HM4 addresses a selection of classical quotations from sources including Virgil's *Aeneid*, Cicero, and Plautus 'vnto the children of the / Reuells and of Powles' (fol. 5ʳ). The directions aimed at child actors in *The Aphrodysial* make reference only to the Children of Paul's, and the play's musical directions, such as the use of the 'consort' after the end of each Act, together with the seven songs that are supplied for the play, are fitting for a children's company.[63] The alternative directions that are found in *The Aphrodysial* that distinguish between costuming and action 'for Powles' and 'for Actors' (also referred to as 'Some'), must have been added to the play sometime between its composition and the apparent cessation of the Children of Paul's performances after summer

---

[59] Dodds, 'The Aphrodysial', 237. Also see n. 36.

[60] An audience of gentlemen is also implied in ll. 1848–9 and 1856, and Harpax addresses the audience as 'my Masters' in ll. 892–3.

[61] Hillebrand, 'Elizabethan Amateur', 407.

[62] Wiggins's entry on *The Aphrodysial* also notes 'a hint at a court performance', although the evidence for this hint comes largely from the presence of a 'Prologue for the Court' in *The Faery Pastorall* (HM4, fol. 63ʳ). See Wiggins, *A Catalogue*, vol. 4, no. 1357, 421.

[63] Other dramatists such as John Lyly and John Marston also frequently included songs in plays written for performance by the children's companies (see e.g. Hentschell, *St Paul's Cathedral*, 144–82). On music in Percy's plays, see John H. Long, 'The Music in Percy's Play Manuscripts', *Renaissance Papers* (1980), 39–44.

1606. It is possible that Percy might have sent a copy of his first five plays to the choirmaster at Paul's, since HM4 contains the following note:

> A Note
> To the Master of children of Powles
> Memorandum that if any of the fiue and fore
> most of these Pastoralls and Comædyes conteyne\d/
> in this volume shall but ouereach in lengh (The
> children not to begin before Foure after Prayers
> And the gates of Powles shutting at Six) the Tyme of
> Supper, that then in tyme and place conuenient,
> you do let passe some of the Songs and make the
> consort the shorter, For I suppose these Plaies
> be somewhat too long for that Place – Howsoeue\<r\>
> on your own Experience and at your \best/ directi
> on be it. Fare well to you all.
> W. P. Esq. (fol. 191ʳ)

The 'Master' Percy was addressing was likely Edward Pearce, who became choirmaster in May 1599 and served in this role until 1612, or else Thomas Woodford or Edward Kirkham, who were variously involved in the business affairs of the company between 1603 and 1606.[64] By the time that Percy was copying and revising his plays in the 1640s, the Children of Paul's must have been a distant memory, so it appears that the note included in Huntington MS HM4 is likely a record of a much earlier note that Percy may or may not have sent along to Pearce with a copy of his plays. It is tempting to imagine that at least some of the plays, perhaps in adapted form, were indeed performed at Paul's prior to 1606–8, but there is no evidence to firm up such a possibility. Nevertheless, Percy's stage directions and note have been cited as evidence of performance at Paul's by some previous scholars, while others have argued against the possibly that the plays can reveal anything useful about early modern staging practices.[65] Matteo Pangallo has more recently discussed Percy as a 'play-writing playgoer' in a much wider context of such playwriters, offering a more nuanced understanding of what Percy's plays can reveal about a theatregoer's understanding of professional performance.[66] There is plenty of evidence throughout Percy's plays to suggest that he considered in detail how his drama *could* have been performed by both children and adult actors, even if no such performances were ever staged.

---

[64] See Shapiro, 'Boy Companies', 273, and Gair, *The Children of Paul's*, 184–5.

[65] See n. 5, also Charles William Wallace, *Children of the Chapel of Blackfriars, 1597–1603* (Nebraska, 1908), Felix Schelling, *Elizabethan Drama* (Boston and New York, 1908), and Gair, *The Children of St Paul's*. See also José A. Pérez Díez, 'The 'Playhouse at St Paul's: What We Know of the Theatre in the Almonry', in *Old St Paul's and Culture*, eds. Shanyn Altman and Jonathan Buckner (London, 2021), 197–220, pp. 201–2, 208.

[66] Pangallo, *Playwriting Playgoers*, 128–39.

The Aphrodysial's list of 'Properties' (fol. 120ᵛ) gives an account of how Percy envisaged the stage being set, calling for locality boards announcing the title of the play and the setting as 'Oceanus Pallace', together with a list of large properties, and the use of a trapdoor in the middle of the stage (presumably used by Leander to pull Hero 'underwater' at line 345). *The Aphrodysial* also calls for an extensive array of costumes, as well as large and small properties, including furniture, metalware, jewellery, fishing equipment, books, a staff, and a collection of trinkets representing Proteus's 'dreams'.[67] The play likewise calls for a considerable range of food items, including a variety of fish dishes, bread, and 'a showre of Rose-water and confits, as was acted / in Christ church in Oxford in Dido and Aeneas' (ll. 551–2).[68] Longer descriptions of setting and action are given in the main body of the text under the heading 'The Direction', while shorter directions calling for action that is concurrent with the dialogue are supplied in the left margin; their place in the main text is indicated by means of asterisks. Percy offers different costuming requirements for some characters, depending on whether they are to be played by boys ('for Powles') or men ('for Actors' or 'for some'), whereby Arion and Talus are indicated as 'Bearded' (ll. 36 and 37), but a marginal note clarifies 'Thus For / Actors; For / Powles with= / out' (l. 36 SD.1–4).

The alternative directions for child and adult players in *The Aphrodysial* reveal an understanding of, or at least a familiarity with, the different performance environments and companies that Percy had in mind when envisaging professional performance. In distinguishing between different courses of action for boys and adults, Percy shows what he thought would be most feasible or appropriate for those companies and their performance contexts. For instance, when Cytheræa arrives at the underwater court, the direction calls for 'Chambers ([or] noise supposd For Powles), For Actors' (l. 550). In other cases, directions allow for differences in the degree of complexity attached to particular sequences, as can be seen at the end of Act 3 Scene 9:

---

[67] The properties are itemized by Wiggins in *A Catalogue*, vol. 4, no. 1357, 420–1, although whereas Wiggins supposes that a whale prop large enough to contain Coüs is implicitly called for, the text suggests that the creature is not visible to the audience. See Dodds, 'Aphrodysial', 260 and Shmygol, 'Protean Objects', 218–19.

[68] Referring to William Gager's play, *Dido*, performed in Christ Church, Oxford, on 12 June 1583. The shower of comfits at this performance is recorded in Holinshed: 'the tempest wherein it hailed small confects, rained rosewater, and snew an artificiall kind of snow, all strange, maruellous, & abundant' (*The first and second volumes of Chronicles* (London, 1587), sig. 6O4ᵛ). On the possible use of comfits in another of Gager's plays, *Ulysses Redux* (performed at Christ Church in early 1592), see Percy's Epigram 188: 'An Audience catching at / comfits at a Playe' (HM4, fol. 206ᵛ).

	He playd, then a Daunce of Ceales and of Porpusyes, Then the Hall opening, was seene a|summer Noone day couch of Sand cullour, with a Sort of dreames Animate and Inani= mate of diuers cullours hanging by Inuisible or on Ash cullou\r/ Threds of Sylk ouer bol\s/ter of the Couch (it bolt and erect)
Ceston	being but bigge as Pawns of chesse. Or Proteus with sundry such in a Mawnd about his neck. Thus for some, The Rest to be omitted, sauing the daunce of the Ceales and Por= pusses. (ll. 1795–1803)

Pangallo posits that directions such as this show that 'Percy assumed that certain effects were within the capabilities of an adult company but either beyond the boys' means or, perhaps reflecting Percy's own experience as a spectator at Paul's, not in accord with what the boys' audience wanted'.[69] In this instance, it would seem that Percy insists on the dance to accompany Arion's music, but leaves the use of a discovery space optional for housing Proteus's collection of 'dreams', suggesting a much simpler staging option whereby the trinkets can be displayed as hanging around Proteus's neck.

As the note to the choirmaster of Paul's suggests, Percy's stage directions allow for non-authorial interventions that might serve to accommodate the length of his play to the restrictions of a particular performance environment. There are numerous instances in *The Aphrodysial*, as there are in all of Percy's plays, that offer alternative courses of action and invite the actor or producer to choose the most suitable option at their own discretion. This is evident, for example, in the direction that accompanies the seventh song:

> Here went furth the whole chorus in a shuffle as after a Play in a Lords howse, Hermes wafting them furth with his winged wand. Vulcan and Proteus after them. Or went furth in state all, as riding vpon Dolphins, Hermes wafting them about the stage with his wand. Whither the bet= ter you may chuse the better, all singing the 7th Song following. (ll. 3027–34)

The first option, which calls for action that Percy associates with private house performance, offers a less physically complex accompaniment to the song than does the alternative, which implies that dolphin props (probably akin to hobby-horses) would be required. Percy leaves it up to the players to 'chuse the better' based on their knowledge of what is most suitable. Another example of alternative means of staging can be found in the opening direction of Act 3 Scene 2:

---

[69] Pangallo, *Playwriting Playgoers*, 133. Pangallo mainly discusses the directions attached to *Mahomet and his Heaven*, which has a much more substantial difference in song and alternative action for adults and children at the beginning of Act 4. This is discussed in detail, together with a glossed, modernized version of the scene in question, in Teramura, 'William Percy's Logical Song', 180–93.

> Vulcan Brontes Steropes Pyracmon with ham
> mers and Aprones, Goldsmith Hammers, Els Iron-work
> Hammers for better Propertie of mouing their Armes, whi=
> ther the better you may chuse. The stithie supposd as Also
> their Hammers by mouing of their Armes onely, or Hamm=
> ers Reall, whither the better. The Longer Hammer I think. (ll. 1194–9)

Pangallo describes these sorts of permissive directions as part of Percy's invitation for actors to make a performance choice based on their experience of what would work best 'while at the same time attempting to impose some degree of control over that staging'.[70] In the aforementioned example, Percy offers a range of possibilities that take into account the presence or absence of both large and small stage props, inviting the performers to make their best judgement, but ending the direction with an indication of his own preference. These long and detailed directions are by no means evidence that the play was ever performed, but they certainly reveal that Percy thought at length about how different troupes of professional players might put his material into action within the given restrictions and limitations of their playing venues.

The quoted stage directions offer alternative staging possibilities, but they do so by expressing the action in the past tense while in fact looking forward to future performance. At other times, as with the copious shorter directions that accompany Vulcan's attempts to woo Humida (ll. 1677–96) and Arida (ll. 1890–1912), both present tense and past tense are used. Generally, there appears to be a preference for the past tense in *The Aphrodysial*, and early commentators who remarked on Percy's plays took this as a sign that they had, in fact, been performed. Chambers certainly assumed this to be the case, but Hillebrand discounted this possibility, suggesting instead that Percy might have adopted the use of the past tense for directions from printed accounts of masque texts, which would account for the fact that some of Percy's past tense directions also look to future performance.[71] Pangallo cites a similar practice of past tense direction in other amateur drama, which demonstrates that Percy was not alone in his puzzling choice of tense.[72]

Percy's exact motivations for copying out the plays and poems written mostly in his youth remain unclear. His holographs were copied out and revised at a time when professional performance was an unlikely possibil-

---

[70] Pangallo, *Playwriting Playgoers*, 128. Pangallo's incisive consideration of Percy's stage directions focuses mainly on *Mahomet and his Heaven*, approaching such seemingly idiosyncratic features as alternative, permissive, and conditional directions in the context of both amateur and professional drama. On the last point, he notes that conditional phrasing in directions can be found in plays written by professional dramatists and published 'in or around 1590, making it possible that Percy encountered this style by reading some of these plays' (p. 132).

[71] Chambers, *The Elizabethan Stage*, vol. 3, 197; 464–5. Hillebrand, 'Elizabethan Amateur', 406–7.

[72] Pangallo, *Playwriting Playgoers*, 135, n. 127.

ity on account of the ban on playing and the dissolution of the children's companies, and Dimmock suggests that the revisions carried out on *Mahomet and His Heaven* move that play toward a more 'readerly' model.[73] The revisions and stage directions in *The Aphrodysial* do not appear to suggest a concern with moving towards a 'readerly' text in this way. Whatever were Percy's motivations or intentions in his late copying and subsequent revision of his plays, the preoccupations with staging and stage business found in *The Aphrodysial* certainly 'provide further insight into the kind of deep, though inflected, understanding of the professional industry that an attentive audience member might develop'.[74]

Editorial Conventions

In this semi-diplomatic edition the following conventions have been observed. Irregular spacing between letters and punctuation has been silently regularized, and is noted only in extreme cases. Variations in size of text have been preserved, with some degree of regularization. In the manuscript there is a general tendency to use a larger hand for text such as speech prefixes (SPs) and headings, and a smaller hand for marginal stage directions (SDs), although there is sometimes variation in sizing within these general conventions (e.g. some SP text is larger than the norm). In this edition, marginal SD text is consistently given in a smaller size than the main text to reflect the general tendency for smaller script for SDs in the manuscript. Other marginal text, such as the word 'dilue' and words intended to be added in place of deleted material are represented in the same size as the main text. A larger size of font is used throughout for SPs, headings, musical directions supplied in the main body of the text, act and scene divisions, first words of certain speeches, and reported inscriptions, in keeping with the conventions generally adopted in the manuscript. Deletions are indicated by square brackets: [Loue-rolle], and the exact means by which Percy marks text for deletion is described in the notes (sometimes text is underlined for deletion and preceded by a high ink point, other times it is marked for deletion with vertical strokes). Angle brackets enclose material which is illegible (e.g. because of paper damage or blotting); stops indicate illegible characters <.>, where each illegible letter is represented by a stop. Interlineations of letters, words, and full lines are enclosed within slashes \ /; two sets of slashes \\ // are used to signal an interlined addition to an interlineation (the only example of this occurs on l. 1820). Whole line interlineations are counted in the line count. In the manuscript some interlineations are inserted above carets; others are not. Where carets are used, they are shown in the text at the point where the interlineation needs to be inserted. This does not always reflect the actual position of the caret in the manuscript; where the

---

[73] Dimmock, ed., *Mahomet and His Heaven*, 49, 52.
[74] Pangallo, *Playwriting Playgoers*, 128.

original position is different it is recorded in the notes. In some cases where carets are used in the MS they are bracketed by stops or have a stop on one side; such stops are reproduced in the text in the position in which they appear. Asterisks used in the MS are also reproduced in the text, although their size has been regularized throughout. Percy uses a punctuation symbol like a question mark for both questions and exclamations. This punctuation mark does not consistently have a curve at the top in either form of usage; a standard *?* has been used in the text to represent this symbol. Sometimes this mark has a comma instead of a point; such instances are described in the textual notes.

The position of text in the left margin is reproduced when it is a distinct addition (such as an SD or a supplementary description, as in the 'Names of the Persons'). When marginal text in the manuscript is intended as a correction to replace a deleted word or words, it is incorporated into the text following the deleted material and its original position is noted. Foliation is not authorial; it follows the foliation added to HM4 by a later hand and is placed in the right-hand margin in this edition. Original lineation has been preserved as far as possible, saving several instances where the insertion of a marginal correction has shifted the original lineation, such instances are recorded in the notes (e.g. see l. 2096, and ll. 2581–2 and notes). Where the constraints of this edition's format have necessitated a turned-over line due to lack of sufficient space, the turned-over text is aligned left and indented (unlike Percy's turned lines, which hang below the right end of the line in question). Percy's copious marginal stage directions frequently present problems for lineation, since multiple lines of marginal text are often cramped in next to one line of main text, or else long marginal SDs stretch into otherwise vacant space on the page, and thus make it difficult to lineate consistently. For that reason, this edition does not include marginal text in the through line count. Instead, where lines of SD and other marginal text are referred to in the textual notes or collation notes in Appendix 2, the SD is keyed to the main line of text at which the marginal text begins (or, if marginal text appears in between lines, it is keyed to the preceding line of main text). Decimals are then used to refer to specific lines of marginal annotations or multi-line SDs (e.g. see ll. 32, 266, 345, 1120, 1208, and notes).

SPs and act and scene divisions are reproduced, as far as possible, as they appear in the manuscript, though spacing between scenes and acts has been regularized. Line breaks have been inserted between acts and scenes. Line breaks have been retained where significant blank space is left in the manuscript (i.e. in some songs, and on some pasted slips). Each line of text, including deleted lines, inserted lines, and act and scene divisions, is numbered separately and the lines are numbered continuously from the first line of the play's title at the top of fol. 120^r. Original spelling, punctuation, and contraction signs have been retained (saving for the 'q' brevigraph described on p. xxxviii). Abbreviations and capitalization have also been preserved, although determining whether letters are capitalized in words in initial position has, in many cases, been a matter of editorial judgement, as the author's majuscule and miniscule forms of characters such as *c, o, k, s, u, v, w*, and *y*, are often difficult to distinguish. Where one of these letters appears at the beginning of a verse line, it is represented as a majuscule in the text, since other letters are consistently capitalized at the beginnings of lines, unless it is clearly written as a miniscule. A detailed account of Percy's hand and the difficulties that some letterforms present is outlined under 'Hand', and imperfect letterforms are only noted where they present potential ambiguity in meaning or where they concern a letterform that generally appears in a clear form elsewhere in the text, or if the nature of the imperfection differs from the general tendencies outlined under 'Hand'.

Apostrophes are reproduced here, although their occasional positioning above, rather than between, letters is not shown, but noted. There are variations in Percy's handling of compound words, since his tendency to form each letter separately makes it difficult in many cases to distinguish whether a space appears between two parts of a compound word, such as *everything*, *anything*, *nothing*, and *today*, and the various '-self' compounds (e.g. *myself*). Where such compound words are taken by the editor to be represented as separate words in the manuscript they are shown as separate in this edition.

The transcription preserves *u* for medial *v*; likewise *v* for initial *u*, and *i* for *j*, in majuscule and miniscule forms. Superscript letters are represented in superscript form. Percy rarely uses contraction symbols or brevigraphs, but a 'q' brevigraph appears six times in the epigraph on fol. 120ʳ, where the 'q' is followed by a wavy or curved downward stroke that resembles a low comma to indicate a 'que' contraction. In the text this brevigraph is represented by 'q' in the following words: *camposq* (l. 6), *Lucentempq* and *Titaniaq* (l. 7), *totamq* (l. 8), *Pecudumq* and *vitæq* (l. 10). Tildes, which occur only twice in *The Aphrodysial*, are represented by a small line over the letter immediately before the omitted letter(s), even when this is not the actual position of the tilde in the manuscript; where their actual position is different, the exact position is described in a note. Ligature *æ* has been retained. Examples of overwriting and alterations to individual characters and words, and corrections made in a different coloured ink, are recorded in the notes.

The
Aphrodysial
or
Sea — Feast 1602.
A Marinall.

Principio cœlum terras camposq, liquentes
Lucentemq, globum Lunæ Titaniaq, Astra
Spiritus intus alit, totamq, infusa per artus
Mens agitat Molem et magno se corpore miscet
Inde hominum Pecudumq, genus, vitæq, volantum
Et quæ marmoreo fert monstra sub æquore Pontus. *Virg.*
Æneid.

The Names of the persons.

Harpax alias Cupid, Prologus et Apologus, A Fisherman

Cytherea.

Oceanus A graue old man with crowne of gold and brayded haire, crowne white and blew enamell'd. And long white Beard, also.

Nereus with blewe Bearde and blewe peruke.

Proteus with coate of diuers cullours and sundry shapes of things and creatures.

Vulcan Apparrelld lyke a Lord, Apron and Hammer with all, knit scull-cap called a Night-cap, chuff and oldish. His ordinary suite in this Marinall gold lace whitelye.

Aglaia wife vnto Vulcan, And one of the three Graces.

Euphrosyne } The Two other of the Graces.
Thalia } Jocular.

Glauce A lusty Nymphe of the sea, Nereus daughter, Goddesse lyke and Taller then Hero. A Sunburnt Lady.

Thetis yet a virgin.

Humida A Nymphe of the sea } Proteus daughters
Arida A Nymphe of the dry land } the one in sealow cullour, the other in sand cullour sattin

Hero with golden Seal about her neck, venus prints.

Arion otherwise Jupiter in his youthfull dayes Bearded

Tasus otherwise Neptune in his youthfull dayes, Bearded

Leander with long golden haire lyke Absolon, loose to the Elbowes.

Rudens
Ponticus } Fishermen.
Gripus

Brontes
Steropes } Cyclops and Smiths vnto Vulcan.
Pyracmon

A Nymphe of the sea.

PLATE I: HUNTINGTON MS HM4, FOL. 120R

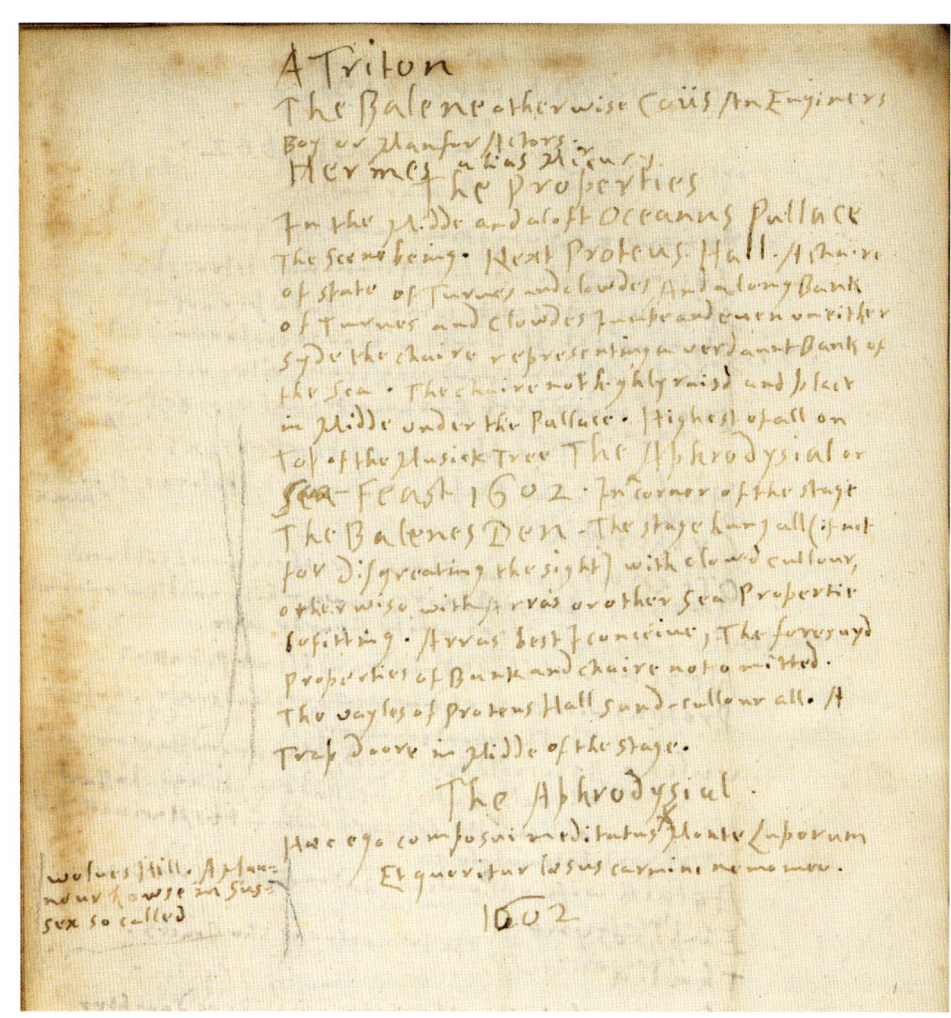

A Triton
The Baleene otherwise Caüs An Enginers
Boy or Manser Actors.
Hermes alias Mercury.
The Properties
In the middle and aloft Oceanus Pallace
The scene being. Next Proteus Hall. A chaire
of state of Turves and clowdes And along Bank
of Turves and clowdes from hand euen on either
syde the chaire representing a verdant Bank of
the Sea. The chaire not highly raisd and ½ feet
in Middle under the Pallace. Highest of all on
top of the Musick Tree. The Aphrodysial or
Sea-Feast 1602. In corner of the stage
The Baleenes Den. The stage hung all (if not
for disgreeating the sight) with cloud cullour,
otherwise withstr vas or other Sea Properties
befitting. Arras best I conceive, The foresayd
Properties of Bank and chaire not omitted.
The sayles of Proteus Hall sand-cullour all. A
Trap doore in Middle of the stage.

 The Aphrodysial.

Hæc ego composui meditatus pondere laborum
Et queritur lusus carmine mæsto meo.

 1602

wolues Hille, A Man-
ner or howse in Sus-
sex so called

Ar. do beseech you
     saye.
                The Second Song
                Two women having Husbands of contrary com-
                plexions.
                        1
Both   Ladyes, resolve us this one doubt
          which both wee longe about,
          whither the Twoyst or the Drye,
          Do better with yow agree.
                        2
1.   The woman that chuseth the Moyst
          May not thinke of other foist.
2.   The Drye, it is not any Lye,
          will nurse us no Jelouzie.
                        3
1.   To Moyst, Do very well know
          How er do wee say o ho.
2.   vnto the Drye, as I do wisse
          wee say, till soone keepe your kisse.
                        4
1.   How should wee by the Moyst learne
          whither wee sitt little carne
2.   The Drye will say, to us, againe
          Trye againe, there is no paine
                        5
1.   My Goodman, is she but a sound
          I breech him for it sound.
2.   My husband, if he wanton Drye
          I recure him by Cookerye.
restore   6
1.   The Moyst will refresh us too Drye
          And poope us all the carrye.
2.   The Drye will hate us no chaffee
too   And save us much Hurse-money.
                        7
Both   Now Ladyes, resolve us our doubt
          which wee both to you put out
          whither the Twoyst or the Drye
          Be, to yow, a better for —
Hum.   Sirrha shalt see the Foole, rightly anow, dressed in his col-
          lours, all, yfaith. But come away now, and follow mee, to come
          to dinner.
Ar.   I follow you.
                Act 2 Scen 7.
                Oceanus Leander in Godlyke attyre.

PLATE 3: HUNTINGTON MS HM4, FOL. 131R

Silue Modicum vnto your ese &c. Now notwithstanding, one
Thing most Impatiently doth affright mee. I dreamt
this last night, I lay with Humida and she lept mee. Dear
ye Foole, she did it according her complexion, therefo=
re she is to be Pardoned. And yet my Leg hath this once in=
to some hope of her, omnia munda mundis, say our
Sacrifiques, for so peremptory is the conceite of a trew
Puritaine so nice, they say, of himself, lightly he findeth not
any one thing to be in him amisse: what though this
the now, the stiffer joint of mee, which vnderhand
now I do Imagine to my self, be crookt as is a sickle
lykwise, yet most vpon and Mechanicall Demonstra=
tions (such as is that of my Lady Humid[it]y) will thir
perfecter be Resolved by a crookeder deuice, then
by that of a straite, I a trewe Theoricke do also know.
Iupiter thou breakest my Leg once I am sure, yet that
thy sonne, that he, that the trew & soare setter of
Olympus, the lord Phoebus Apollo, shall not now so soo=
ne set it straite into his former Ioint againe
therefore, for as long as I may but walke, with such
earthly paragons on shoare, I will neuer after pur=
le to Heauen more. Call in thy conceited affection yne
Ican, for me thinkes thou fallest out of that the
loue of Humida into this the loue of thy Leg, where=
fore could wish, thou wouldest but ease him vntill so=
one, so come now to the platter, And here is the Mat=
ter, for here comes Humida.

Harp.	upon her, noble Sir.
Hum	Dost flye mee now thou hast my Love?
vul.	I am notichuse, thou smellest drye, as is the Earth, my gentlr.
He stoupeth backe	Heigh ☓
the followes	Harp. I haue not lightly seene Hiue thaw downe so Rostif. ☓
or submitely	Hum. I will my selfe eauiron thee.
	vul. Get further from off mee, for Gods sake, Heigh ☓
He setts a syde it	Hum) Come mixe thyne armes with myne.
so he may.	
	vul. Fast as I may. But
He stoops	Hum. Be these thy Protestations? whot?
	vul. whoope ☓
He stoops	Hum. And shall I escape this seruice at thy hand?
	vul. No, Humida, No; Heigh
He setts backe	Hum Come on thy wayes and follow mee.
	vul. Lord, Lord, Lord
He stoops)	Hum. Come on, I say.
	vul. I come, I come, I come to thee. Ho.
He stoops	Hum I see thou hast deluded mee. Therefore thus I begin unto
& lowe.	thee. villaine.
Harp.	Iumpe.
Hum.	Sowe mee not. ☓
She start backe	vul) Busse, Busse a Busse.
or flownd. He	Hum) Nay nay I'ndeed mee not.
followed	vul. O yes.
& flue	Hum. wast oft, I say.
vul.	Nay nay.
Hum.	Get thee hence.
vul.	No no, my wench.
Hum.	kisse my Tayle, you foole.
vul.	Ho ho, Regard my Toole.
Hum	out out, you Rogue.
vul	oh ho, my Fub.
Hum:	Hadst none, in this circumference? know, say,
	To play upon but mee a water Nymphe?
	But euen a daughter of wise Proteus?
	That sayes that Thetis shall haue a Sonne greater
	Then be the Gods of high olympus all?
	I vowe, from euery vain, thou shalt repent it.
	Cytherea wonder of th'uniuers
	Is hither come to keepe her Festiuall,
	where, before her, I shall so blazon thee.
Harp.	In a Muttley I beseech you, lady
Hum.	That the whole court shall wonder at the Fact,
	Till when I doe leaue thee to chewe on this
	The Foulest Rascall that euer I mett with. (Harp)
vul.	And misse to prouide the cloake-bag for him.
	Hei mihi.
Harp.	why bleede you, my Lord?

PLATE 5: HUNTINGTON MS HM4, FOL. 138R

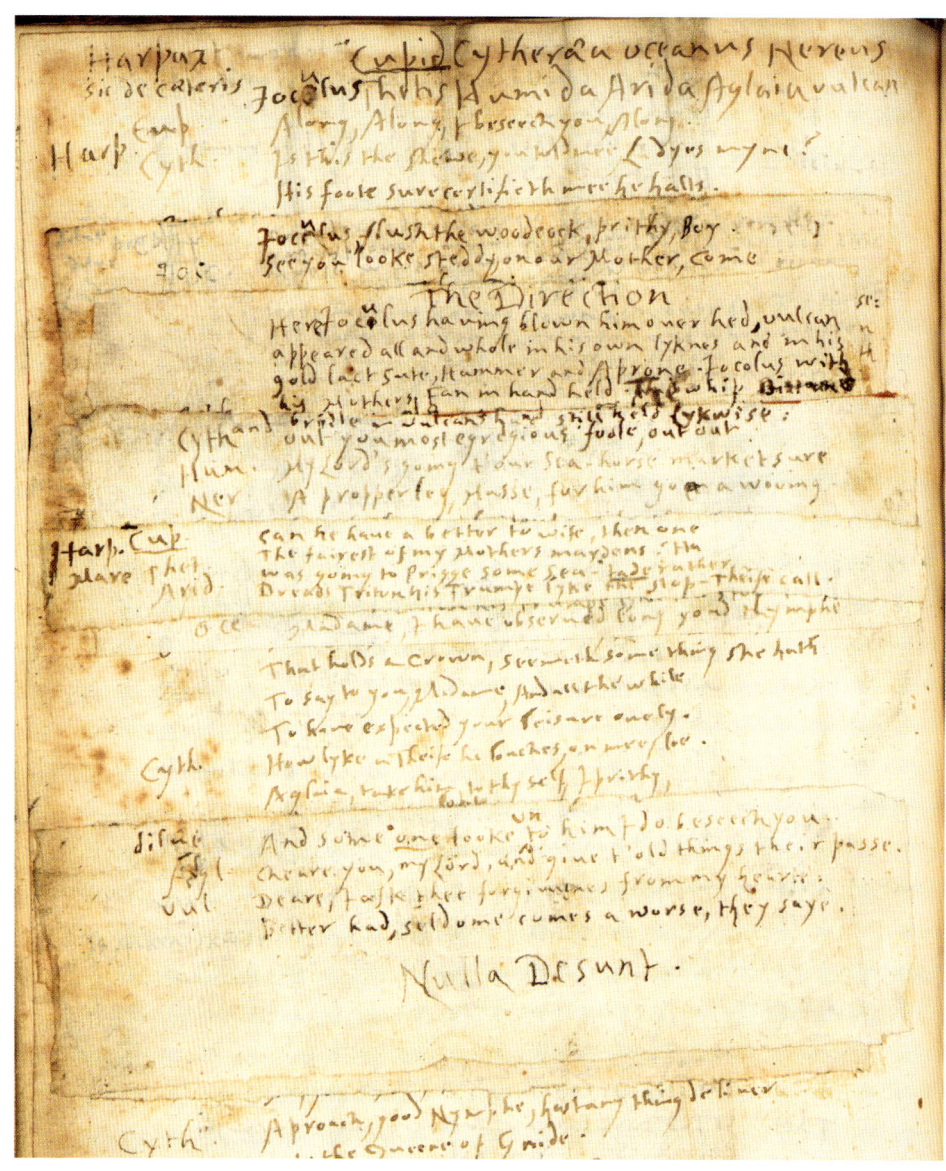

PLATE 6: HUNTINGTON MS HM4, DETAIL OF FOL. 146V

[Fol. 120ʳ]

The
Aphrodysial
or
Sea-Feast 1602.
A Marinall.

Principio cælum, terras, camposq, liquentes
Lucentemq, globum Lunæ Titaniaq, Astra
Spiritus intus alit, totamq, infusa per artus
Mens agitat Molem et magno se corpore miscet
Inde hominum Pecudumq, genus, vitæq, volant<u>m
Et quæ marmoreo fert monstra sub æquore Pontus. Virg
                                          Ae. 6.

    The Names of the Persons.

Harpax alias Cupid prologus et Apologus, A Fisher
Cytheræa.   (man
Oceanus A graue old man with crown of gold and brayded
      haire, Crown white and blew enameld And long white
      Bearde also.
Nereus with blewe Bearde and blewe Peruke.
Proteus with coate of diuers cullours and sundry shapes
      of Things and creatures.
Vulcan Apparreld lyke a Lord, Aprone and Hammer with
      all, knit scull-cap called a Night-cap, chuff and
      oldish. His ordinary suite in this Marinall, Gold
      lace wholelye.
Aglaia wife vnt\o/ Vulcan, And one of the Three Graces.
Euphrosyne } The Two other of the Graces.
Thalia   Ioculus

---

7 *Titaniaq*] ²*a* possibly altered   9 *Molem*] otiose stroke follows *o*   10 *volant<u>m*] <u> altered from illegible letter   15 *(man*] implicitly continues previous line   26 *vnt\o/*] imperfect altered *o* written above *t* in darker ink   28 *Ioculus*] possibly later addition; fainter and larger

Glauce A Lusty Nymphe of the Sea, Nereus daughter, Goddesse lyke and Taller then Hero. A Sunbur=nt Lady.   30

Thetis yet a virgin.

Humida A Nymphe of the Sea   } Proteus daughters the one in [sea blew
Arida A Nymphe of the drye Land   } the other in sand cul\l/our satten

Hero with golden Scalop about her neck, Venus Preist.

Arion otherwise Iupiter in his youthfull days* Bearded

Talus otherwise Neptune in his youthfull dayes,* Bearded

Leander with long golden haire lyke Absolon, loose to the Elbowes.

Rudens
Ponticus   } Fishermen.   40
Gripus

Brontes
Steropes   } cyclops and Smiths vnto Vulcan.
Pyracmon

A Nymphe of the Sea.

[FOL. 120ᵛ]

A Triton

The Balene otherwise Coüs An Enginers Boy or Man for Actors.

\Hermes alias Me\r/cury./   50

Marginal notes:
- cloth of syl=uer blewe. or clowde cull=our, the Best.
- Thus For Actors; For Powles with=out.

33 SD.1 *cloth*] c retraced SD.2 *sea blew*] underlined for deletion; preceded by high ink point SD.3 *other*] o possibly altered; t possibly written over ?r SD.4 *cul\l/our*] ²l written above o   35 *Scalop*] c altered   50 *Me\r/cury*] c possibly altered

　　　　　The Properties
In the Midde and aloft Oceanus Pallace
The Scene being. Next Proteus Hall. A chaire
of state of Turues and clowdes, And a long Bank
of Turues and Clowdes Iumpe and euen on either
Syde the chaire representing a verdaunt Bank of
the Sea. The chaire not highly raisd and plact
in Midde vnder the Pallace. Highest of all on
Top of the Musick Tree The Aphrodysial or
Sea-Feast 1602. In \a/ corner of the stage   60
The Balenes Den. The stage hung all (if not
for disgreating the sight) with clowd cullour,
otherwise with Arras or other Sea Propertie
befitting. Arras best I conceiue, The foresayd
Properties of Bank and chaire not omitted.
The vayles of Proteus Hall Sand-cullour all. A
Trap doore in Midde of the Stage.
　　　　　The Aphrodysial.
Hæc ego composui meditatus */ Monte Luporum
　　Et queritur læsus carmini nemo meo.   70

_{Wolues Hill. A Mannour howse in Sussex so called}

---

60 *Sea-Feast*] *Sea* written in larger letters over *sea*　　63 *otherwise*] *t* altered from *r*　　69 SD.1 *Hill*.] ink mark under stop possibly bottom point of colon　　70 *carmini*] ²*i* lacking point

1602

[Fol. 121ʳ]

The
Aphrodysial
or
Sea-Feast 1602.

Harpax The Prologue after second sounding.
Gentlemen, Albeit it hath so happend ˄\that/ I am descen=
ded to you, loe, from court of King Saturnus in Forme of
a Fisherman, notwithstanding, in this place, wherein you be
now, you must apprehend mee a God, That God I assure you   80
that   maketh the flintiest Heartes among you now and then to re=
solue. But let that passe, And listen all to cause of my comm=
ing from aboue, From King Saturnus his Court you must conceiue. Once eury yeare be held vnder these Seas, in Court of
King Oceanus, in honour of my Lady and Mother Cytheræa, Aphro
dysialls. This is the day, and here this day, Cytheræa intendeth
to dine. Vulcan is sent before from aboue, by Aglaia, one
of Cytheræa her Graces, and his new bedded spowse (From
King Saturnus his Court you must suppose) to work Platters
and standing Bolles against the Feast. I her cosen Cupid   90
am sent after him, As now you see mee, in lyknesse of
one Harpax a Fisherman to obserue his Haunt. This is
the Summe of that I know, And this now you all know.
Other Accidents, of which these be ˄\but/ Scruples, the Sequell of
our Marinall shall declare them all vnto you. Onely our
desire is, as euer, hencefurth, you ˄\would/ but obteyne your
Long-wisht Mistrisses, Gentlemen, each of you would
but vouchsafe accept of a Fresh and fragrant ghirlond, of
water Cressies, distributed to him on his browe, to sitt qui=
et the whiles, and with [o]vs to concelebrate our Aphrody=   100
siall in same manner and order. This is the summe of
my Argument vnto you. Loue and Cytheræa both, be at
your seruice, Gentlemen.

Here they sounded the Third

71 *1602*] 6 altered   77 ˄*that*/] *a* altered; caret imperfect   78 *from*] m altered   80 *assure*]
r altered; word smudged by blotting   81 *that*] added in darker ink to left of line   92 *Haunt.*
This] headstroke of *T* obscures stop   96 ˄*would*/ *but*] *would* interlined in darker ink; caret below *b*
of *but*   100 *vs*] written over *our*; *o* deleted with vertical stroke

10

Act 1 Scen 1.
The Direction.

The Speakers and Mutes were Oceanus, Nereus, Triton,
Arion, Talus, Glauce. Humida, Arida, Thetis, Leander[s]
naked and bound about the Priuities with blewe weedes,
And led by the arme by Glauce, Bound in a Scarfe of Sea   110
blewe. Vulcan, Proteus. Triton sitting by Oceanus and
writ[ti]ing in a Toale Booke on his thigh, Oceanus now
sitting in the chaire of state. They came in suddenly
(as it were) without Pompe or order, Oceanus lead=
ing the way, The rest placing them, on the Bank on
either syde of him. Arion his Speech is translated,

[FOL. 121ᵛ]

worde for worde, out of the first weeke and fifth
day of Seigneur du Bartas. Talus his felloWe straye.

        Oceanus Arion Talus. Arion with an
        Orpharian, Talus with a large Paire of Compas=   120
        ses of copper. **Triton Glauce Nereus.**

Oce. Gentlemen, since seasd you be both our strayes
      Now relate us from point to point, The
      Whole Processe of your Aduentrous Lucks,
      And first the Cytharæde begin to saye.
Ar.   Now had I gold and honour in content
      That I had purchasd by my Instrument,
      When in a Coue'tous Bark, a greedy Traitresse
      I did embark mee to sup the Aire of Greece.
      Straite, loe, the shoare went back, Tarentum steeple   130
      Forsooke our Sight, And from each diuers People
      Nothing was seene but waue and Aire, while on
      The liquid Sea the Pilot had but one
      The pointing Compasse to his Guide, when soone,

---

108 *Leander*[*s*]] *s* deleted with vertical stroke   110 *And*] *A* smudged   112 *writ*[*ti*]*ing*] ²*t* blotted, ²*i* deleted with vertical stroke; *n* possibly retraced and overlaps slightly with previous letter   114 *were)*] bracket extends down to the bottom of page   115 *rest placing*] headstroke of *t* extends across first two letters of following word; *c* possibly altered from *r*   116 *his*] *h* retraced   117 *fifth*] *ft* altered   120 *Compas*=] strokes in = are short, lower stroke very faint   122 *Gentlemen*] ³altered; *n* imperfect, looks like *m*   *both*] otiose stroke under *o*   127 *That*] *h* altered   129 *to*] *t* written over *s*   *Greece.*] stop in darker ink, possibly added   130 *shoare*] *o* possibly altered from *a*   *steeple*] ³*e* possibly altered   132 *while*] *w* altered   133 *but*] *b* possibly altered   134 *his*] *h* possibly altered

The Mariners, who oft tyme hatch more Treason
Then doe the waues, then does the wandring wind,
Stripped my coate, vndid my cloake resignd,
Riffeld hie and lowe mee to finde my Treasure
That I had wun by cunning of my measure, .
Haling mee, which had, vnto the chaine there by   140
To fling mee into water. Sonnes, quod I,
With weep[p]ing eye, that haue the Sea your Syre,
That of the Raging waues do tame the Ire,
That now the Moyst and \now/ the Drye inhabite,
My Suppliaunt Voice, with wordes intrupt, I [scope not,] ope not
\For this small gold I haue to saue I scope not/
My cheifest Threasure sisting in my Song,
Wherewith I cherish the Maydes of Helicon,
With conquering foote suppressing humaine Pelf,
But to your humaine selues pray for my self,   150
Onely you would not cast your murdring Armes
On one, whom Ioue and Gods hugge in their armes.
(So may the faire witches of Phare Messine
Stop, in fauour of you, their Mouthes diuine,
So may the Trumpe of Triton appease the wrath
That Iust Neptune 'gainst you præpared hath)
Alas, though I may not obteyne sayd grace
(As already I reade it in your Face)
Yet suffer I marry my funrall finger
Vnto the number of my vocall singer,   160
That Troopes of Marine dietyes at least
Admiring the sweetnes of the Feast
A shoare may bring my corps with teare
And in a heape of oaze enterre it there.

[FOL. 122ʳ]

135 *tyme*] smudged headstroke on *t*; gap between *ty* and *me*   139 *measure,*] otiose point under ²*e*; stop otiose, possibly in different ink   141 *water*] *w* retraced   142 *weep[p]ing*] ²*p* deleted by vertical stroke in darker ink   145 *scope not,*] underlined for deletion; preceded by high ink point   *ope not*] added in left margin to replace [*scope not*]   148 *Wherewith*] ²*e* imperfect   149 *conquering*] *c* retraced and preceded by otiose ink mark   151 *Armes*] *A* written over *a*   156 *hath)*] bracket extends downward through next line   158 *Face)* bracket extends downward through next line   159 *suffer*] '*f* lacking cross-stroke   *marry*] otiose stroke over ¹*r*   *finger*] *f* written over *s*, possible false start for *singer* which appears at the end of the following line   162 *sweetnes*] ²*e* altered

Strike vp, Arion, quoth the felon crewe
Of saylours then, Strike vp and giue vs now
Gold and Mirth in one. Beating then, them fore,
These Twynd wyres with my harmonius foure
The waues so charmed with my Harmony
The Congers lined, in one companie, 170
With Lampreys crookt, Mullet and Shark
Left off their Naturall hatreds to heark,
The Lobster too, vpon the Back of Teth',
The Theif Pourcountrill did, with loue, entreate,
When amid the Troopes of thousand Fishes
That waite vpon the call of Proteus whisses,
A Dolphin, Better, then the Rest, Recording
Her motion, to the Harmony, according,
Coasting the Bark with flowing flowe and slack
Summoneth mee now to [heape] leape vpon her Back. 180
Thrice did they thrust mee onto Sea, Thrice did I
Giue back, Thrice, againe, they on thrust mee,
And thrice I did recoyle, when in the end
Not hable to forebeare what they intend
I got vpon the Misers back, who now
Seemeth rather to flye then swim, I vowe,
The charge she had on her made so light,
The least Flat she feares, the least Shelf, I weete,
Not for her self but charge, And with Flight sport
Seeketh to bring her Phæbus to his Port, 190
The while thus to my deare Monture I,
In Pickt Passages, pay my my fare Perdy.
O Mighty Lord[s] of Sea that whilom hast,
To drench this world, made thousand seas one wast,
Præseruing but one spotles Paire from Crime,
To celebrate thy name in|after Tyme,
Alas cast eye on him that hath one Sight
Of body drencht in Sea, My horse, o Spright,

165 *Strike*] S retraced   167 *in*] otiose second point over *i*; *n* retraced   *them*] *m* imperfect   180 *to*] three dots in triangle formation above *o*   *heape*] underlined for deletion, curved stroke through *h*   *leape*] added in left margin to replace [*heape*]   191 *Monture*] *o* imperfect, looks like stop   193 *Lord*[*s*]] *s* marked for deletion with a vertical stroke   196 *in*|*after*] vertical rule separates words   198 *horse,*] *s* altered; comma below *e*   *Spright,*] comma obscured by ascender of *d* in *Guide* on the line below

   And ship without a guide be thou their Guide,
   If conquerour I be of Wind and Tyde,   200
   Or that on Græcian shoare my Foote I print,
   With sollume vowe my Iu'ry Harpe I stint,
   My hearte, my hand, my voice vnto thy lore.
   The Spuming Sea now straite his rage forbore,
   Heauens blackt before from Browe wipt off his teares,
   And winds changd sudden their Mouths into eares.
   The Courser discouring this court at lengh,
   (Seemeth intend) now blamd her hasty strengh,
   And longer to enioy this Harmonye
   Wisht ˄\yet/ hundreth mile of the Hostlerye,   210
   Yet præferring the health of ˄\her/ deare Lord

               [Fol. 122ᵛ]

   Before of his sweet tunes the rare Accord
   She wafts him safe to you, And which I
   Prise, Life I gaue her that gaue life to mee.
Oce. Arion, a strange mishap thou hast scaped,
   Which with satisfactory vowes needes must
   Be appaid the Gods, But of that anone
   Whiles th'opportunity shall serue its turne.
   But now th'Inginer lay furth his storye.
Tal. Before I fell to this Aduersity   220
   I liued in the Isle of Creete, and was
   A famous Enginer, Vulcan my Father,
   And name is Talus. No sooner had I wun
   My fifteene yeare of Age, when, loe, my Syre
   Did bind mee Prentice to a Man of Creete
   Hight Dædale, vnder whom I did so profitt,
   I equalld not, but more excelld him farr,
   And found the sawe and needfull compasses;
   He bore mee grudge, withall did sweare reuenge,
   When now the Minotaure now borne, begot 230
   In incest of a Bull, he did Impeach mee
   T'haue holpe Pasiphae t'her lust by Iin,

---

201 *print*] *p* and *in* possibly altered 202 *Iu'ry*] apostrophe over *r* 211 *health*] *t* altered 212 *of his*] *f* written over *t*; no gap between words *his*] *is* possibly written over *e* *Accord*] '*c* altered 216 *vowes*] *v* formed from *w* 218 *turne.*] stop formed from two dots and a short stroke 219 *storye*] *s* possibly altered 224 *loe,*] *e* written over otiose comma *Syre*] *y* altered from *u* 226 *whom*] *h* has extra downward stroke on limb 228 *sawe*] *w* possibly altered

        The King was mou'd, straite sent him with a Band
        To apprehend mee sure, The Fight was long,
        And many were the wounds, till in the end,
        By Fortune of the warr, the Hold was tayne,
        Goods sackt, And I hurld headlong into Sea.
        What of the rest became I may not saye,
        Mee Pallas wound in armes as down I fell,
        So brought mee safe, this morne, here where you dwell.   240

Oce. The sad stories of your strange Aduentures
        Haue so bewitcht the soule of Oceanus,
        That willing with his hearte, He could remit
        Your bodyes to the world, But so it is,
        No liuing soule salutes these Regions
        But payes an vsuall Toale before it parts
        (Your's an hundreth crowns a peice, Sirrha, set
        Them down an hundreth Crownes a peice) And it
        Once payd you may, when please returne to shoure,
        Till when, being held th'Aphrodysiall   250
        This day within our court, whither at Noone
        Cytheræa descends with her white Trayne
        To Iudge the Pleas of the Gods and Mortalls eake,
        I giue you leaue, your liberties excepted,
        To Court and Reuell where your selues you please.
        Leander, loe, whom for his golden haire,
        The stout daughter of Dore and Nereus

[FOL. 123ʳ]

        Glauce rauisht this morne, he shall not back,
        But waite, Immortally, vpon our Cup,
        While she, the whiles, holds th'Ambrosia t'us,   260
        And so, you Captiues, see you hencefurth tell
        Oceanus, in these Seas, vsd you well.

Ar.   Wee can no other, for he is honourable.
Oce. Triton, Lets see. Hast set them down their Toale.
Trit. Fast as Pen may walk, my Lord (Oce) There, Foole, there*

Pointing him to a higher blank

233 *Band*] *d* altered   237 *hurld*] *u* possibly altered   238 *became*] gap between *be* and *came*
239 *wound*] *n* possibly altered   *armes*] *s* possibly altered   242 *so*] *s* possibly altered   243 *remit*]
e imperfect   249 *Once*] *c* altered from *e*   250 *held*] *e* altered, possibly from *o*   255 *Reuell*]
'*e* possibly altered   257 *Nereus*] '*e* possibly altered   258 *rauisht this*] no gap between words
260 *While*] *W* possibly altered   265 SD.2 *a*] *a* extends into next word   *higher*] *e* possibly
altered   *blank*] two otiose strokes over *an*

   Glau) Come come, my sweet Leander, Let us in both.
Ner. And the Lords, of each our Sea, giue you ioy both.

    Act 1. Scen 2.
   Hero with a Torch put out and fyrie smoaking.
Her. Leander, Leander, Leander hoa,   270
  Why answerst not, Leander, to my call?
  Leander, I say, tis thy Hero calls,
  Leander, Leander, my Leander.
  Nay then, I see, Leander's lost, For that
  This coast, these many tymes, I'haue trauesed
  Still hallowing on Leanders name
  And none hath answered, These many Tymes
  Sent shoutes and \none/ Returnd, Then, oh Gods, oh,
  Ops, Vesta, Ceres, Iuno, Iupiter,
  Cythe\<ræ\>a and the Rest, Poure down,   280
  With armed armes, your full bent Vengeaunces
  On this Breast of ours, For what auayleth her
  One howre to liue Leander once bereft her.
  Euen as that Sparrowe, once, in Aulis Port,
  Her chicks deuourd before her eyen, at last
  Gaue vp her self, to fill the number vp,
  Vnto her Foe, so I, vpon the Fall
  Of my stout Ilion, do offer, loe,
  A constant hearte, besprent with goures of blood,
  Vnto my raging Foe the Sea, vnto   290
  My raging Foe the Sea, I say, For if
  He had loued hero well, he would then
  Haue wound Leander in his armes and borne
  Him safe vnto my Bed, He would haue layne
  The Miser on a heape of Oaze. But oh,
  The greedy Gulph hath wrapt him in his Mawe
  And left not Boanes for Preist of Venus share.
  I know lykwise the water dietyes,

274 *Leander's*] apostrophe over *r*   275 *This*] *T* possibly altered   278 *shoutes*] imperfect *u* might be *o*   *Returnd*] *R* altered from *r* and possibly caret; *t* altered   280 *Cythe\<ræ\>a*] blotting and smudging obscures \<ræ\>; possibly an altered *r* above blotted letters   282 *her*] *h* possibly altered   285 *Her*] cross-stroke does not join two mainstrokes of *H*; looks like *It*   *deuourd*] *'d* formed from *b*, possible false start for *before*   292 *hero*] *h* possibly altered   297 *share.*] stop smudged horizontally   298 *dietyes*] *t* possibly altered

> They had but seene Leander on their waues
> They would haue crownd his browes with Flags and Sedges, 300
> With Minths, with water Cressies and with Lillyes,

[FOL. 123ᵛ]

> And brought him so on shoare. Oh, No,
> I find it was some Monster, flown from Rock,
> That fouly swallowd him, not any els,
> For surely cast your Count, the dietyes
> Be rapt with beautye, And do fauour those
> That most, in Countnance, do resemble them,
> And such Leander was, in all his Parts
> And features, framed, For had you but seene
> His copious Rayes drawn furth in Longitude, 310
> His Pelop shoulder caru'd of Iuourye,
> His glorious Heauen with Two starrs set,
> His fragrant bosome and his Hony-suckles
> Or Loue or voluptas you would haue deemd him.
> And find you then such Fault, you Gods and Men,
> I wayle, so Impatiently, my Leander!
> Leander, Leander, my Leander!

Act 1 Scen 3.
The Direction.
> He appeared aboue water wan and naked crownd 320
> with blewe sea weedes, Hed and Priuities.

Leander Hero.

Lean. Hero (Her) Whom do I behold? Leander?
      Alas how Pale and wan the Poore Hearte lookes.
Lean. Call no more Leander, A God he is.
      Glauce tangeld mee labring in Nereus warde,
      And there, gainst my will, pluckt mee into Sea.
Her. O Tyde of woe, o Mell of Miserye.
Lean. Why didst not hold the Fannal furth on high?
Her. Alas, I did, But wind did murder it. 330
Lean. Hadst thou, but one while maintaynd his Light

---

300 *would*] d altered   301 *Minths*] M possibly altered   306 *favour those*] r touches t
311 *caru'd*] apostrophe over u   *Iuourye*] o imperfect, looks like imperfect v   314 *voluptas*] l altered
316 *Impatiently*] e possibly altered   321 *blewe*] w imperfect   *weedes*] w imperfect

	I had beene sau'd (Her) O sillie mee forlore.
Lean.	I neuer shall enioy thee, Hero, more.
Her.	I'll giue my Iewells, vnto Sea, to pleasure thee.
Lean	Not all the Treasure, in the deepe, will measure mee.
Her.	By powrfull spelles, I'll loose thee from thy Thrall.
Lean.	[Thou] So mayst thou enthrall thy self withall.
Her.	Share I will with Glauce so I ransome you.
Lean.	I? Shall I find my Hero so vntrewe?
Her.	Is lost for euer my Leanders kisse?
Lean	Neuer the Gods, once stalld, returne from Blisse.
Her.	My case is desprate, and I Flye to you.
Lean	Come hast, and yeild thee in my armes (Her) I come.
Lean	Hero (Her) I come (Lean) Hero, my Hero, I say (Her) I come Leander, I come to thee.*

He pluckt her vn=
der water to him.

Act 1 Scen 4.

[FOL. 124ʳ]

Harpax Rudens Ponticus Gripus Prote=
vs.

Harp.	Mʳ Proteus, I do assure your worship, if you quell not the Rage of yond Leuiathan, wee shall roust all wee shall take hencefurth vpon the superficies of our two Thumbes I swe= are.
Rud.	It is a Thing Absonaunt in Nature, see what Fegaries the vil= laine will fetch. He roareth lyke Thirty Barril of gun= powder, He springeth at a spring Three Acres of water, He squirteth Fyre not onely before but also behind.
Prot.	Pia Mater præserue thy virginity.
Pont.	More, he roareth Latin, Hebrew, Greeke, Caldee, Italian French, Spanish, German, Dutch, Welch to boote.
Grip.	He keepeth the Aphrodysial in his belly.
Prot.	Monstrum Horrendum, informe, ingens, cuitut sunt cor= pore Plumæ.
Rud.	Zounds he hath not vnderstood vs the while. Plumæ, Sir, your Fowle is a Fish, Sir

332 *had*] h possibly altered   *sau'd*] apostrophe over *u*   337 *Thou*] underlined for deletion; short horizontal stroke above *T*   *So*] added in left margin to replace [*Thou*]   *self*] *l* small, like apostrophe   339 *Hero*] otiose ink stroke above *ro*   341 *once*] *ce* altered in a darker ink   345 SD.1–.2 *vn=/der* *e* altered   349] SP high   358 *Latin*] *t* written over ?*d*

Prot. Plumæ quasi plumie, For because before he part he shall
     be plumed.
Pont Deare Sir, set vs a course.
Harp. Thinkst? he will set his dogs on him?
Pont. To you wee be come, as to an Asyle
Prot. His combe shall be curryde.   370
Grip. For loe you, Sir, he deuoureth all where he cometh lyke
     vnto your Iron Milles in Sussex[<.>], Ho[a].
Prot. I haue not any one there. Describe mee the Beast. Come.
Harp. Has a Hed lyke my Fathers Potage-pot.
Prot. O the Tinkerlye Pot-hed. Mouth?
Harp. Lyke a Mule when she pisseth.
Prot Eyes?
Harp. Beacons oynted with Bacon.
Prot. Nose?
Harp. A Grater with a whistle in him.   380
Prot. Eares?
Harp. A Paire of Baskit Hilts.
Prot. Bulk?
Harp. Why, A well trussed Chronicle.
Prot. Gilles?
Harp. The Flaps of an Atorneys capcase.
Prot. Passe ouer the rest, And vayle you all Foure to his Tayle
     now All.
Harp. It is not much vnlyke to your worships Bearde, Mr Proteus

He toucht his bearde.
     Prot) His Properties? come, say.   390
     Wel. First he will leape you, lightly, ouer a Mast, as M^r
     Iohn will do ouer his chaine.
Prot. Who's the Gentleman? say.

[Fol. 124^v]

Rud. Iohn an Apes, Sir.
Prot. Oh, Iohn a Napes.
Rud. Secondly, He will foame you at Mouth one thousand
     six hundreth threescore and six kilderkins of Brine
     at a Breath, and sup you in as many at another.

---

369 *Pont.*] dark ink spot above *t*   *come*] *o possibly altered*   372 *Sussex*[<.>],] *illegible letter follows x, deleted with vertical stroke; comma possibly formed from stop*   *Ho*[a]] *a deleted with vertical stroke*   388 *now*] *o possibly written over* ?e   390 *Properties*] *P altered from imperfect p*   397 *threescore*] ²*e altered*   *Brine*] *n imperfect, looks like m*

Prot. What store of greace hath the villaine?
Pont Why do you ask? 400
Prot. For my shoemakers benefit I do it.
Rud. Fowre thousand, six hundreth, forty foure Tuns, one
hundreth fifty fiue Hogsheds, one quintal and one
half
Prot. It is reasonably well.
Rud Thirdly, ^\he/ writeth with his nose.
Prot A Text?
Rud. A Text. Fourthlye will tell you what the money is in
thy Purse, Proteus.
Prot. A bad Propertie, by my Faith. 410
Rud. Fifthly, dances Trenchmore either to drum or droane.
Prot. O the Gallant.
Rud. Sixthly singeth Prick-song.
Prot. Passion of mee.
Rud. Seauenthly, speaketh Greeke.
Prot. And keepeth the Accent?
Rud. An keepeth the Accent. Finally and lastly will tell you
as infallible Oracles as a Three-footed stoole.
Prot. A Three-footed stoole?
Rud. That is at Delphos. 420
Prot When comes he furth to his repast? Say
Rud. About Noone.
Prot. Thus it shall be, with a Net shall be layd furth first for him,
wee will, in the manner, with our full mights and force,
hale him, Incontinently, to Court.
Rud. Sir, I thank you for high wisdome.
Grip. But how.? if by chaunce, as all things be mortall, he do
escape vs?
Prot. A Harping-yron may then, chaunce, cleaue his Sconce
into two Parts. 430
Grip. I doe easily agree with you int, Mr Proteus.
Harp. But is this all wee shall doe about the Beast? Sir.
Prot. Yes very verily, and in deed, Sir.

403 *and*] *d* possibly altered from *?o*, with long horizontal ascender stretching leftwards   405 *It*] *t* written over *s*   406 *Thirdly*] *d* possibly altered   *he/ writeth*] caret under *w*   408 *Fourthlye*] *l* altered from *t*; *e* imperfect   411 *dances*] *ce* possibly altered   412 *Prot.*] stop faint   417 *Accent.*] stop smudged horizontally   418 *Oracles*] *e* possibly altered   420 *is*] *s* altered   424 *force*] *e* imperfect

Rud. For the Net, let mee alone with him.
Pont Mee for the Roapes.
Grip. Mee with my grapple to hold him sure by the nose with it
Prot Breif, each now to his Boothe, and meet wee here again
      soone. So præpare vs against \t/his villaine you talk.
Harp. Pithyly.

[FOL. 125^r]

Prot And let vs haue a song, before wee Part, withall.   440
Rud. So, Sir.
Pont. Most excellent.
Grip. Begin, Sirs, Hoa.

The First Song.

1

Will you buye, will you buye
Any Sea fare of mee?
Playce, Cod, Haddock or faire whiting,
Cockles, Oysters, Mussells, Ling,
Either from Grauell or sliming,   450
Shall haue, of each, for a Farthing,
Without your further Rewarding,
All Fine

2

Will you buye, will you buye?
Any Sea ware of mee?
That may agree with your Pallate,
That beene so fine in the Carrate,
Lobster, Shrimpe, Sturgeon or Turbate,
Flounder, Sole, Thorneback or Herring,   460
Shall haue, of each, for a Farthing
Without their further Regarding
All Fine.

---

435 *Roapes*] imperfect *a* looks like *u*   436] SP low   437] SP low   *Boothe*] ¹*o* possibly altered; ²*o* imperfect, looks like *v*   455 *Will*] otiose inks marks around *W*   ²*buye*] *b* possibly altered   458 *Carrate*] ²*a* possibly altered   460 *Herring*] *H* possibly retraced or altered; otiose extra stroke on ¹*r*   462 *Regarding*] *g* retraced

     3
  Will you buye, will you buye,
  These flight wantons of mee
  Filme, nor boane shall you molest,
  By St Peter I protest,
  Conger of the Thick Arrest,
  Gurnet, Smelt, Crab, or Sweet Powting,   470
  Shall haue, of each, for a Farthing
  Without your further Retarding,
   All Fine.

Prot. Now come your wayes all and . . . . follow mee *

In stately manner
and high Maiesti=
call stalking.

   Act 1. Scen 5.
  Vulcan Harpax Cyclops.

Vul. Whoope, Sirrha.
Harp. My Lord.
Vul. Harpax, Adesdum paucis te volo.
Harp. So and shall lyke you.   480
Vul. Come on thy ways. That I am thy Lord and Master thou
   Knowest it, my Boy.
Harp. To myne own charge that I doe, I do assure you, my Lord
Vul. That a Master hath for his Relatiue a seruant to do him

[FOL. 125^v]

   his Buisines? say.
Harp. Trewe.
Vul. That Buisinesses be of diuers sort also?
Harp. Trewe againe.
Vul.. Of which sortes, bearing Letters is one.
Harp. Whither rides your Lordship? To my Lady Aglaia your   490
   newe bedded Spowse?
Vul. Why speakst not?
Harp. I
Vul.. Well. Come on. I inferre, soritically, by these the Premi-
   ses, that thou must needes beare mee now two letters,

481 *thou*] t lacks headstroke   483 *do assure*] retraced in darker ink used for final lines on this page
486 *Harp.*] stop faint and high   *Trewe*] otiose mark follows *r*   487 *sort also*] otiose ink point
between words   488 *Harp.*] stop faint and high   489 *Vul..*] extra stop probably otiose *Letters*]
ink spot below *er*   490 *Harp.*] stop faint and high   494 *Vul..*] second stop high, probably
otiose   *inferre,*] comma below line, extends into next line

22

    The one to Humida a Mayde of the ^\moyst/ Sea, the other to Ari=
    da a Mayde of the Drye Land, Proteus daughters, For
    Arithmetically I am falln in Loue with both the Two,
    The one or the other, I care not which.
Harp. My Lord, what needed this Net-work to Packstaff?   500
    I would haue done it with half the cost.
Vul. I that am winding into my Mistresses fauours must
    vse winding Arguments Boye, winding Arguments
    be of diuers sorts, of diuers Sorts the readiest is to be
    chosen, Now therefore before I do wind into my Ladyes
    Sanctuaries I am Practising that ready Argument
    surnamed the Mowse, See.
Harp. Giue mee your Letters.
Vul. Hold thee.
Harp. When must this be done?   510
Vul: Soone.
Harp. You haue no other Buisinesse to employ mee?
Vul. Be gone, Returne, God blesse my Sonne.
Harp. And you, as Cæsar, betweene two Bayes the oakes [blood] Bud.
    May beare, betweene your honours hornes the koaks hood.
    Farewell, my Lord.
Vul. Et tu. He was a calf dared first affirme Phisically
    Two contraries might not be conteyned in one and the self
dilue [same] subiect at one and the same tyme. For I; who|am
    a Phisicall subiect now, A humaine Body viz. And by   520
    a Metaphore, as shall straite loe appeare to you, An
    Apothecaryes Gally pot, haue swallowd, into this one pot
    of myne down, one Humida, who is as Moyst as a
    Plum, And one other Arida who is as drye as is a chich
    So there, as I say, let the Knaue now thunder thump
    his, Cannon, long as it shall please him so to doe, against
    this old Trunk of myne, yet he shall neuer remoue

496 ^\moyst/ Sea] caret placed under S of Sea 500 Packstaff] P possibly altered; 'f retraced 505 wind] w altered Ladyes] e imperfect, lacks second stroke 506 am] m altered or retraced 512 You] u imperfect, like a dash 514 oakes] short dash above s blood] underlined for deletion Bud.] added in left margin to replace [blood]; stop is likely otiose 519 same] underlined for deletion; preceded by high ink point I;] point over comma possibly otiose who|am] vertical rule separates words; a altered 520 subiect] lobe on b indistinct, looks like l 521 loe] o imperfect, looks like v; e imperfect, looks like o 524 drye] indistinct lobe on d 525 there] re written over r and illegible letter deleted by vertical strokes the] otiose point over e 527 this] point on i merges with comma after his on previous line

         mee from the Fast of him, For my Hearte moueth it,
         my gutt plucketh it, and my Toung telleth it lykwise.
         But why shouldst yet be in loue, Vulcan? As in eury thing   530
         lyke a trewe chymick, as thou beest, thou dost Vulcan,
         so now in this, Vulcan, run back to the cause of
         him. My face I do pronounce him bacon, My leg

[FOL. 126ʳ]

         I find bad, But my witt I account worse, Therefore I do
         inferre, by these the Premises, that the whole Parliament
         of cælestiall dietyes, For those the durty Parts, my gallant
         wife, my lady Aglaia hath played silly down halting
         mee, haue in this one now new Match, all of them
         Sung Osanna in Excelsis, to come, before mee now.
         Madame, looke to your saddle, Madame, For I haue   540
         charged my Pot-gun of defyance against you, Madame,
         Subandiendum est, by Atorney, on others, Madame,
         you haue sent mee before but to work a Bolle for you,
         Madame, But I will work him thourough out vpon
         your Polle, Madame. Come thou Nemesis with thy
         Bit, then I do not any thing doubt but that then
         I shall very well hit. But heark, as I conciue
         Cytheræa is now new landed at Court.

                             The Direction.

dilue   Chambers ([or] noise supposd For Powles), For Actors.   550
         Also a showre of Rose-water and confits, as was acted
         in Christ church, in Oxford in Dido and Aeneas. Guns
         withall and Thunder thereto.

Vul.   I must now in, fall to woork, els chaunce at dinner
         sweet Cytheræa may be serued in oyster shells, all, els
         in Mussell dishes, in lieu of them, to mend her or=
         dinary moreouer and besyde.

Cyclops   My Lord, my Lord.*
within fro.

---

528 *Fast*] *a* imperfect, looks like *u*   529 *telleth*] ¹*e* imperfect, looks like *o*   531 *Vulcan*] *V* imperfect, looks like *O*   532 *Vulcan,*] comma retraced, looks like two commas   *back*] *b* altered   534 *bad*] *b* altered   536 *cælestiall*] otiose stroke betweel *cæ*   537 *silly*] *s* altered   539 *before*] *f* altered   547 *heark,*] *k* altered; comma placed below next word   550 *dilue*] faint   *or*] underlined for deletion; preceded by high ink point   552 *church*] *c* obscured by ink smudge   *Oxford*] ²*o* indistinct, merged with cross-stroke of *f*   554–7 *Vul. ... besyde.*] added on pasted slip in darker ink   558] SP high

Vul. I come, I come; I come to you presently, my Sonnes, I come 560
     Here they knockt vp the consort.

     Act 2 Scen 1.
      The Direction
 A Transcension of Saylours and Tritons with Bagge
and Baggage, Trinkets and Cables, loose and broaken, Mu=
sick still playing on the whiles. Here Arion and Talus
stood on either hand of Thetis, not walking in Tayle
of one the other, bending but now and then vnto her.
     Talus Arion Thetis.

Tal. Graunt mee thy Loue, faire virgin of the deepe.
Ar. To mee thy Loue that in the waters keepe. 570
Tal. What would not Talus doe to sack such Roses.
Ar. What would [A] not greater Arion to pluck those Poseys?
Tal. Though Enginer my father Vulcan is.
Ar. I'haue bound in Wyres a thousand Mistrissis.
Tal. Corydon brown Thestilis wins at last.
Ar. The saylour sing, on shoare, the storme once past.
          [FOL. 126ᵛ]
Tal. Lyke Proportion I neuer found before.
Ar. Lyke Harmony my Harpe-string neuer bore.
Tal. Thy lockes be sheene as Sun in morning Plight
Ar. Thy Feete be pure as the Diamonds light. 580
Tal. Neuer ^\were/ heauenly ioyes, on Earth, before.
Ar. I deeme the Skies be of their Saints forlore.
Tal. When Gods do meete they chuse their Pallace here.
Ar. Thou art Panthæon of all heauenly cheare.
Tal. Happie the Man, whom first thou makst a Father.
Ar. But three tymes he that first the fruit shall gather.
Tal. O graunt mee loue, thou virgin faire and bright.
Ar. O graunt me loue, thou with the syluer feet.
Thet. Thus long, with Patience, haue I hearde your suite,

559 *come;*] point on semi-colon heavily inked   561 *Act*] *A* retraced   564 *Trinkets*] *ts* obscured by ink smudge   *loose*] ²*o* blotted   566 *walking*] *l* short and curled, looks like *c*   568 *Arion*] *A* lacks cross-stroke   571 *sack*] *a* could possibly be *u*; *k* altered   572 *A*] crossed out   *Poseys*] ¹*s* possibly altered; ²*s* possibly retraced   579 *lockes*] *c* altered, possibly from *o*   580 *Diamonds*] *s* added in darker ink   581 *were*/] *r* possibly altered   583 *Pallace*] otiose ink mark above ²*a*   586 *gather*] ink transfer above to right of word, from text on pasted slip on facing page (line 634)   589] SP low

	And by your woo\r/des do find the same as ardent,	590
	Yet if so it be, in deede, you make shewe oft,	
	Fullfill one task, and haue my loue there with.	
Tal.	What Thetis giues in charge will Talus doe.	
Ar.	And what she bidds Arion sweares vnto.	
The	I take your Bonds, and on the same do thus	
	Begin. I had[e] now many yeares agone	
	[A Loue-rolle] A Ceston for my wrests, which long I held	
	As pretious as my eyes, with this I quelld	
	The waues, with this the waues I lykwise raised,	
	When at any tyme I swom the Maine,	600
	Raisd lykwise with this th'Affections of loue;	
	The same I lent, one day, to Vlysses,	
	Moued with compassion on the Man,	
	Whilst he in dangrous perill was of life,	
	To bring him safe on shoare, which since the Tyme	
	Neuer my eyes could see it more, Now if	
	You loue mee, as you say, procure it mee,	
	For I haue vowd to marry none but him	
	Shall bringt to mee, So bee you gone, I pray both.	
Tal.	Is this your finall Resolution? Virgin.	610
Thet.	It is, my wisdome and my dainty Deare.	
Ar.	Wilt not otherwise be persuaded? (The) No.	
Tal.	Hard virgin thou, dost on shittenesse	
	This, to torture mee, I will do it yet.	
	Albee I do leaue my soule in gage, So thou	

He rounded her in the eare:

	The Flint-heartest Virgin, that liues, Adieu.*	
Thet.	Adieu, good Sir, commend mee to your Father.	
Ar.	Nor will I returne, till I bring him you *	

starde her in the face

Thet)	I do thank you for your diligence too,	
	So take the tyde, along with you, I pray, too.	620
	Be they flown?. A Puff of winde flowe after,	
	A Iuster case of combes did neuer meet.	
	Why did the woodcoaks think it possible?	

591 *oft*] t imperfect   595] SP low   596 *had[e]*] word altered from *haue*; d written over u; e deleted with vertical stroke; h possibly altered   597 *A Loue-rolle*] underlined for deletion; preceded by blotted high ink point   *A Ceston*] added on pasted slip in left margin to replace [*A Loue-rolle*]   609 *bringt*] t lacks headstroke   614 *This,*] comma added in darker ink   *yet.*] large gap before stop; stop is below line   615 *gage*] otiose mark above ²g   619 SD *starde*] a imperfect, looks like u   621 *flown?.*] stop otiose   623 *woodcoaks*] a could be imperfect c

[Fol. 127ʳ]

  T'obtaynd Thetis, th'one an Enginer,
  Th'other but a Cythəræde. It is decreed,
  By Prophesye of old Themis, should spring one
  From Thetis Loynes, should be greater
  Then Syre or Mother, Besyde one that should
  Conquer Townes, Cities and Nations,
  Wherefore refusd young Ioue my loue For   630
  Feare of Crosse to his aspiring to Olympus,
  Held now in rigour vnder Saturnus,
  For who may be more greate then youthfull he?
  Cause, I say, Ioue might ˰\not/ haue [this Loue-rolle,] This Ceston
  Nor Neptune eake, though he commaunds the waues.
  But let these Raunge, in the name of Dagon,
  The Sea, and home returne without their bootie,
  For such a task I haue Imposd on them
  The Toyle they'll spend shall not procure the same
  Though they should ransack the whole watry Maine.   640
  Onely Florish, and see thou, hence, disdeyne
  The base embracments of such lowly men.
  But I must attend on Cytheraea.

     Act 2 Scen 2.
In their sea attyres. * Euphrosyne Aglaia Thalia.

Euph. Aglaia and Thalia, loe and see,
  Wee be now happily ariued all
  At Court of Oceanus, Had wee but
  Little how euer stayd longer on Sea,
  Wee should not haue celebrated, I wusse,   650
  Cytheræas Aphrodysial this day.
Thal. Oh Gods, what a storme hath beene raysd this morne?
  I think my sweet Lady Cytheræa
  Be moyled well as any of the Three;

---

624 *Enginer*] ¹n altered, possibly from false start of *g* 628 *Then*] followed by high otiose stroke 634 ˰*not*/] caret written over illegible characters *this Loue-rolle,*] underlined for deletion; high ink point above *t* of *this* *This Ceston*] written on pasted slip in left margin to replace [*this Loue-rolle,*]; edges of ?two other pasted slips visible beneath. 637 *bootie*] ²*o* altered possibly from *e* 645 SD.1 *In*] *I* heavily inked 650 *should*] *d* lacks lobe 651 *Aphrodysial*] otiose stroke like apostrophe above *s* 652] SP high *raysd*] *s* written over another character, possibly *e* 654 *Three;*] point above comma added in darker ink

     I neuer beheld, in dayes of my life, such
     Surging waues, Euphrosyne, to haue beate
     So 'gainst Ribbes of our shallop, I assure thee.
  Agl. I persuade mee, some Marine dietye
     Hath assest some faire Paramour this morne,
     So that they struggling both for the Masterye   660
     They haue raisd that sudden storme wee endurde.
  Euph. Well I do beleeue thee, Aglaia,
     For what might the cause be, I pray now,
     That my Lady Glauce, who is but a
     Sun-burnt Impe, you see, should deck her
     As she were but now going to the game?
  Thal. I think my sister Aglaia and she
     Haue layd a wager, whither of the Two
     Shall beare the Bucklers, this day, for Brau'rye,

                       [Fol. 127ᵛ]
     I find her so affectionately   670
     Long for the chuck other sweet hearte Vulcan.
  Agl. Goodly Lords, why not for my sweet hearte Vulcan?
  Thal. For cause, I see not any thing in him
     For thee so to affect him, Aglaia.
  Euph. Not for his Gold, I am sure, Thalia.
  Agl. For there be things, in him, better then is
     His Gold, I assure thee, Euphrosyne.
  Euph. But what, I prithy, say sweet Aglaia?
  Agl. The vertues of his mind do exceede far
     Those his Indewments of Fortune, I assure mee. 680
dilue Thal. But what, [I prithy] bee those his vertues? ^[\good/] sister say.
dilue Agl. Item and Imprimis, that constant Loue
     He beares mee, doth counteruayle that the wealth
     He hath obteyned by knock of his Hammer.
  Thal. For all that finesse of yours, Faire Mistris
     Aglaia, he may, chaunce, fall into lapse
     Yet of some of the watery Element.

---

660 *struggling*] *u* retraced 661 *that*] ²*t* missing headstroke 662] SP high 666 *now*] ink spot under *w* 668 *wager*] imperfect *a* looks like *u* 675 *Euph.*] stop high *sure*] *s* possibly altered 677 *Euphrosyne*] *r* possibly written over *o* 678 *Euph.*] stop high 681 *I prithy*] underlined for deletion; preceded by high ink point ^*good*/] caret placed below *s* in next word; interlined word then partially underlined for deletion; preceded by faint high ink point

Agl.	Not for the gemmes of the Sea I assure mee.	
Euph.	How if he should, what course might you then haue	
	To frustrate him of his faithles attempt?	690
Agl.	I should so beseige him with lure of my lookes,	
	And with harmony of Toung that will he	
	Nil he, he should in a Trice, aspire but	

dilue Vnto [the\se/] kisses of ˄ \these/ my lips (Thal) That will
          Confound that smell, mary, \that/ he shall bring,
          With him, of that garlick, he shall haue eate
          Next his hearte, that morning, deare Aglaia.
Agl.   Fye, vpon thee, sister, Fye, vpon thee.
Euph.Why, whats the Matter now? Aglaia.
Agl.   Nay, I haue an Antidote for that, Sister.   700
Euph.What? I prithy (Agl) Nay Pardon mee for that:
Thal. Hee'rs such a coyle with vs now. Come away,
          Come, my Lady is so dank, with the storme,
          She will call away, for the Three, straite, loe.
Agl.   And well rememberd, Thalia, mary,
          For neuer diue-dapper hath beene so sousd
          As she hath beene sousd, by the waues, I troe.
Euph.Then, with speede, come and see, that each thing
          Be in readines against her Indewing.
Agl.   With the best speede, I may, Euphrosyne.   710
Thal. Hast you, Lady Aglaia (Euph) you too.

                    Act 2 Scen 3.
             [C]   * Glauce Graces.
standing* Glau. Come away, Ladyes, come away, Cytheræa hath such
at the doore   neede of you as passes, come away, come away, Hoa.
             Grac. Wee come.

[Fol. 128ʳ]

694 *dilue*] d possibly retraced   *the\se/*] *se* interlined, *the* underlined for deletion; *se* not underlined but presumably intended for deletion with the rest of the word   698–702] SPs low   702 *Thal.*] h written over *a*   703 *dank*] imperfect *a* looks like *u*   707 *the*] *t* possibly retraced   714 SD.1 *standing* *] asterisk is above *ing*   SP] high   *Come*] crossed out C appears above C, likely false start to line

29

Act 2 Scen 4.
Proteus Rudens Harpax Ponticus Gripus.

Prot. Masters, is the Toyle set?
Rud. It will giue him a Iolt on the Bulk, I feare it will cause him   720
      rebound to his Den, Proteus.
Prot. Take thou heede to that, Harpax.
Harp. Feare not, I will steale betweene him and home, And in steede of my
      Harping-yron will employ my whole Talonds on the Iack of him,
      And if it shall so lyke you, Mr Proteus.
Pont. Where I will be bold, Trip his worships Tayle, so swingue him a
      shoare.
Harp. Mee on his back, Ponticus.
Rud Mee with my Roapes to clewe them fast together both.
Pont. I then after them to leape vpon the Iacks of both the Twayne.   730
Grip. I, to leade you ashoare all with my grapple in his nose, I wusse.
Prot. Here is his Den, And here let vs begin to waite the Toyle all.
Pont. Come on.
Prot. He is not to be had, by Sword or by Corde, so soone, Therefore Aliam
      vitam, alios mores Tempus postulat, A Fresh Barril must be set
      on Broach first. Can you make faces? saye.
Harp. God hath made each vs one face, And wee can make no more then
      he hath made vs.
Prot Neither So nor So. Can you squint? can you gloate? can you grin?
      lowre, leere, Powt, Pouch, strout, stare, scip and squint, simul?   740
Rud Wee haue practisd the Matachine since wee could scrall Mr Proteus.
Grip. Why asketh your worship?
Prot. Possible the villaine hath some priuie Token by the which he knows
      his freind from his Foe.
Grip. I vnderstand you. Making thus seuerall Anticks on him, wee may
      chaunce, so hap on the freinds token, so entice him furth his
      hole.
Prot. You haue entrapt mee, Father Gripus.

---

722 *thou*] h possibly altered   723 *Harp*.] stop merges with lobe of *p*   *steede of my*] gap between *d* and *e* of *steede*; no gap between *steede* and *of*; no gap between *of* and *my*   728 *Harp*.] stop merges with lobe of *p*   *Ponticus*] *u* imperfect   730 *Pont*.] stop high   *then*] otiose stroke below *t*   731 *ashoare*] *r* possibly altered or retraced   734 *soone*] ²*o* altered   736 *faces?*] ? missing point   737 *Harp*.] indistinctive lobe on imperfect *p*   *made*] *e* possibly altered   *then*] *e* altered in a darker ink, *n* possibly added   739 *Can*] *a* possibly altered   743 *Possible*] *o* retraced   *hath*] indistinct limb on *h*, otiose mark appears above letter   745 *vnderstand*] *n* possibly altered

Pont. For squinting let mee alone with him.
Rud. Mee for strouting   750
Grip. Mee for gloating.
Harp. Mee, for all [of them] them, at self and one Instant, I do verily a=
uouch it to you all, My Masters all.
Prot. I, to interpret the Toungs.
Grip. Withall but to rem\ẽ/mber tell him wee be your worships Anticks,
too, Mʳ Proteus.
Prot. I will remember it. Set, Masters.

Act 2 Scen 5.
Balene Harpax Rudens Ponticus Gripus Pro=
Bal. [I do Prop]   teus.   760
dilue   I do Prophesye the comming hither of Rogues.
Harp. Your freinds and seruaunts be come take measure of the
capacity of your sconce, my Lord. Know you, Sir, this To=
ken? Ha.

[Fol. 128ᵛ]

Rud. Or This?
Pont This?
Rud. Now this?
Grip. Lastly ˄ \Sir/ This?*
Thus farr but they ma=   The Apes of Cataia may not remoue his Resolution, I
de the faces.   Prot. do now perceiue him well.   770
Bal. I will send you Tokens to Lucifer all.
Rud. I pray, be not angrye, The Greeke is villanously slit
since comming of the Turk, wee onely desire your
Lordships rules, for the making a Grammer, whereby
wee may restore her to her better health.
Bal. Gnosi seauton.
Prot. Greeke, by our Lord God.
Rud. What sayd he? Proteus.
Prot. Know you Shafton?
Pont Lord, Sir, he was a Cathegoricall Knitter of Nets, as   780

752 *of them*] underlined for deletion; preceded by blotted high ink point   *them*] written in different ink to left of line 753 to replace [*of them*]   *verily*] v possibly retraced   756 *too,*] added to left of line   757 *Prot.*] stop high   760] SP high   *I do Prop*] underlined for deletion; preceded by high ink point   770 *him*] i lacks point, mainstroke short   *Prot.*] SP precedes previous line in MS, positioned here on l. 770 due to lack of space on l. 769   771 *send*] e imperfect, strokes look like cc   772 *slit*] i lacks point; t missing headstroke

	was any, in Cyprus, I wisse.	
Bal.	A Cathegoricall Knitter of Cyprus caps he was	
Harp.	If you abuse the wiues of Cyprus, Sir, wee will be bold	
	play vpon your whistle, Sir.	
Bal.	Grapsato ton cripton coly kirkseny cockseny cupton	
	Grapsato ton religo para Bim para Bom para Bombos.	
Rud.	What sayes he now? Proteus	
Prot.	Ask him thou thy self, Rudens.	
Grip.	I beleeue it be the language of the damned.	
Prot.	Possible, For it is a wicked, detestable, and most damna=	790
	ble language.	
Harp.	I pray, you would turne your Mother Toung into a Sy=	
	prisse Crespe, ˌ \<b>ut,/ wee may consyder her, whither she be	
	scuruye, or no.	
Bal.	Graspe, gripe, kick, coll, Cut my Combe,	
	I come, on you, with a Bi, with a Bo, with a B[o]\u/mb.	
Harp.	Most scuruy she is I do promise you, Sirs.	
Pont.	I thought the greate Baselyke had beene on Fyre, he rat=	
	tled so in the Throate, I \do/ assure you all, my Masters all	
Bal.	Walram he con rague.	800
Prot.	Welch, by the Lord, also.	
Rud.	What, I prithy, sayd he?	
Prot.	He will tattar you to raggs all.	
Grip.	A most louzie Infliction it is, I wusse.	
Harp.	Now shalt see mee play noble Curtius with him and Ram	
	this [t]his gutter of Perdition straite. *Please you,	

Here he squinted

	my Lord, tast a Pippin? Ha.	
Bal.	Ne mange point, Ie vous remercie.	
Prot.	Sayes, in French, he shall be maungie with it.	
Harp.	Will you none?	810

pronounced nown in French.

| Bal. | Non.* |

[FOL. 129ʳ]

782 *Bal.*] altered from *Har.*   787 *now? Proteus*] ? added, or altered from false start for *P*   789 *Grip.*] stop high   790 *Possible*] P formed from F, possibly false start for *For wicked*] imperfect limb on *k* makes letter look like *ll*   792 *Harp.*] short descender on *p*   793 \<b>ut/] *b* altered; caret obscures comma after preceding word   795 *Cut my*] smudged by blotting; *t* altered   796 *you,*] comma very faint   *Bi, with*] first three letters smudged by blotting   *Bo\u/mb*] *u* written above crossed out *o*   797 *promise*] *e* altered from *i*   798–9 *rat=/tled*] top stroke of = faint   799 ²*all*] *a* imperfect, *ll* retraced   803 *He*] *H* with imperfect cross-bar, looks like *It*   804 *wusse*] smudged by blotting   805 *with*] ink spot above *w*   806 [*t*]*his*] *t* cancelled with vertical stroke

	Prot.	Sayes, tis now high Noone.	
	Grip.	I vnderstood that, Proteus.	
	Bal.	Quid vobiscum ille Nebulo?	
	Harp.	Proteus he calls thee Knaue in Latin.	
	Prot.	Sir, you lye, For albeit I be [but] Master of Oceanus his Antick\s/	
dilue		yet know that [Antique] Persons be, euer, men of greatest Ac=	
[Antick]		count there.	
	Rud	Displease not the Beast.	
	Prot.	If it were not for shame ———————	820
	Pont	Thou't not lay seige to the Rock with thy Fist? Proteus.	
	Prot.	I will be quiet, But ———————	
	Pont	Be quiet then and Butt at him another whiles.	
	Prot	Well.	
	Rud.	Before wee shall take our leaues of this Babel or Tower of	
		confusion, know, Sir, wee be come tast a Bolle of your wis=	
		dome, For they report you haue two faces vnder one hood	
		lyke Ianus, yet can wee decerne but one face and one whis=	
		tle. Now if, as they say, you can tell things Past and Things	
		to come, Sir, Saye what did my wife, last night, in my Kitchin	830
	Bal.	She lighted a Candle at wrong end to obey thy bidding.	
	Rud	Admirable.	
	Grip.	I went yesterday to pick Oysters for Oceanus his dinner, Say	
		what befell.	
	Bal.	An Oyster gript thee, by the nose, Gripus.	
	Grip.	Iust as a pair of sheeres, I assure you.	
	Pont.	But what, now for mee, Sir, I pray you.	
dilue	Bal.	A shark hath bereft thee of both [thy] Cods, Ponticus.	
	Pont.	You lye, Sir, verily	
	Prot.	Sauing our quarrell, I haue two daughters, Two wonders of their	840
		sexe, say, what shall become?	
	Bal.	Cynthius Aonia redimitus tempora lauro	
		Pocula Castuliæ plena ministretaquæ.	
	Prot.	Glewe thy clouen Toungs and answere mee in one [but], what shall	
dilue		become my daughters? say.	

816 *but*] underlined for deletion; preceded by high ink point   *Antick\s/*] *s* written above *k*
817 *Antique*] underlined for deletion; preceded by high ink point   *Persons*] otiose ink stroke above *o*
818 *Antick*] written in left margin and struck out by a series of vertical strokes   823 *whiles*] *w* possibly altered   837 *mee*] *ee* altered   838 *thy*] underlined for deletion; preceded by high ink point   844 *but*] underlined for deletion; preceded by high ink point   *what shall*] added in darker ink at end of line

Bal. They shall marry with Two thyne Anticks, Proteus.
Prot. I neuer thought other of them notwithstanding.
Grip. King Saturnus, what shall be his destinie? say, I pray you.
Bal. She his wife shall beguile him in his Accounts.
Rud My Lady Thetis too, what shall her lot be? say.   850
Bal. Fore foure and twenty howres be run their courses ˄\she/ shall sing
     a newe song, Full well I do know it, sweet Gentlemen my=
     ne.
Harp. Now once more for the token * But my Master what to day
He made hornes   shall be his Fortune?
Bal. His wife shall take him by the Bearde, I suppose.
Harp. Sir, I giue you thanks, for the Three, right heartily.
Prot. Not the Apes, as I sayd before, of Cataia may remoue his
     Resolution.

[FOL. 129ᵛ]

Pont. Please your Lordship now come furth receiue the   860
     wyne at our hands? say.
Bal. Pardonnes moy.
Rud. One wrench of your back as also ˄\but/ one Swing of ˄\your/ Tayle
     will bring you thither straite, Full well you do know
     so, Sir, I beleeue.
Bal. Monsieur ie boy qu'eau.
Rud. Hang thy self.
Bal. It is thy destinie, Rudens.
Rud. Since wee can not hit the signe.
Grip. Eury Almanack will tell you.   870
Rud. What course is to be taken now?
Prot. The Remora or Torpedo haue possessed mee, see.
Harp. Lift the Two hind wheeles, Man, and wind forward [luis-]
dilue   Lustily, Ha. Hey gee, drawe.
Prot. One Ounce of Galbanon., Three of Mithridate, Diacost
dilue   on fiue, [Dialac\c/|a] Dialacca six, Calamus Aromati=
     cus Two, Hermodactyles one Scruple, Diacolum=
     entum, Diacappuris, Diacurcuma, Diaphenicon.

851 ˄\she/] interlined word written above *shall* and smudged by blotting   854 *But*] *B* altered   855 *be*] ink mark between letters possibly false start for imperfect *e*   863 ˄\but/ *one*] caret under *o* of *one*   ˄\your/ *Tayle*] caret under *T* of *Tayle*   873 *luis-*] underlined for deletion; ink mark like dash above *l*; no point on *i*; possibly false start for *lustily*   875–6 *Diacost/on*] end of word on next line but no hyphen at end of line   876 *Dialac\c/|a*] underlined for deletion; preceded by high ink point; vertical rule separates last two letters

Grip. Now runneth he as he were greasd.
Rud. What the Pox art ambling on? Sirrha.   880
Prot I am numbring those the drugs, I must take in into
      mee first.
Rud. Art quick as thyne Anticks, Proteus.
Prot. Thou slowe as my Calues, Rudens. Two ounce oft haue
      it,∧ \and/ of I haue it.
Pont. Now eury one to his Booth, And meet wee here againe
      as wee haue now done, And with Instruments and
      with Tooles lykwise.
Prot. Agreed, For by then I shall haue got a drug for his Lord=
      ship, so whale whale, now looke vnto thy Tayle, Hoa.   890
Pont. Harpax, come along.
Harp. Ponticus, goe on before, I will follow you. Now my Mas-
      ters all, obserue mee but you. I must contort the whole
      Ingenie I haue against my Polt-footed Master his Blo=
      ck howse now, For behold I haue, According that the
      Commission was giuen mee by my cosen Aglaia,
      perused his letters, which such pure stuff they be, it
      is not possible but that as pure stuff thereon should
      follow, For let mee but consyder what I shall distin=
      guish, in them, the cheifest; Here be cro\o/[<c>]kt letters,   900
      crookt lines, crookt orthography, crookt Inuention, croo=
      kt Inditing, crookt all, wherefore, in breife, that I may,
      but in countercambio, not deale so Indirectly, with his
      honour as he hath done with himself
      I will first and foremost deliuer his letters to the super=
      scribed, then Imediately will returne to my fellows,
      after to begin that Paugeaunt, vpon him, which I haue
      now on foote. But, loe, here, in Pudding tyme they
      come.

                                              [Fol. 130ʳ]

---

881 *take*] *t* altered, possibly formed from illegible letter   885 *it,*∧ *and*/ *of*] comma obscured by caret; *and* added above *of*   886 *meet wee*] *t* added into gap between *mee wee*   892 *Mas-*] dash faint, near bottom of line   896 *Commission*] *'s* retraced   900 *cro**o*/[<*c*>]*kt*] *o* interlined above ?*c* deleted with vertical stroke   904] blank space at end of line filled with series of vertical strokes and cross hatchings   908 *here*] ²*e* possibly altered   *in*] point on *i* merges with mainstroke of *p* in *vpon* on line above

Act 2. Scen 6.
The Direction
910

Arida, Humida in their ordinary habits, vide names
of Persons, Perukes and Rabates of the same. The one
dilue cloth of Syluer blewe, The other ˄ \cloth of Gold/ yelow. [Satten] for expre=
sions of the sheene – blewe water Sea and the yelowe dry=
land shoare.

Humida Arida Harpax.

	Ar.	Sister Humida, though your reasons were this morning
		at our rising so Pregnaunt, you shall neuer persuade mee
		though, but that, in some things, wee do excell you. 920
	Hum	I tell thee, Arida, in each thing, the moyst is to be præfer\e/d
		before the Drye, In as much, Man, some Philosophers
		haue affirmed him the Element of all. But let that passe,
		And tell mee, how sits my wyre, Sister.
	Ar.	Passing well, in my conceit, it does, Sister.
	Hum.	But how? this Iewel.
[\<glistring>]	Ar.	Well. But how [blewe] doth your Band looke? Barbara.
[\<Trew>]	Hum.	It looketh of the [verteous] complexion ˄ \cullour,/ Honestye.
[\<....>]	Ar.	Nay but myne of the Ieleous complexion cullour, verily.
	Hum.	See, here is one doth obserue our talk, whoore. 930
	Ar.	I, by my Troth, does he, whoore.
	Hum.	Let's quæstion him, deare Sister myne.
	Ar.	Agreed, yfaith, Come.
	Hum	Faire youth, hast any Thing? say to vs.
	Harp.	Yes Madame.
	Hum	What? I prithy.
	Harp.	I am to deliuer each your Ladiships a letter.
	Hum	From whom?
	Harp.	From my Master.
	Hum	Who's thy Master? Sweet. 940

911–17] written on pasted slip, in darker ink; text is visible after the scene direction, possibly the top of *h, D, i,* and *r* from the original *The Direction* line   914 *Satten*] underlined for deletion   916 *land*] *d* possibly altered   927 \<*glistring*>] word added in left margin and smudged for deletion *blewe*] underlined for deletion; preceded by high ink point; deletion presumably cancelled   928 \<*Trew*>] word added in left margin and smudged for deletion *verteous*] underlined for deletion; preceded by high ink point; deletion presumably cancelled   929 \<....>] illegible word added in left margin and smudged for deletion   931 *I, by*] comma and *b* altered   935 *Harp.*] *H* possibly altered

    Harp. Vulcan.
    Hum. Requireth he an Answere?
    Harp. Yes, Madame.
    Hum. Imediately?
    Harp. So and shall lyke your honours?
    Hum. That's a pretie Boy. Come again but by and by, shalt haue them
          Adieu.
    Harp. And you, Madames *

Here they reade their letters to themselues fir=st.

          Hum) Pure Rogue. Sirrah, in good sadnes la, shall
    I heare thy letter? In recompense shalt heare myne.   950
Ar. With my whole hearte, good sister Humida
Hum. List now.
    Moyst Humida, moyst as is a Spunge, I haue fed so much
    on the Curst of thy soule, it lyeth on my stomach heauy
    as does Crust, wherefore I do adiure thee, wench, by ˄\all/ those
    the Potations, in our childhood, wee haue beene both toge=
    ther at, thou yeild, vp to mee, thee now my [concu\<bi\>ne] concubine

[Fol. 130ᵛ]

    That I shall obteyne thee I do obserue by the Dawes,
    Then, Humida, but breifly list to my deuice, whereas
    thou being the water, I the Fyar, wee shall neuer agree   960
    (For Fyar and water, they say, will neuer agree) by much
    feeding, as Possible I may, I will engrosse mee, for thy loue
    into that the aerye Element, By the which meane, I
    shall not onely gather, being now but a scrag, corpulence,
    But also wee shall then commix, both vs, so the better,
    our two greaces ˄ \in one/ which possible, I may not now so do, for
    want.
              Thyne neuer if not for one night
                    Vulcan.
    Send mee your answere and pay the Porter.   970
Ar. Worde for worde the same, but where he must needes.

---

949 *Rogue.*] stop smudged   954 *Curst*] *u* written over another character, possibly *r*, in darker ink
955 *all*/] caret under *t* of *those*; *ll* altered or retraced   957 *yeild*] *l* altered *concu<bi>ne*] underlined for deletion; preceded by blotted high ink point; *o* imperfect, looks like *v*; *bi* altered *concubine*] added in left margin to replace [*concu<bi>ne*]   958 *shall*] ²*l* altered, possibly from *t*   959 *deuice*] ²*e* possibly altered *whereas*] *s* possibly altered   961 *much*] *m* altered from another character, possibly *s*
962 *may,*] comma merges with descender of *y* in *they* on line above   *thy*] *y* altered or smeared
963 *By*] *B* altered   971 *needes*] *d* possibly altered

Hum. Lets heare him, Prithy.
Ar. Come.
     Drye Arida, drye as is a Spung, I haue fed so much on
     the Curst of thy soule, it lyeth on my stomach heauye
     as does Crust, wherefore I do adiure thee, wench, by
     all those the Potations, in our childhood, wee haue both
     beene together at, thou yeild, vp to mee, thee \now/ my concubine.
     That I shall obteyne thee, I do obserue by the Dawes. Then,
     Arida, but breifly list to my deuice. whereas thou being   980
     the Drye land, I sometyme the Aire, wee shall not agree (
For The Earth and the Aire, they say, will neuer Agree) I am
     determined come, to thee, anone, in my glorie of Fyar,
     By meane of the which, euen as the heate of my Fyre shall
     allay the cold of thy Earth, Arida, so also shall the cold of
     thy Earth allay the heate of my Fyre, Arida.
                Thyne neuer if not for one night
                        Vulcan.
     Send mee your answere and pay the Porter.
Hum. Had the Codshed no other work his fopperye on but vs   990
     Oceanides? But vs wise Proteus daughters? He that
     sayes Thetis shall haue a Sonne greater then be the Gods of
     Olympus? Ha. How shall both vs thouroughly be reuengd
     on him, Sister, saye.
Ar. Let vs but Metamorphe vs, the drye land into the Sea, and
     the Sea into drye Land, wee shall perfourme vpon him a
     right Ridiculous Ieast, Sister.
Hum. I vnderstand you; But when shall this be? Say.
Ar. Soone.
Hum. Betweene the one and the Two after dinner.   1000
Ar. No better howre.
Hum. So be it too. But goe wee now in both, allure him on,
     with our letters, Sister.
Ar. Agreed.

972 *heare*] *a* altered   978 *\now/*] *n* possibly altered   979 *Dawes*] *s* altered   *Then,*] *n* altered; comma retraced   981 *agree (*] *(* imperfect   982 *For*] added to left of line; *o* altered   983 *Fyar,*] comma imperfect, short   984 *heate*] gap between *he* and *ate*   *shall*] otiose stroke under *s*   985 *Earth*] *h* possibly altered from *t*   990 *fopperye*] '*p* altered   *but*] *t* written over another character, possibly *s*   993 *Olympus*] *s* possibly altered   995 *land*] *l* altered from ?*s*, possibly false start for *Sea*   999 *Soone*] *e* possibly altered   1002 *too*] *t* possibly altered from *s*   1004 *Agreed.*] stop faint

Hum Your song, Sister, first of the Moyst and of the Drye, I
     do beseech you [Fol. 131ʳ]
Ar. Saye.
The Second Song
Two women hauing Husbands of contrary com=
plexions.   1010

1

Both Ladyes, resolue vs this one doubt
     Which both wee be now about,
  Whither the Two, Moyst or the Drye,
     Do better with you agree

2

1. The woman that chuseth the Moyst
     May not thinke of other Foist.
2. The Drye, it is not any Lye,
     Will nurse no Ielouzie.   1020

3

1. To Moyst, I do very well know
     Neuer do wee say o ho.
2. Vnto the Drye, as I do wisse
     Wee say, till soone keepe your kisse.

4.

1. How should wee by the Moyst learne
     Whither wee but little earne
2. The Drye will say, to vs, againe
     Trye againe, there is no paine   1030

1012] SP high   1013 *now*] *w* altered; ink mark under *o*   1014 *Whither*] *h* possibly altered   1020 *Ielouzie*] *z* possibly altered   1024 *the*] *e* possibly altered   1025 *Wee*] *W* possibly altered   *keepe*] ³*e* possibly altered   1029 *againe*] point on *i* over *a*

                             5
1.   My Goodman, if he but abound
          I breech him for it sound.
2.   My husband, if he wax too drye
          I [recure] restore him by Cookrye.
                             6
1.   The Moyst will refresh vs too drye
          And Poope vs all the coneye.
2.   The Drye will bate vs much of yee
          And saue vs [much] too Nurse-money.   1040
                             7
Both. Now, Ladyes, resolue vs our doubt
          Which wee both to you put out
       Whither the Two, Moyst or the Drye
          Be, to you, a better fee.
Hum Sirrha shalt see the Foole, rightly anone, ydressed, in his cul=
       lours, all, yfaith. But come away now, and follow mee, to Court
       to dinner.
Ar.   I follow you.

             Act 2 Scen 7   1050
         Oceanus Leander in Godlyke attyre.
                                                    [FOL. 131ᵛ]
Oce. Leander, thou Knowst, what haue beene the loues
       Of Marine dietyes to thee, First, by
       That burning Feruency, where with Nereus
       Daughter, this morning, tooke thee on the Sea, Next,
       By my bestowing that Blessing on thee,
       Of all the greatest, Immortallity.
       This I do not recapitulate to thee,
       As I would send thee againe to shoare,

1032 *he*] *e* possibly altered   1035 *recure*] underlined for deletion; preceded by high ink point; ²*e* imperfect, looks like *o*   *restore*] added in left margin in lighter ink to replace [*recure*]   1040 *And*] poorly formed, cross-stroke faint   *much*] underlined for deletion; preceded by faint, blotted high ink point   *too*] added in left margin in lighter ink to replace [*much*]   1042] SP high   1045 *Be*] both letters altered   1046 *anone*] *e* possibly altered   1051 *Godlyke*] *l* possibly altered   1054 *That*] *h* possibly altered

40

	As one vnmeet for this high Dignitye,	1060
	But that thou wouldst requite one loue for other.	
	Then, good Leander, this is that I do	
	Say to thee, thou wouldst helpe mee in a suite,	
dilue	To which thou, and none but thou, mayst further [thee] mee.	
	This the Breif, so thou, in breif, now answere mee.	
Lean.	Sir, what needed these Protestations?	
	Vnto that Man that loues and honours you.	
	Your Bounties be to mee, as leaues that fall	
	In th'Haruest season, or Spots cælestiall,	
	Then boldly say your mind, If any Thing	1070
	It be in compasse of Leanders Powre.	
Oce.	Come, must haue thy oathe too (Lean) I will, by Ioue.	
Oce.	Then Know, I loue thy Here, and none but Here,	
	And to thy Promise here I chalenge Here.	
Lean.	Gods, ere' who would haue thought, Oceanus	
	T'haue gone about to taint his Seruaunts Bed?	
Oc.	Shall I haue her according that thy oath?	
Lean	To sell his ioye Leander would be loath.	
Oce.	What would not th'one freind do to please the other.	
Lean.	If Freind vnfreindly craues wee must be other.	1080
Oce.	Some loue Community, then why not some?	
Lean.	Some be some, some be some, How now your doome?	
Oce.	The Spartan gaue his wife the gallantst Man.	
Lean.	Should a trewe Louer sell his heartes ioy than?	
Oce.	Boue all the Gods do hate Ingratitude.	
Lean.	So when in others corne wee Sythes intrude.	
Oce.	Better left in place it is no Theeuerye.	
Lean.	Anything tenderer then Here to mee.	
Oce.	Thou wilt \not/ aduance my burning Suite? seye.	
Lean.	I can not, Sir, I pray you Pardon mee.	1090
Oce.	Well. I will trye an other way with thee.	
	Wilt beare her a gemme, as token, from mee?	
Lean.	Sir, that most willingly (Oce) Reade thou this now. *

1060 *Dignitye*] 'i altered or added in darker ink by high ink point   1064 *thee*] underlined for deletion; preceded   1068 *that*] *ha* retraced   1072 *(Lean)* high ink spot precedes bracket   1075 *ere'*] apostrophe merges with descender of *y* in *thy* on previous line

41

  some gemme encha= Leand) Thyne by the styx.
  sed in shell of a Fish   Oce) Ha? Hast thou sworn by the Poole of styx, she's myne?
  with Posye about him Then la, Sir Boy, vpon the Penaltie
          I claime thy Promise (Lean) I haue I do|graunt,
          [But withall] There withall desire to be remitted
  Oce. The world shall not vnbind thee, Leander.

[FOL. 132ʳ]

Lean. Good Sir, consyder mee (Oce) Speake [no more, Boy,] not to mee 1101
   Behold I charge thee on the Penaltie
   That on the default depends, which is losse
   Of thy Immortallity, thou bring mee,
   And that without [any] Longer Tardation,
   Faire Hero to my bed, think thou on it,
   And say Oceanus hath forewarned thee,
   Till then I leaue thee, what Lyons can not
   Cunning Foxes may. But now I must waite
   On Cytheræa. (Lean) Hard choice, Leander,
   To loose Immortallity or Loue. 1110
   The one is deare to mee as is my soule,
   Th'other the Spire of our Beatitude,
   I'll persuade her ˰\though/ according my Bond
   Till she find meane to cancell it, By hap,
   May she saue Immortallity and Loue.
   Onely, for the Fact, if thou displeased be,
   O Cytheræa deare, o Pardon mee.
     Here they knockt vp the consort.

1095 *sworn*] *s* possibly altered 1097 *do|graunt*] vertical rule separates words 1098 *But withall*] underlined for deletion; preceded by high ink point *There withall*] added in left margin in different ink to replace [*But withall*] 1100 *no more, Boy,*] underlined for deletion; high ink point and otiose vertical stroke above *no* *not to mee*] added in left margin in different ink to replace [*no more, Boy,*] 1104 *any*] underlined for deletion *Longer*] added on pasted slip in left margin, in different ink and in larger writing, to replace [*any*] 1107 *then*] *t* written over *w* 1109 *Lean*)] bracket descends through line below 1111 '*is*] *s* possibly altered *deare*] 'e altered 1112 *Beatitude,*] comma partially obscured by ascender of *d* in *Bond* in line below

       Act 3 Scen 1.
Braue and glo= Oceanus* Cytheræa Nereus Thetis   1120
rious to behold. Glauce, The Three Graces, Attendaunts, sauing
       Leander and Hero.

Oce. Cytheræa, Queene of the heauenly orbes,
   As wee all well may now say, happily
   To this our Court welcome you be, For such
   Be the defects of our Element here,
   Wee had neede the Generall Parliament
   Of Gods had descended, to vs, from aboue,
   To haue discust our wrongs, yet since, alone,
   In you be conteynd what of them is sayd,   1130
   Wee humbly beseech your diety diuine,
   You would but streighten vs in these our Paths,
   And see redresse to each that is a misse.
Cyth. My Lord, such is the Power Loue hath infusde
   Into this Breast of ours from the Beginning
   Of the World, that as it is my bounden dewtye
   I may not gainesay you in what I may,
   So what so ere it be that your Lordship
   shall Impose vpon mee, I shall be ready,
   With all that strengh and Powre lyeth in mee,   1140
   Obey you to th'vtmost of what I can.
Oce. Honour and Thanks to the sacred Person
   Of thy noble self, my Petition too
   Be it to the Parliament of Heauen,
   [They would] That haue indewd thee with ˄\that/ sapience
                [FOL. 132ᵛ]
   That is in them conteynd; (For as [thou saydst] I sayd it,
   (Thou wert, at first, the Mother of vs all),

1120 SD.2 *behold*] *l* possibly altered   1121 *Graces*] *c* possibly altered *sauing*] *s* altered from ?*a*
1129 *our*] *o* possibly retraced   1130 *conteynd*] *d* possibly altered   1132 *Paths*] lobe of *P*
possibly altered or retraced   1133 *misse*] otiose point above *se*   1137 *you*] stain of blotted letter
from other side of folio shows through below *u*   1138 *what*] otiose ink mark below *w*   1144
Heauen,] comma altered from stop   1145 *They would*] underlined for deletion; preceded by high ink
point *That haue*] added in left margin to replace [*They would*] *indewd*] ²*d* formed from *e* *sapience*]
c possibly altered   1146 *conteynd;*] semi-colon merges with bracket *thou saydst*] underlined for
deletion; preceded by high ink point *I sayd*] added in left margin to replace [*thou saydst*]; *say* possibly
retraced   1147 *all),*] bracket merges with comma

43

        [So beseech wee] Wee may beseech their good dietyes all,
        The last thou mayst be vnto them and vs.
Cyth. What is your suite to vs, Lord Nereus,   1150
        For by your looke, it seemeth vnto mee,
        You haue, in hand, some match, the which without
        Our helpe, may not be perfourmed so well.
Ner. Noble Cytheræa, thus it is, loe,
        (Without Cæremony I tell you trewe)
        Glauce my daughter, whom you behold here,
        Whilst Auster, this morne, vented his rage
        On th'Hellespont, by force and strengh of armes
        Sest on faire Leander as he crossd
        Our warde vnto his Make, who since, by doome   1160
        Of our Marine dietyes, as also
        By our Priuiledge of Place, in which he's now,
        He's adiudgd to Glauces Bed, wee beseech
        You would but present be at the Diuorce,
        And with your sacred hands knit to the Knot.
Cyth. A Lusty Lasse, mary, to Counterwrastle
        With such a lusty young man to her bed.
        How say you, Glauce, be you contented
        I do make vp this Bond betweene you? Ha
Glau. Madame, what thanks Glauce may yeild vnto you   1170
        For the same, most willingly she subscribeth.
Thet. Trust mee, Madame, my sister Glauce, in this,
        Hath got th'aduantage ore mee, yet I hope sure
        My case will be better though long in breeding.
Cyth. Trewe haue you spoken, Lady Thetis, trewe,
        For your destinie is th'haue a worthier
        Make then she. But be you content, Glauce,
        I make vp this Match betweene you? (Glau) I am.
Cyth. Much good do it you I wooe the Gods than.
Glau. And the Gods reward Cytheræa for it.   1180
Oce. In the Behalf of both, I do giue thanks

1148 *So beseech wee*] underlined for deletion; ink blot or blotted letter above *S*   *Wee may beseech*] added in left margin to replace [*So beseech wee*]   *all,*] comma merges with ascender of *d* in *and* on line below   1153 *well*] *w* retraced   1158 *armes*] small ink mark at end of line, preceded by a large gap; probably otiose   1159 *crossd*] followed by otiose blotted letter or ink mark in right margin   1165 *hands*] *h* possibly altered   1170 *thanks*] *s* possibly retraced   1176 *destinie*] ¹*e* possibly altered from *i*   1177 *Make*] *M* altered, possibly from *I* in false start for next line

    To your Sacrednes, as of my children both.
    The while, to you, my suite let it be this,
    If any there shall be default here,
    In this your now Aphrodysial, Madame,
    Either in Cheare or in Sport, you would not
    Impute it a Fault vnto vs, But to
    The hasty comming, of yourself, vpon vs.
Cyth. So, and shall lyke you, good Lord Ocean.
Oce. So let vs all to dinner, Come (Cyth) Your Lordship   1190
    Would but leade the way, wee will follow you.

   Act 3 Scen 2.

                    [FOL.133ʳ]
    The Direction
    Vulcan Brontes Steropes Pyracmon with ham
    mers and Aprones, Goldsmith Hammers, Els Iron-work
    Hammers for better Propertie of mouing their Armes, whi=
    ther the better you may chuse. The stithie supposd as Also
    their Hammers by mouing of their Armes onely, or Hamm=
    ers Reall, whither the better. The Longer Hammer I think.
      Vulcan Brontes Steropes Pyracmon.   1200
Vul. Pyracmon, Brontes, Steropes (All) My Lord.
Vu. Bring wee furth the stithye and fall to work,
    This Present will not be done, By the Tyme, els.
Bront. The labour will be in the beating, The
    Rest is nothing (Vul) Then Tymely let vs beate it.
Pyr. In a Pythagæran Round, I wisse
Vul. So. Sett, Masters. *

They moued their armes as had been working. No song here.

     Ster) I wonder Cytheræa, that drinketh lyke a Sparrowe so,
    The Gods of the Sea should bespeake her a Posset Bolle would
    water an Oxe, my Lord.   1210
Vul. It was my Lady Aglaia her own Proiect, not any theires, I do assure
    you, Gentlemen.
Pyr. As how? I pray you.
Vul. I haue a wife, The Lord be praised for her, of the Element of other

	whoores, sober abroade and Rauenous at home, that is the very cause she bespake him so.	

Ster.   Why then, in a Pox, bespake she not an engin too, to heaue it to her Mouth?
Vul.   For she vses mich it away all, from her Lady, by the Tap.
Bront So you conclude your wife to be a whoore, my Lord?   1220
Vul.   Dost not see it?
Bront. Yes, very well.
Vul.   Yet, when I do tell her of it, euer and anone she breakes my heade, with a rusty Hammer, for it.
Bront But how? and shall lyke you.
Vul.   Sine Cerere et Baccho friget Venus, without wyne and good cheare, Venus waxes cold.
Pyr.   Can you not breake hers with another? my Lord.
Vul.   As how? say you.
Pyr.   Temperet appositum Lympha refusa merum. Put but full   1230 water into your wyne you shall be safe.
Vul.   No sore, yet now and then she and I be at quarter blowes.
Ster.   Where she is Quarter-Master ouer you.
Vul.   Oncc the quarter but
Ster.   As when? my Lord.
Vul.   In Bucking Tyme but.
Ster   Videlicet euer.
Bront. I shall tell you, Sir, If I had such a wife, I should haue beate her hed and the stithye together, sure.
Vul.   Possible, by Force of Hammer, there is not to be beate ⌃\Furth/ such an other, sure.   1241

[FOL. 133ᵛ]

Pyr.   A Pox on her, she is good for naught.
Vul.   Trewe, for she is good to be naught, For I shall tell you, Gentle= men, she hath pickt my Pocket many and oft.
Bront A good Repairer of his wiues Creuis he is.
Ster.   Faith, good My Lord, how oft, the yeare, doth your Lordship lye with her.

1223 *heade*] ²*e* possibly altered   1226 *Vul.*] ink spot above *V*   *Cerere*] ¹*e* and ³*e* possibly retraced   1227 *waxes*] *w* imperfectly formed   1231 *your*] otiose ink mark precedes word   1232 *quarter*] *q* possibly retraced   1244 *oft.*] stop possibly retraced   1246 *lye*] *l* retraced

Vul. But once the yeare.
Ster. As when?
Vul. Vpon her Marriage day but.   1250
Pyr. She shutts him vp her stallion I beleeue.
Vul. I will trick her a coate to her Father.
Bront She, with her tricks will trick you an other.
Vul. I will Anathomise the Carrian vnto him.
Ster. Sing wee, and be merry, and let the Carrian gad, whither her
      Hed will leade her, well.
Pyr. Well sayd, by my Fa, For wee haue, euen, Smoake enough,
      in the howse, without her.
Bront.Yes, by our Lady, and sweet St Anne too.
Vul. But come, Now let vs round it, in a Syluer Round, All foure   1260
      Men wee. Come.
Bront.A Thing, at this Tyme, not vnrequisite, therefore not to
      be omitted. Saye.

Here shorter hammers or hands.

            * The Third Song.
                 1

    To stithye, to stithye, you Cyclops soone,
        Now let vs take this Bolle in hand.
    It will be high Noone before it be done,
        I doe Protest by Cupids Brand.
      Pit a pat, pit a pat strike it sound,   1270
      Pit a pat pit a pat, clip him round.
               2.
    This Metall of Gold, loe it is but brittle,
        Giue him chaunce, that it to vs sold,
    The drosse is much and the substance but little
        Giue him Bane that [that] thus has vs polld.
      Pit a pat pit a pat strike it sound
      Pit a pat Pit a pat, clip him round.

1253 *tricks*] s altered; additional stroke may be intended as comma   1255 *Ster.*] otiose ink mark beneath *S*   *whither*] i imperfect, lacking point; r written over illegible letter   1257 *Smoake*] S possibly altered; o written over smaller o   1258 *without*] 't possibly retraced   1260 *Vul.*] otiose point above stop   1264 SD 1.–2. *hamm/ers*] a altered, imperfect   1269] otiose ink point in right margin   1271] ink mark in right margin, transfer from f of *floore* on next folio (l. 1322)   1272 *2.*] gap precedes stop   1276 *that*] underlined for deletion; preceded by high ink point   *thus*] added in left margin to replace [*that*]   1277 *sound*] d altered

        3
  Well sayd, my Mates, and lusty Masters all,   1280
    Strike the Iron while it is hot,
  If after dinner you come to my Hall
    You shall be repayd eury groate.
    Pit a pat Pit a pat strike it sound,
    Pit a pat pit a pat clip him round.
        4.
  Noble Aglaia my darling deare,
    Now that thou art exalted faire,
  If thou hearest on that syde of ˄\the/ eare,
    Thou wouldest but pay mee my fare.   1290
    Pit a pat pit a pat strike it sound,
    Pit a pat [a pit ˄\a/ pat] Pit a pat clip him round.
                 [FOL. 134ʳ]

Ster. Loe, your Sonne Talus commeth toward vs with an oare
   on his shoulder, seemeth by his Countenaunce, he would haue
   some Priuate conference with your Lordship.
Vul. Well it may so be, The Boy hath not beene well since morning,
   Goe, get you in all, Rest an howre, then do you fall, againe, to
   your work; all.
Pyr. Feare not, my Lord, wee shall.

     Act 3 Scen 3.   1300
    Talus with an oare **Vulcan**
Tal. Father, [good day] God speede your hand, I pray the Gods
dilue So prosper you in your cheifest wish, Sir,
   As I haue neede of succour at your hand.
Vul. How now? Man, what makes thee looke thus sad?
   And with an oare too, on thy shoulder? say.
Tal. Father, the Paphian God hath struck mee.
Vul. Gods pretious, Knaue, if that be it, wee'le haue her,

1287 *Noble*] indistinct lobe on *b*   1288 *exalted*] *t* lacks headstroke   1290 *wouldest*] *l* possibly altered   1292 *a pit* ˄*a*/ *pat*] underlined for deletion; preceded by high ink point; *pit* altered or retraced; *a* in *pat* written over *e*; *t* in *pat* retraced *Pit a pat*] added in left margin to replace [*a pit* ˄*a*/ *pat*] *clip*] *c* altered   1296 *Well*] *e* possibly altered *since*] *e* altered   1302 *good day*] underlined for deletion; preceded by high ink point   1303 *prosper*] *prospe* retraced *cheifest*] ²*e* possibly altered   1308 *wee'le*] apostrophe above ²*e*

		I, and it were Aglaia for thy Loue,	
		For blither then she is she cannot be.	1310
	Tal.	Not all the Toungs that be from Pole to Pole,	
		Not all those charmes that be conteynd in Veste,	
		Nor all the Powres that come from Erebus	
		May either ease or comfort mee (Vul) And why?	
		I pray you (Tal) so difficult I'haue found	
		This pretious Purchase (Vul) The woman? say.	
	Tal.	Thetis begot of Dore and Nereus.	
Pointing [<a>]to	Vul.	Thetis I'haue known as light as is that Froth, *	
some corner		And would she not graunt? (Tal) In deed she graunted mee,	
of the stage or		But with such a condition, Father ————	1320
floore rather	Vul.	Relate the circumstance from point to point.	
	Tal.	I had, quod she, now many yeares agone	
		[A Loue-rolle] A Ceston for my wrests, which long I held	
		As pretious as these eyes, with it I queld	
		The waues, with it the waues I lykwise raised,	
		When as at any Tyme, I crossd the Maine,	
		Raisd lykwise with this th' Affections of Loue.	
		The same I lent one day to Vlysses,	
		Mou'd with compassion on the Man,	
		Whilst he in dangrous Perill was of life,	1330
		To bring him safe on shoare, which since the Tyme	
		Neuer my eyes could see it more (W|vl) And then?	
	Tal.	She sayd, she vowd to marry none but him	
		Should bring it her, withall she ˰\did/ Impose	
		The Task vpon mee. So, with vnpartiall	
		Eye, Behold, Sir, how I haue toyled.	
	Vul.	I smell her drift, her queint and delicate	
		Stomach will digest no Fish but Cod[<s>] Fish	
	dilue	They say, what wouldst haue [\m/thee] mee do for thee? say.	

1310 *blither*] *bl* retraced; *t* possibly altered   1312 *charmes*] *h* possibly altered   1316 *The*] *e* possibly altered   1318 SD.1 [<a>]*to*] <a> cancelled with vertical strokes, possible false start for *at   is*] letters possibly formed from *w*, in false start for *woman* two lines above   1323 *A Loue-rolle*] underlined for deletion   *A Ceston*] added in darker ink on pasted slip in left margin to replace [*A Loue-rolle*]; *A* retraced   1327 *Raisd*] *a* possibly altered   1330 *Whilst*] otiose ink strokes above *W*   1331 *shoare*] otiose ink spot below *oa*   1332 *more*] ink spot below *m*   *W*\|*vl*] *W*\|*v* written over or formed from illegible letters   1333 *him*] *i* imperfect, missing point   1334 *her*] *e* altered   1336 *toyled*] *t* retraced   1337 *Vul.*] SP high; otiose point follows stop   *drift*] *t* smudged, imperfect   1338 *Cod*[<s>]] *s* deleted with vertical stroke   1339 \m/*thee*] *thee* underlined for deletion; *m* written above *t*

[FOL. 134ᵛ]

Tal. The Bolts of Iupiter be made you know 1340
     Of Scalding Austers, of Freezing Aquiloes,
     Of Fyre, of Hayle and Rayne, Now of Same stuff
     If you might work lyke [Bracelet] Ceston vnder gold
     Enameld to bleare her sight I would not
     Doubt but t'obteyne the fruite of my long suite.
Vul. This all hast say to mee? (Tal) Sir, this is all.
Vul. How if I be depriud of heauenly Blisse?
     To pleasure thee. (Tal) Rather let Talus dye.
Vul. Thy suite is graunt, though Possible it be
     I shall be hurld down the Skie for it, Come 1350
     Thy wayes, and gather thy Spirit, Since the
     One leg I haue already broake, I will,
     As well, aduenture th'other for thy sake.
     I'll teach her a Trick for aspiring make
     Men greater then ˬ \be/ the Gods, I warrant her.
Tal. I thank you, Sir, your Liberallitye
     Hath redeemed mee from the Iawe of Hell.
Vul. Come dispatch, For I haue buisinesse now
     Concerning myne own very self, in hand.
     Come. 1360

Act 3 Scen 4.
Proteus Harpax Rudens Ponticus
Gripus.

Prot. Come, come, my Mates, let mee embattle you my
     self, come.
Pont. Wee be too grosse for thy Batteling, Proteus.
Prot. Come, come, Harpax, present thou, here, Neptune with
     thy Trident, Rudens, thou here behind him with thy
     Roapes, Ponticus on thy left syde with his leauer, Grip-
     pus, thou, here, on the right hand with thy Grapple, so. 1370
     where be the rest all?

1340 *Bolts*] *o* imperfect, looks like *v*; *l* poorly formed, looks like imperfect *s*   1341 *Aquiloes*] *es* imperfect   1343–4] written in darker ink on pasted slip   1343 *Bracelet*] underlined for deletion; preceded by high ink point above upper edge of pasted slip   *Ceston*] added in left margin of pasted slip bearing lines 1343–4 to replace [*Bracelet*]   1362 *Ponticus*] *c* possibly altered   1364 *Mates*] otiose ink stroke below *s*   *embattle*] '*e* possibly altered   1366 *too*] headstroke on *t* extends into possible false start for an imperfect *o*, followed by *oo*   1370 *so.*] otiose point above *o*

Grip. I do know of none els that you haue, vnles it be honest Glau
    cus, that keepes, at home, the Cats from burning, Mr Pro=
    teus.
Prot. I, in the armes of this circle.
The Direction.
He had about him, lyke a scarff, A Blank list, beset with
black Figures, and now placed on the floore. Book and
wand too. The Signes of the Zodiake mixt with other
of a Fashion more strange, The Figures being, both   1380
together, of this list.
Pont. I, mary, Sir, he hath plact himself lyke vnto a Pole=
    tick and warie Captaine I auowe.
Prot. Captaine Hannibal did the lyke, Sirs, I do assure you trew.
Harp. I am persuaded, I shall egregiously anger the villaine
    now, I do so stand puting Hornes at him, loe.
                                                              [FOL. 135^r]
Pont. Rather thou standst, lyke one, should stick a Brawn, Harpax
Harp. Thou lyke an Oxe-sumner, Ponticus, the rather.
Rud. I will gird him faith.
Grip. Sir, when begin wee? I pray you.   1390
Prot Now, Sir
Harp. So, Sir.
Prot Buckle in your sel[f]ues.
Rud. With doe, Sir.
Prot Feare not, and I warrant you.
Pont. Wee Troe, Sir.
Prot Call, when you see him.
Grip. Who ho ho, Sir.
Prot Come not within my Circle, I reade you.
Harp. No no no, Sir.   1400

1373 *burning*] u could be *a*; *ing* blotted   1377 *about him*] headstroke of *t* touches ascender of *h*   *Blank*] *B* imperfect and possibly altered   *list,*] comma retraced   *beset*] *se* altered or retraced   1378 *placed*] *p* possibly formed from long *s*; *l* altered   1379 *too*] '*o* possibly altered   *other*] *o* altered, possibly from *w*; *h* possibly altered   1382 *himself*] *el* imperfect; *f* smudged   *lyke*] *l* smudged   *a*] otiose ink mark to top right of *a*   1382–3 *Pole=/tick*] *t* imperfect, possibly altered   *warie*] *w* possibly altered   *auowe.*] *e* imperfect; stop merges with ascender of *d* in *do* on line below   1385 *egregiously*] '*e* imperfect   1388 *Oxe-sumner*] *n* possibly altered from *m*   1393 *sel[f]ues*] *f* cancelled with vertical stroke   1399 *within*] *w* possibly altered   1400 *Harp*] *H* imperfect, cross-stroke is faint; otiose point above stop

The Direction.
At eury Cupplets end passed an Antick ouer the stage with a dish
of Fish, Musick still playing on. And from this place to the
later end of the next Scene The still Musick playing on, both
the Scenes through.

Prot.)   Oysters and Musell,
By sise a Bushell,
Before my Lord,
Vpon his Borde,
Wee you entreate,   1410
By Ioues high seate,
Do not repent you
But see present you,
Ere he be sett
Vnto his Meate.

Harp. Your humble Seruaunts, consydering your manifold ver=
tues, my Lord, be come, Sir, to present you, with a boate
full of their caption, See.

Act 3 Scen 5.
Balene Harpax Rudens Ponticus Gripus   1420
Proteus.

Bal. What's the store?
Harp. Mary, my Lord, first and Imprimis, before your entrance to Ta=
ble, here is a huge, and well and trewly measurd Bushell
of oysters for you.
Bal. There be too fewe, for my feeding, here.
Rud. Wee haue chosen them, as neare as wee could, to the sise
Of your Mawe, my Lord.
Bal. I shall not be filled with them now, I assure you.
Pont. The more sorie wee.   1430
Grip. Since it will be no other with you, what other Remedy? Sir,
I pray you now.
Bal. Why, some other dish, I beseech you now.

1403 *Fish*] s altered or retraced   1405 *through.*] stop added in darker ink above faint stop
1406 *Prot.)*] bracket overlaps stop   1415 *Meate*] ²e possibly altered   1416 *consydering*]
g partially faint   *manifold*] otiose point between l and d, possibly intended as an extension of l
1416–17 *ver=/tues*] t possibly altered   1420 *Rudens*] n altered   1423–4 *Ta=/ble*] b and e possibly
altered   1424 *huge*] u imperfect, looks like dash   *trewly*] y retraced

Prot)   Meate for King,
        A dish of Ling
        As I deuine,
        By yond Sunshine,
        A Forraine State,
        Awaites to bate,
        Hasten thee soone,   1440
        Ere he be gone,
        Els will he soone,
        Thee call greate Lown.

Bal.   Ling, Ling, stand thou [<c>]neare, that I may ⌃ \but/ smack thee now.

Rud. Trewly, Sir, most chu⌃\re/lously, he, loe, now fumeth vpon you, See.

Grip. The villaine thinketh more of his Letcherye then he does of his Belly, I perceiue him trewe.

Pont For did you not obserue with what whot assaults of em=   1450
bracements he came vpon the Ling? Hoa.

Bal.   I haue Smackt him and smackt him, suffiently, I troe.

Harp. He will be ⌃ \much/ made on for it, I do assure you, my Lord.

Grip. Both by Male and by Female, I assure you, Sir.

Rud   Now, Sirrha, Baite him ⌃ \thou/ with the vieu of a Codshed, Hoa.

Prot. Let mee alone with him, Come.

        Prot)   Capacious Cod,
              I pray my God,
              In goodly tune,   1460
              As Cabbage done,
              May wax thy Polle,
              As huge as Poule,
              As it is sayd,
              In Ancient Reade,
              My Lord be fed
              With thy greate hed.

[FOL. 135ᵛ]

1444 [<c>]*neare*] letter cancelled with vertical stroke; *a* imperfect, possibly formed from *e* *but*] *b* retraced; *u* altered   1446 *fumeth*] *e* possibly altered   *vpon*] otiose ink mark follows word   1453 *Lord.*] two points above stop, probably otiose   1455 ⌃*thou*/ *with*] *h* of *thou* written over *y*; caret below *i* of *with*   1457] SP low   1458 *Prot)*] bracket extends down to bottom of line 1459   1459 *I*] retraced

	Harp.	Looke you, Sir, A most comely and venerable Codshed
		presents him now vnto you.
	Bal.	I haue but tasted of him.	1470
dilue.	Pont.	[Nof] Not of him, I am sure you haue.
	Bal.	For my Belly is full of the foresayd Ling, I assure you
	Grip.	That I perceiued well by that the salt Rheume he bel=
		cht vpon thee, Ponticus.
	Rud.	Trewly, Sir, wee haue taken maruellous paine in
		the taking same Cod, for your Lordship.
	Bal.	Some other Dish, I beseech you now.
	Harp.	Proteus, A iolle of Sturgeon hath not his fellow, for
		a Princes boarde, they say.
	Prot	Come on, by my Troth, come.	1480

        Prot)   Sturgeon, to whom,

[FOL. 136ʳ]

    People of Rome,
    Wonted to Fum,
    Trumpet and Bum,
    When he came in,
    Their Lords to dine,
    My Lord not Fright
    With fearefull Sight,
    As if that Sight,
    Were ghastly Spright.   1490

Harp Loe you, my Lord, a sturgeon keepeth now in his Mouth, for
      feare least he should displease your honour with it, loe.
Rud. He frighted a King with it once, but he kisses your Lordship
      with it now.
Bal.   I will none of him, For he smells ˄\too/ rank of the Marine; Foh.
Rud. He will consume for it, If I may be bold saye it to you, my
      Lord, I dare well say.
Bal.   Second course, Hoa.
Harp. Zounds, I think thou liuest on the sauour of broyled meates,
      as do the Gods of Olympus, Sirrha.   1500

1468 *venerable*] *a* retraced; *b* possibly altered   1469 *presents*] *nt* smudged by blotting   1470
Bal.] *B* retraced   *him*] point on *i* retraced   1471 *Nof*] underlined for deletion; preceded by high
point   *am*] *a* imperfect, possibly altered   1477 *now*] *o* altered or retraced   1481 *Sturgeon*] gap
between *g* and *e*; *o* possibly formed from *e*   1488 *With*] *W* possibly altered

Grip. By your leaue, I perceiued yet, that his Mouth much did wa=
ter after the Salt-Fish, Sirs.
Rud. So, Man, he did after the Rest.
Bal. Second course, I saye.
Harp. To dresser, Proteus.
Bal. Gentlemen and yeomen, waite you on the Sewer all, Hoa.
Grip. Thou art the merriest Piece, as euer Man delt with, Sirrha.

*Prot   Fishes and Wantons,
        From diuers Cantons,
        You be so wimble,   1510
        You be so nimble,
        But once the yeare
        Wee see you here,
        Passe by in shoales,
        Forsake your holes,
        As you next yeare,
        Encrease would here.

Thick with dishes.

Harp. Loe you, Sir, a whole Shoale of them floate in vpon you
dilue [now], So that you may come furth, chuse you, according
your own good lyking, now.   1520
Bal. Reach mee but a note of them.
Harp. Here be Herrings, Gurnets, Mackrills, Congers, Whitings,
Playces, Puffins, Powtins, Greate Crab and little Crab,
Anchoues, Greene Fish cum multis alijs quos nunc Per=
scribere longam est.
Bal. I am satisfyd, with them all, see.
Pont. Neuer a whit you be.
Grip. Trewe, for omne quod est nimium vertitur in vitium
say the Philosophers, Gentlemen.
Pont. Old Sawe and trewe Sawe, Goodman Gripus, it is.   1530

[FOL. 136ᵛ]

Bal. Cheese and fruite, Hoa.
Harp. Of all baites, a peice of cheese is the surest.
Rud. So it be toasted.

1503 *the*] *e* altered, formed from imperfect *e*   1506 *Sewer*] *w* imperfect, possibly altered   1507 *delt*] *l* altered   1508 *Wantons*] *W* possibly altered   1511 *nimble*] *l* altered   1518] SP high   1519 *now*] underlined for deletion; preceded by high ink point   1523 *Playces*] *P* possibly altered   1526 *satisfyd*] ink spot between ²s and *f*   1527 *Neuer*] otiose ink mark follows word below line *whit*] otiose point above *i*   1529 *the*] *h* retraced   1530 *Pont.*] *P* retraced; stop is faint   1531 *Bal.*] stop very faint   1532 *surest*] *e* imperfect   1533 *be*] *b* possibly altered

Grip. So to be translated, sure.
Prot Come on, come, let vs but [all] see the euent thereof; Come.
dilue   Prot) Porpisse and Antick,
                That daunce it and Prank it,
                Telling the weather,,
                Ere it get hither,
                Say that I say it,   1540
                And not delay it,
                To close Mawe vp,
                Whiles he doth sup,
                Before my Lord,
                Bring Cheese to boarde.
            The Direction.
      Here they brought in Sea fruite and cheese. Quicquid
      nascatur in parte vlla Naturæ et in mari est, Plinius
      lib. 8 Cap. 2. Some Analogicall resemblances to the
      same fruites they be that growe on the grownd.   1550
Harp. Now stand you all close, Sirs.
Pont. Be ready with thy Roapes Rudens.
Rud. Hold vp thy Leauer, Man.
Pont. I I, let mee alone with him.
Prot. You, Gripus, Hoa, Hold furth thy Grapple more stiff
      vnto him, Foole.
Grip. I I, I wusse.
Prot. Now stand close, I say.
Harp. Now, or neuer.
Bal. There is not one yet, for my dyet, I assure you.   1560
Prot. No?
Bal. No.
Rud. Fyeth, wee shall neuer do it, I auowe.
Pont. I thought verily wee should haue had him, this Tyme, Fel=
      lowe Proteus.

1535 *all*] underlined for deletion; preceded by high ink point   1537 *Prank*] k imperfect
1538 *weather,*] attempt to retrace comma has rendered secondary comma, probably not intentional
1547 *they*] h altered   1549 *resemblances*] r possibly retraced   1550 *same*] m has extra set of minims   1559 *Harp.*] stop high   1564 *wee*] w retraced   *him*] m imperfect; partly blotted
1564–5 *Fel=/lowe*] otiose stroke above F   1565] otiose ink marks in left margin

Harp. A Pox followe the Rascall.
Grip. And the Greene Canker consume him eake.
Prot Nay now, Sirs, wee will either haue him, or be frighted
      furth our witts all.
Grip. Let vs see it, Prithy.   1570
Pont. Come Come, I pray you, Sir, come.
Harp. Sir, please you wash, For loe you now, the Viccar is
      comming toward you, say grace to your Lordship.
Bal. I will sing Salutation to him first.
Grip. This is notable, by my Troth.
Pont. Come come, begin Proteus, begin, Hoa.

The Direction.
The Balene whisteld the Spanish Pauen to them

[FOL. 137ʳ]

From within. Then enterd an Antick lyke an ill fauourd Herm=
ite of the Sea: A Bason and Towell before him, with capouch,   1580
Long Bearde, Finnye feet and hands, And Exit passing ouer
the stage.

Rud. Proteus, make vp thou, the odd Crotchet vnto him, Hoa.
Prot. Come on.

> Prot)   Thou in my Hearte,
>   Who ere thou art,
>   Nor for thy Spite,
>   I care one mite,
>   The drag I find,
>   Is farr behind,   1590
>   Then be not nice,
>   If thou beest wise,
>   But come to banquit,
>   And God be thankit.

The Direction.
Here the foresayd Hermite appeared to them againe stan=
ding at doore, with Fyre, storme, and Crakers from Skie. They
all fled but Proteus.

1567 *eake*] ʹe altered or retraced   1570 *see*] s possibly altered from another character; otiose point above ʹe   1571 *Sir*] otiose extra point on i   1572 *now*] no possibly formed from m
1578 *Pauen*] P possibly altered; e imperfect   1595 *The*] T altered

Bal. Ho, ho ho ho ho ho ho * ho.
All. Aie, Aie, Aie, Aie, Aie.   1600
Prot. Now if I be not, with thee, to bring yet, before night Sirrha,
     Call me Cutt. I goe.

          Act 3 Scen 6.
           The Direction.
Vulcan in an Aire-cullour, [Light] syluer dead Ash-cullour, or shep=
pards Graye cullour suite, bigger in the body then he was before
farr. [Light] syluer Dead sheppard-Graye I deeme the best, His extraor=
dinary suite for this Scene. For his other extraordinarye
suite vide ˰ \vt/ infra Act 3. Scen 10. Then sayes as followes
        Vulcan Solus.   1610
Quid non mortalia Pectora cogis?
Dure Puer veneris comp\u/lsor totius orbis?
I haue fed so much on the cold meate of Humida her
Loue, That the vitall spirits of my blood, From that the
Alacrity, they were wonted to haue, be turned, see, into
Refuse Kitchin stuff all, which otherwise is to say, From
that the pure Flame, that I was once, I haue Metamorpho
sed mee into this the thick Aire, that I am now. Where=
fore, Humida, I come, vpon thy seuerall now, sub intel=
l[<.>]\i/gendum est, If thou hast any. For before I was   1620
drye as the Fyre, But now I am Moyst as is the Aire,
Before I was hot as is the Fyre, But now I am, loe,
but some what hot as is the Fyre, For the super abon=
dant Quality I haue, I haue Præserud him but some

                                                        [FOL. 137ᵛ]
dilue Modicum vnto your vse. \Yet/ Now ˰ [\yet/] notwithstanding, one
     Thing most Impatiently doth affright mee. I dreamt,
     this last night, I lay with Humida, and she bepisd mee. Dea=
     re Foole, she did it according her complexion, Therefo=

1601 *night Sirrha*] imperfect *t* formed from comma; no gap between *t* and *S*   1605 *Light*] underlined for deletion; preceded by high ink point   *syluer dead*] added in left margin to replace [*Light*]   1606 *in*] ink spot above *n*   1607 *Light*] underlined for deletion; preceded by high ink point   *syluer Dead*] added in left margin to replace [*Light*]   1611 *cogis*] *c* imperfect   1614 *That*] *t* altered or retraced   1617 *once*] *o* possibly altered   1620 *l[<.>]\i/gendum*] *i* interlined above illegible letter marked for deletion with vertical strokes   1621 *now*] otiose ink mark above *n*   1625 *Yet*] added, possibly in different ink   *yet*] underlined in darker ink for deletion; preceded by high ink point   1626 *affright mee*] no gap between words   1628 *according*] ²*c* possibly retraced

re she is to be Pardoned, And yet my Leg putteth mee in=
to some hope of her, omnia munda mundis, say our   1630
sacrifiques, For so Peremptory is the conceite of a trew
Puritaine Louer, they say, of himself, lightly he findeth not
any one thing to be in him Amisse. What though this
the now, the stiffer Ioint of mee, which vnder hand
now I do Imagine to my self, be crookt as is a sickle
lykwise, yet most open and Mechanicall Demonstra=
tions (such as is that of my Lady Humida\es/) will the
perfecter be Resolued by a crookeder deuice, then
by that of a Straite, I a trewe Theorike do also know.
Iupiter thou broakest my Leg once I am sure, yet that   1640
thy Sonne, that he, that \same/ the trewe boane setter of
Olympus, the Lord Phæbus Apollo, shall not now so soo=
ne pluck him straite into his former Ioint againe
therefore, For as long as I may but walk, with such
earthly Paragons on shoare, I will neuer after pur=
le to Heauen more. Call in thy conceited affection, Vu=
lcan, For mee thinks thou fallest out of that the
Loue of Humida into this the loue of thy Leg, where=
fore could wish, thou wouldest but case him vntill so=
one, So come now to the Matter, And here is the Mat   1650
ter, For here comes Humida.

    Act 3 Scen 7.
       The Direction.
Humida in Aridaes gown, Peruke and Ruff, all of gold
sand cullour, squird in by Harpax to his Lord and
Master.
      Harpax Vulcan Humida.
      Harpax Vulcan Humida.

1629 *mee*] *m* possibly altered   1630 *omnia*] otiose extra point on *i*   1633 *What*] *h* imperfect, possibly altered   1641 *same*] *s* merges with descender of *y* in *my* on preceding line   *trewe boane*] *e* and *b* written over blotted otiose ink marks   1643 *pluck*] *k* possibly altered or retraced   1645 *will*] *w* formed from *s*   1649 *vntill*] *n* poorly formed, looks like *m*   1653 *Direction*.] stop obscured by blotting   1654 *Peruke*] ²*e* possibly altered   1658–63] written in darker ink on a pasted slip; *Lord and* visible beneath upper edge of slip; *The Direction* partially visible beneath bottom of slip; *H* visible to left of the bottom left corner of slip   1658 *Vulcan*] *l* possibly altered

Harp. Loe my faire Lord and Master, I haue lured you
      hither the Haggard, Sero tamen, I vowe   1660
Vul. Humida? my lip? my eye? my kid? my doue? my honey?

Here he started back.   Gods body, Heigh *

The Direction.

    Here Vulcan starting vp his body from a far as would
    haue leapt her and could not and starting back withall,
    Then reade \you/ the worde Restif for Liuely in the line
    B. viz. vt infra. Otherwise he scipping (whither
    the better) syde way from Humida (if that he may
    so doe without wrenching his Foote, As some say he
    may by a deuice in his shooe) Then contrarywise   1670
    reade the worde Liuely for Restif in the sayd Fifth
    line B videlicet following.

Hum. What ayles, my Loue?

                                                      [FOL. 138ʳ]

Harp. Vpon her, noble Sir.
Hum Dost fly mee now thou hast my Loue?
Vul. I can not chuse, thou smellest drye, as is the Earth, my gerle.

He starteth back she followes.   Heigh.*

or so liuely.   Harp. I haue not lightly seene Aire t'haue beene so Restif. *
Hum. I will my self enuiron thee.
Vul. Get further from off mee, For Gods sake, Heigh *   1680

He scips asyde if so he may.   Hum) Come mix thyne armes with myne.

He stopt.   Vul. Fast as I may. But
Hum. Be these thy \vowes and/ Protestations? what?
Vul. Whoope.*

He stopt.   Hum And shall I reape this seruice at thy hand?
Vul. No, Humida, No; Heigh

He scips back.   Hum Come on thy wayes and follow mee.

He stopt.   Vul. Lord, Lord, Lord
Hum Come on, I say.

1659] partial letter visible in left margin at outer edge of pasted slip   1660 *Haggard*] H retraced   1661 *Humida*] H possibly retraced   1662 SD.1 *Here*] H imperfect, possibly retraced   1666] caret retraced   1674–5] SPs high   1677 *Heigh*] H imperfect; cross-stroke does not join mainstrokes   1678–9] SPs low   1684 *Whoope.**] stop merges with asterisk   1685] SP high   1686] SP high   *No;*] *o* altered or retraced   1689 *say*.] stop blotted

He stopt.	Vul.	[I come,] I come, I come to thee. Ho.	1690
dilue	Hum	I see thou hast deluded mee. Therefore thus do begin vnto
		thee. Villaine.
	Harp.	Iumpe.
	Hum.	Sewe me not. X
She start back or flowd. He followd.	Vul)	[Busse,] Busse o Busse.
	Hum)	Nay nay Touch mee not.
dilue	Vul.	O yes.
	Hum.	Waft of, I say.
	Vul.	Nay nay.
	Hum	Get thee hence.	1700
	Vul	No no, my wench.
	Hum	Kisse my Tayle, you Foole.
	Vul.	Ho ho, Regard my Toole.
	Hum.	Out out, you Rogue.
	Vul.	Oh ho, my Fub.
	Hum.	Hadst none, in this circumference? Knaue, say,
		To play vpon but mee a water Nymphe?
		But mee a daughter of wise Proteus?
		That sayes that Thetis shall haue a Sonne greater
		Then be the Gods of high Olympus all?	1710
		I vowe, from eury vaine, thou shalt repent it.
		Cytheræa wonder of th'vnivers
		Is hither come to keepe her Festiuall,
		Where, before hor, I shall so blazon thee.
	Harp.	In a Mottley I beseech you, Lady
	Hum.	That the whole Court shall wonder at the Fact,
		Till when I do leaue thee to chewe on this
		The Foulest Rascall that euer I mett with. (Harp)
		\And mee to prouide the cloak-bag for him./
	Vul.	Hei mihi.	1720
	Harp.	Why bleede you? my Lord.

1690] SP high   *I come,*] underlined for deletion; preceded by high ink point; comma not underlined but presumably intended for deletion   1691 *hast*] h imperfect, extra downward stroke on limb is separate from letter and looks like comma   *do*] *o* imperfect, looks like point   1694 *X*] probably an incomplete asterisk   1695 *Busse,*] *Busse* underlined for deletion; preceded by high ink point; comma not underlined but presumably also intended for deletion   *Busse*] B altered or retraced   1706 *Hum.*] stop high; otiose point below stop   1713 *Festiuall*] otiose ink stroke obscures *a*; another otiose ink stroke between *ll*   1716] SP high   1721 *Harp.*] short descender on *p*   *Lord.*] otiose ink stroke precedes stop

[FOL. 138ᵛ]

Vul. Why did greate Pan from liuer bleed?
      When, for his Loue, he caught a Reede.
Harp. Pan piped for his Loue; and you Squeake.
Vul. No conserue is able to conserue mee.
Harp. A Consolidum would close your hearte yet.
Vul. Already the Apple of Anguish hath closd it.
Harp. How say you to a Cup of Helebore to mitigate your madnes
      though?
Vul. Well Boy, if for each gullet I might but haue a comfit to   1730
      him, For Amor et fælle et melle est fæcundissimus.
Harp. Shall I be your Phisitian? say.
Vul. I do graunt thee a License [of] for the same.
Harp. I shall be a mighty gainer by it.
Vul. God giue thee Ioy of it.
Harp One woman, they say, is good Phisick for another wo=
      man.
Vul. I do beleeue thee well.
Harp. Therefore raise your Sprights, and do you coniure mee
      vp the other woman now.   1740
Vul. I shall be blazoned.
Harp. I warrant you.
Vul. Persuadst thou mee?
Harp. I do.
Vul. What's the forfaite if thou faylst?
Harp My credit.
Vul. It is [a] little as May, yet notwithstanding, I will now
dilue suddenly transforme mee, [lykwise,] into my Flame-cul=
      lourd Habitude, and according thy bidding will assay
      the other.   1750
Harp. Whiles I shall fan the Fyre vnto your Lordship and at=
      end you.

1724 *Loue;*] point on semi-colon possibly unintentional   *Squeake*] k possibly altered   1731 *fæcundissimus*] ³s possibly altered   1733 *of*] underlined for deletion; preceded by high ink point   *for*] added in left margin to replace [*of*]   1739 *mee*] 'e possibly altered   1740 *vp*] added to left of line   1742 *warrant*] extra set of minims on w   *you*] otiose ink spot above u   1743 *mee?*] otiose ink mark like stop follows ?   1744 *do*] d possibly retraced   1745 *What's*] h possibly altered   1747 *a*] blotted with ink smudge, presumably for deletion as false start for *as*   1748 *lykwise,*] underlined for deletion; preceded by high ink point

Vul.   I do thank thee for it by my Troth. Come on, Harpax,
      come on.

          Act 3 Scen .8.
        Arion with an orpharian. Solus.

Ar.   O Gods, when will you set a Periode
      Vnto my watry toyle? When will you fixe
      The center to my wandring? or where will
      Pitch my Rock to rest vpon? As Gods be Iust   1760
      To frustrate Theeues, so should they benefite
      The Harmeles wanderer in what he seekes.
      For tell mee, Lords, when did Arion euer
      Prophane your rites or reaking Hecatombes?
      When did Arion frustrate you of fat
      Of Beeues or of the Bloods of offerings?
      Haue I not sung, vpon my seuen-string Lute,
      Vpon your days your gestes Heroicall?
      Haue I not heaued to your golden shrynes

                                            [FOL. 139ʳ]

      My fragrant wreathes of Thyme and Eglantine   1770
      Obteyned by my skill? Yea haue not built
      You Altars with my rimes? Then, o good Gods,
      Vnloose this yoake, and graunt mee, at the last,
      My longd Tranquilitye, For know you, Lords,
      I'haue swom these Seas both Heighth and Longitude,
      Haue diu'd each Poole, each creeke, each Tritons den,
      Th'Alcyons couch, and eury Burton bed,
      Among the golden Sands, and in the Oaze,
      Among the syluer shells, and in the Peeble,
      Nor yet can find this Long-desired [Loue-rolle] Ceston.   1780
      Neuer, I weene was Fortune in these Seas,
      Or if she had, had found, long since, this [Loue-rolle] Ceston.

1753 *thee*] otiose ink strokes above *t*   1754 *come*] *e* possibly altered   1758 *watry*] *t* lacks headstroke   1761 *they*] ink blot partially obscures *y*   1766] blotted ink spot in left margin   1769 *heaued*] *a* formed from *e*   1772 *Altars*] blotted headstroke on *t*   1776 *Poole,*] comma merges with ascender of *d* in *and* on line below   1780 *Loue-rolle*] underlined for deletion; preceded by high ink point   *Ceston*] added in darker ink on pasted slip in left margin to replace [*Loue-rolle*]; edges of another slip visible   1782 *found,*] comma short and faint   *Loue-rolle*] underlined for deletion, preceded by high ink point   *Ceston*] added in darker ink on same pasted slip in left margin as the addition in line 1780 to replace [*Loue-rolle*]

> The greedy [Haulk] Shark pursewes his Pray and finds,
> The Tench the Roach, the woolf the water-swallow,
> The Ork the Dolphin, the greater Fish the lesse,
> And humaine I bereft of sillie [Loue-rolle] Ceston.
> They say, there dwelles, in parcell of these Seas,
> A God, that hath a Dreame for eury Thing
> (He that dreames Thetis shall haue a Sonne more
> Greate then the Gods, if she but wed with them)   1790
> Him will I trye, And (As Orpheus moued
> Grim Dis of Hell) once trye my Art, and see,
> I may obteyne a Dreame vnto this [Loue-Rolle] Ceston.

The Direction

> He playd, then a Daunce of Ceales and of Porpusyes, Then the
> Hall opening, was seene a|summer Noone day couch of
> Sand cullour, with a Sort of dreames Animate and Inani=
> mate of diuers cullours hanging by Inuisible or on Ash cullou\r/
> Threds of Sylk ouer bol\s/ter of the Couch (it bolt and erect)

Ceston   being but bigge as Pawns of chesse. Or Proteus with sundry   1800
> such in a Mawnd about his neck. Thus for some, The Rest
> to be omitted, sauing the daunce of the Ceales and Por=
> pusses.

Act 3 Scen 9.
Proteus Arion.

Prot.   Gods blessing on thy Breast man, thou hast giu'n
> Hippocris to the Soule of Proteus,
> Ask what thou wilt, thou shalt haue it, Sirrha.

Ar.   I thank you, Sir, I craue but one single face,
> For the rest, I let them free to your pleasure..   1810

1783 *Haulk*] underlined for deletion; preceded by high ink point   *Shark*] added in left margin to replace [*Haulk*]; *S* retraced or altered from *s*   1784 *woolf*] *w* imperfect   1786 *Loue-rolle*] underlined for deletion; preceded by high ink point   *Ceston*] added in darker ink on pasted slip in left margin to replace [*Loue-rolle*]; edges of another slip visible   1788 *Dreame*] *D* possibly altered   1793 *Loue-rolle*] underlined for deletion; preceded by high ink point   *Ceston*] added in darker ink on pasted slip in left margin to replace [*Loue-rolle*]; edges of another slip visible   1794 *The*] *T* retraced   1796 *a*|*summer*] vertical rule separates words; ink blot above *e*   1800 *Ceston*] added in darker ink on pasted slip in left margin with no indication of where the word should be inserted   *of*] written over illegible characters   1801 *in*] *n* imperfect   *Mawnd*] *w* is poorly formed, possibly altered   1806 *Prot.*] stop faint   1807 *Hippocris*] cross-stroke on *H* faint   1809 *Ar.*] stop high   1810 *pleasure..*] second stop is probably otiose

	Prot.	Arion thou shalt both diuide and chuse *	

Here he demon=
strates some of
them with his
Rod.

    Prot. Arion thou shalt both diuide and chuse *
           Say, wilt haue this Gentleman with the Peake?
           This sleeke Monkey with the Breade in its Mouth?
           This Catt with his Tabour? Els, this Mongrill
           of Wax? The Iack an Apes with his Fiddle?
           Or please you, Sir, weare this Medaile? Heye [heye] he.

[FOL. 139ᵛ]

    Ar.   This will serue my Turne, the other I remitt.
    Prot. I am libbed of my capitall ware, see.

.The Direction.

Here Arion tooke vp a Bracelet of gold, ˄\\\The// Rolles writhen/ enter=
changeablye the one [Plate] Rolle black the other of   1821
diuers cullours enameld, He tooke him vp as
he hung ouer the Bolster of the Bed, or furth the
Mawnd.

Nulla Desunt.

    Ar.   So, with aboundaunt Thanks, I take my leaue,
           For this greate Benefite y'haue done to mee,
           And if at any tyme you want my skill,
           Commaund and haue Arions wyres at will.
    Prot. Now goe thy wayes, with all my hearte and with all   1830
           my soule after thee, sweet Musitian, For thou hast
           giuen mee the Refection of the soule, I assure thee.
           Yet I can not but muse, how it came to passe, he should
           haue intertayned, aboue the rest, this [Loue-rolle] Ceston,
           I will chewe the cud of his intent. Verily the gallant
           Knaue according the force and vertue that is in

1812 *Peake?*] point on ? looks like comma   1814 *Tabour?*] point on ? looks like comma   1816 *heye*] underlined for deletion; preceded by high ink point   *he*] added in darker ink in left margin to replace [*heye*]   1820–5 written in darker ink on pasted slip   1820 *The … writhen*] interlined above pasted slip; caret above ²*e* in *Bracelet*   1821 *Plate*] underlined for deletion; preceded by high ink point   *Rolle*] added in different ink on separate pasted slip in left margin to replace [*Plate*]; *R* retraced   1826 *So,*] *S* written over illegible character   1830] SP high   1834 *Loue-rolle*] underlined for deletion; preceded by blotted high ink point   *Ceston*] added in darker ink on pasted slip in left margin to replace [*Loue-rolle*]; *C* retraced   1835–40 written in darker ink on pasted slip

     this [Bracelet] Ceston knewe that he wanted a Swashing
     Codpeice (quantum Fæmellis omnibus vna satis)
     For of other Properties that be in him he knows
     not any. So according the complexion of his Fellowe   1840
     Swaggerers of the Bush, he came to ouereach mee
dilue of my Iewell I held so deare. But well fare [\well/] his hearte
     for the one Properie of him, For his hand hath deser=
     ued his other Properties too by my Troth. Yet least
     the other Arions now come too, and do start mee the
     lyke Iack, I will presently in, Bolt all my doores and
     all my windowes I haue in my house vpon all their
     sweet and well featured faces Plat. So sweet cour=
     teous young Gentlemen I wish you to frolick all.

        Act 3 Scen 10.   1850
         The Direction.
     Vulcan in his other extraordinary suite fitted for
     this Scene, Cloth of Gold Flame-cullour or Red
gold coullour.
         Vulcan Solus.
Vul. Gentlemen, behold, I haue soaken furth the whole
     Moysture of my body, And am Metamorphosed again,
     See, from that the grosse Aire, that I was once, into my
     First, and into myne own trewe and naturall E=
     lementary Propertie of Fyre, as I am now. For   1860
     Humida, with her bunch of Candles of Threates, set
     on Fyre my greace, that I fell into coales, [And] so as by
     that meane I lost my Totall and my vniuersall Tal=
     lowe trewly. [Now] for this tyme therefore, my sweet Arida, I co=
     me, loe, to inuite thee but to the burnt leauings of it.
     A villanous cold and dry Mawe I know thou hast

1837 *Bracelet*] underlined for deletion; preceded by high ink point *Ceston*] added in left margin of a large pasted slip bearing lines 1835–40 to replace [*Bracelet*]; *o* possibly altered   1839 *be*] *b* possibly altered   1842 ²*well*] interlined and preceded by high ink point; underlined for deletion   1848 ²*sweet*] *t* imperfect, headstroke added to base of mainstroke   1851 *Direction*.] stop high, faint   1854 *gold*] added in darker ink to left of line *coullour*] *c* retraced in darker ink; ¹*o* imperfect   1856 *haue*] *h* possibly altered   1862 *And*] underlined for deletion; preceded by high ink point *so as*] added in darker ink in left margin to replace [*And*]   1864 *Now*] underlined for deletion; preceded by high ink point *for this tyme*] added in darker ink in left margin to replace [*Now*] *therefore*] *f* possibly altered   1866 *know*] otiose ink strokes below word between *o* and *w*

[FOL. 140ʳ]

    According thy Earthy complexion, wench. yet a good
    Fyre, as I did Intimate the same to thee in my letter,
    which is my self, and the Humidity of the Broth, which is
    my Affection to thee, may well helpe thee, with it, down,   1870
    My Mayde, More I haue reserued mee which
    to say I haue præserued mee for to enhable ^\thee/ the better
dilue thee so to disgest mee. But stay. ^\why fearest [thou] to aproach mee?/
     Am I a Toade?
dilue Wyde. Am I a Baselyk? Besyde. Am I any other
    venemous Insect? Ireland defyde. Thou louest mee I
    know, For thou hast done it, but for to set a keener edge
    vpon my Appetite I know. Most hartily I do thanke thee
    for it, And for the same, now loe, I do rest thy Perpetuall
    seruaunt, yet let mee giue thee but this one Item, by the
    way, my deare Arida, whereas now I am but tenderly ro=   1880
    sted, if that thou hie thee not hither the sooner, For a sum=
    pteous supper, that thou wert lyke now to haue, then thou
    shalt but feede on the coales, as did once my Lady Porcia. But
    here she comes sleeke as a Rabbit, see.

       Act 3 Scen 11.
        The Direction
    Arida in Humidaes gown, Peruke and Ruff, All
     of Syluer-Sea-blewe or clowd cullour, The Best.
       Arida Vulcan Harpax.

Ar. Vulcan? my Lord? my Loue? my Ioye? O Followe mee,   1890
   O follow mee. *

Turnes her tayle and flowes from him.   *stops*

Vul. Oh I come, I come, I come to thee. *
Ar. Man? what aylst? Follow, o Followe
Harp. O follow her, Sir, she is but newe come from the Plump, my Lord
Vul. Masse, I can not yet groape her
Ar. Iumpe vp, on mee, lightly, I say. *

1870 *thee, with it,*] commas partially obscured by top of pasted slip bearing lines 1871–4   1871–4] written in different ink on pasted slip   1872 *thee*] *th* possibly retraced   1873 *thou*] underlined for deletion; preceded by high ink point   1874 *dilue*] unclear what this refers to   *Am*] faint   1876 *hast done*] no gap between words   1880 *whereas*] *h* possibly altered   *but tenderly*] no gap between words   1885 *Scen*] otiose ink strokes above word   1890 *Ar.*] stop high

She flowes from him.	Vul.	Thou beest nimble as the running streame, wench.	
	Harp.	I haue not seene Fyre, so to haue longed for a Bucket of wa= ter in my life, before.	
she flowes and looks back. He sings and followes.	Ar.	Come kisse mee, here, Sirrha.*	1900
		Vul) Tarry, sweet Loue, Tarry one howre *	
		Ar) Looke mee in the face, here, I say *	
Looks back.		Vul) Wype that sweate from of that Face first.	
	Ar.	It will make my kisse but too drye for thee.	
	Vul.	Nay but that, yfaith, I will trye straite. * whoope.	
He stopt and start vp. she flowes he followes.	Ar)	Come along, come along, Sir, I pray you *	
		Vul) Who ho.	
	Ar.	Follow, o Follow, I beseech you, Sir Followe.	
	Vul.	O ho, o ho.	
	Ar.	Courage, Sir, Courage.	1910
	Vul.	Much as I may or can, Madame, But *	
He stopt.	Ar)	Come on, come on, Sir, I say	
	Vul.	Oa.	

[FOL. 140ᵛ]

	Ar.	What wilt giue mee, I come to thee? say.	
	Vul.	A million.	
	Ar.	Of what? say.	
	Vul. Of	Beaten Angells.	
	Harp.	Other wise of Diuells.	
	Ar.	Who's your warrant?	
	Vul.	My Knaue he is.	1920
	Ar.	Will you giue your worde for him? Sir.	
	Harp.	I doe.	
	Ar.	Vpon your credit?	
	Harp.	Vpon my little credit.	
	Ar.	Now come thy wayes and mixe, thy louely armes, with	
She comes, he starts back		myne *	
	Vul.	Notorious strumpet, Fye Fye, how thou stinkest. Heigh	
	Ar.	Come againe, come againe, sweet Loue *	
She sings he starts back	Vul)	I recant, I recant, Heigh.	
	Ar.	O do not, o do not, my Vulcan.	1930
She sings he starts back.			
	Vul.	Yes, Arida, yes, Heigh.	

1906] SP high   1911 *Madame*] ²*a* possibly altered   1912 *come*] *e* possibly altered   1917 *Of*]
added to left of line   1919 *your*] *r* obscured by smudging

Ar. Thou wilt not then be clipt by mee?
Vul. O I may not, I may not, O Arida.
Ar. By thy Faith and Troth? Vulcan.
Vul. By my Faith and Troth, No, Arida.
Ar. Then fare well and be hangd.
Vul. Thou too, and be hangd too.
Harp. How doe you? my Lord.
Vul. I am falln out of Bridewell into Bedlame, sure.
Harp. How so? I beseech you.   1940
Vul. The Furye of ˄\that/ my Longing is now turned, into this the
      Kick of my loathing, See.
Harp. Many gallant Man, of whom your Lordship is one, hath
      lowzd him, ere now, at weeping crosse, my Lord.
Vul. I will strip the Geas of their Feathe\r/s.
Harp. Then stick them in your Cap.
Vul. I will garde them, pretiously, with two dozen whip=
      corde.
Harp. Why Trim.
Vul. I will bugle them with Pepper, with Bay-Salt.   1950
Harp. Spectatum Admissi Risumteneatis Amici?
Vul. They shall be constabled both, for the next voyage toward
      Cuckolds Hauen, Harpax.
Harp. The Matter what you haue præscribed him notably well,
      Now for the Forme how your Lordship had neede your
      learned counsell.
Vul. Who is that counsell? say.
Harp. It is my self, If so you do accept of mee.
Vul. I will ˄\be/ polisht once by the squire of thy Aduice, Sirrha.
Harp. There lyeth hard by a famous Balene, that speaketh   1960
      Oracles.
Vul. I haue hearde of the knaue.
Harp. To him I will leade you, And from him you shall obteyne

[FOL. 141ʳ]

      a Playster for your broken heade.
Vul. My wife will requite mee it, I suppose.

1932 *Thou*] otiose ink mark precedes word   1934] otiose ink spot in left margin   1944 *crosse*] ²s retraced   1954 *well*] *e* imperfect, formed from one stroke   1959 ˄\be/] added in darker ink   1965] SP high

Harp. That's most certaine, my Lord.
Vul. What Blind lane is to be chosen thither? saye.
Harp. This. That you would but Metamorpho\se/ you, into the habit
dilue   and forme of Madame Reuenge ^\of the Sea/, with Whip, Bitt, and
        Bridle [to]
in hand held [boote], and that you would suffer mee [to] leade you thither, in   1970
dilue   manner, forme, and fashion thereunto belonging, my Lord.
Vul. What Transformation would I not put mee into to be reueng\d/
     on the Harlots? Sirrha.
Harp. You say well, come on your ways, you shall see that most
      faithfully and safely in the Manner, I will conduct you thither
      Come.
Vul. I am persuaded.
Harp. Follow mee, my Lord, but.
Vul. I doe.

     Here they knockt vp the consort.   1980

     Act 4 Scen 1.
  Nereus Cytheræa Thetis Glauce Humi
  da Arida Euphrosync Thalia Aglaia.
   All with Angle Rods, Nereus with an Angle-rod
   leading them the waye.
Ner. Graund Madame, since you be disposed take.
     Our poore Fishermens sport in gree, I will
     Leade you to such plenteous stores of Fishes,
     And ^\those/ in copious numbers where they lye,
     That your Ladiship will say there is not,   1990
     In any where of th'vniuersall Mound,
     So greate and noble sport as in this
     The Extent of our watry Element there is,
     Try you th'experience when so you please.

1968–71] written in darker ink on a large pasted slip 1968 *Metamorpho\se/*] ²*o* written over *e*; *se* partially visible underneath pasted slip 1969 *to*] underlined for deletion; preceded by high ink point 1970 *in hand held*] added to left of line on same pasted slip as carries the main text *boote*] underlined for deletion; preceded by high ink point *to*] underlined for deletion; preceded by high ink point 1971 *Lord.*] otiose ink mark follows stop 1981 *Scen*] otiose ink mark below *c* 1982 *Thetis*] otiose ink stroke precedes word; otiose ink strokes above *i* 1983 *Aglaia.*] stop faint; faint otiose ink mark above ²*a* 1984 ¹*with*] *i* missing point 1986 *take.*] stop probably otiose 1988 *plenteous*] heavy inking on *o* 1989 *in*] *i* missing point, possibly obscured by limb of *h* in interlined word *copious*] otiose point over ¹*o* 1991 *th'vniuersall*] otiose ink mark above *s* 1992 *in*] faint otiose point over *n* 1994 *please.*] blotted otiose ink mark follows stop

Cyth. My Lord, so well I lyke the Sport, and it
      with that trewe loue, that I and these my Ladyes
      shall laye deare wagers on it, Each of which
      shall drawe the noblest Fish vnto her line.
      So I for my self (If gracious Fortune
      Allowe my attempt) do chuse first the Herring   2000
      For my Lot, For as th old Ballade doth sing,
      Of Fishes of the Sea Herring's the King.
Thet. For my Part I wish a Puffing might bite
      At baite of my line, For it is a Fish
      Has prickles on him, And I wish a Prickle
      Might prick the Heartes of them shall but attempt
      My Bed, vnles it be the Gods themselues.
Ner. So doe, Lady, for Themis may not erre.
Glau. For my money come Lobster to my line,

                                                [FOL. 141ᵛ]
      For if I win not Leander from Hero,   2010
      I wish I might neuer goe forward in
      Loue of myne, But euer they to crawle backward
      I shall but greet in any case of Loue.
Ner. Well sayd, my gerle, keep thee in that mind still.
Hum. The Gods of the Sea send mee a Mackrell,
      For Mackrell, in French, signifies Bawde,
      And Bawde would I wish mee sooner to be
      Then Bawde should persuade mee forgoe the flowre
      Of my virginity to any one
      Packhed, should but allure mee with his Gold.   2020
Ar. A Playce, A Playce for my Fortune I wish,
      For if I shall not keepe my Place from such one
      Shall but assault him, I wish eury Mouth
      Lyke Playce it self, should wrye their Mouths at mee.

1995] SP high   1996 ²that] otiose ink mark precedes word   these] ²e imperfect   1999 my] otiose point over y   Fortune] otiose ink mark precedes word; e imperfect   2001 old] o imperfect; possibly altered   2003 Thet.] stop high   2006 Heartes] cross-stroke in H does not join mainstrokes   attempt] e possibly altered   2007 themselues] l possibly retraced   2010 For] F faint   2012 to] t missing headstroke   backward] d possibly altered   2014 Ner.] stop high   my] blotted ink smudge precedes word   that mind] no gap between words; d possibly altered   2015 Mackrell] otiose point over e   2016 in] i missing point   French] ink stain below en   Bawde] e imperfect; could be imperfect s   2021 Ar.] stop high   I wish,] cross stroke on I touches w; comma retraced

Euphr. A Conger for mee, For if my Grace giuen
        Congrewe not with my manners, I Implore
        Venus would turne mee to some Monster sooner,
        For that Materia præsupponit
        Habitum do our Philosophers saye.
Thal. I wish a Crab, For as a Crab has clawes,
        So wish I now, had clawes of a Crab too,
        If I clawe not him on the face, that shall
        But offer violence to my Maydenhed.
Agl. Now for mee and my deare Hearte Vulcan, Haa.
        Contrary a Cod would not come to mee
        A misse, then that a Herring Cob? I vowe,
        Madame (**Cyth**) And why not a Herring Cob? Foole
Agl. For had rather my sweet Hearte had turnd Cod
        Then so for to cosen mee for his Gold but,
        Or as the Gypsie serud Antonye once.
Cyth. Good Reason, mary. So come your wayes now,
        And let vs but see the euent of all,
        And the Lords send thee thy Longings, Aglaia,
        So it be not a Herring Cob, you saye.
        But leade the way, my good Lord Nereus.
Ner. Follow (**All**) with our whole Heartes wee doe (**Ner**) Then
                                          (Come

Leander gaue, she reade the Poesye about the gemme.

        * Act 4 Scen 2.
          Hero Leander.
        Thyne By the Styx.
Her. Why? my deare Leander, This be it but,
        I do not doubt, but that by an ouereaching
        Wrench of my cunning, both to set thee free
        And saue thy Immortallity too.
Lean. Nay so, nor so, For the Gods haue decreed

2025 *Grace*] *ce* faint   2030 *Thal.*] stop high, looks like hyphen on *b*   *too,*] comma retraced or possibly altered from a stop   2031 *Crab*] indistinct lobe   2037 *Foole*] *e* possibly altered   2041 *Cyth.*] stop high   2043 *Aglaia,*] comma formed from stop   2046 *Ner.*] otiose point above stop   2047 *(Come*] intended as continuation of previous line   2048 SD.1 *she*] preceded by high ink point   *Act*] otiose ink stroke precedes word   2049 *Hero*] faint otiose point precedes *Hero*   2050 *the*] ink blot between *h* and *e*   *Styx.*] stop high   2051 *Her.*] stop high   2052 *ouereaching*] ²*e* imperfect, written over illegible letter; *a* poorly formed   2054 *And*] *d* possibly retraced   2055–6] ink marks in right margin, transferred from the next folio

On Leanders head to wreake their vengeaunce,

[FOL. 142aʳ]

For what that the meane is may stand, Hero,
And may be inuent may make Leander yeild
His Heartes deare Prize vnto an others Lust?
His soules sole gemme vnto an others trust?   2060
Nay trewly, not all that wealth Disconteynes
Could made him done it, wherefore I charge thee, sweet,
By all those Gods that on our wedding night
Were in our chamber, Venus, Priapus,
By all my paines, and by our wedlock Band,
By Loue, by Faith, as I'haue persuade thee to it,
Hero, so lykwise thou persuade him from it.

Her. My good Leander, art [thou] Ieleous then?
dilue Although by dew of my Profession
     I am bounden my self to Prostitute   2070
     Vnto a faithfull Loues Petition
     Yet well thou [knowst] wee'nst, since first thou hadst the Flowre
     Of my virginity, with what deare care
     I haue maintained it Immaculate
     Vnto thy Sole Fruition, Then, sweet my Loue,
     Present mee to the Man, and for the rest
     Let resolued Hero alone with it.

Lean. Hero, hadst though lou'd mee trewe, thou wouldest
dilue Haue rated mee for my Rashnes, not [t'haue] to
dilue haue Thus counselled [mee] yield my better Half   2080
     Vnto the mercy of anothers Bed.

Her. A Man goes furth, the morne, dispairing life,
     Yet returneth he victor home at night.

Lean. If once the Haulk but find thee in his gist
     How is it possible thou do escape it?

2057 *meane*] 'e imperfect   2058 *Leander*] 'e imperfect   2059 *Lust?*] ? possibly altered from comma   2061 *Disconteynes*] gap between *s* and *c*   2065 *wedlock*] *o* possibly altered   2068] SP high   *thou*] underlined for deletion; preceded by high, darker ink point   2069 *dilue*] added in darker ink   2071 *faithfull*] *h* altered   2072 *knowst*] underlined for deletion; preceded by high, darker ink point   *wee'nst*] added in darker ink in left margin to replace [*knowst*]; apostrophe above ²*e*   *Flowre*] otiose ink mark between *w* and *r*   2075 *Vnto*] *V* possibly retraced   *thy*] *h* possibly altered   2078] SP high   2079 *dilue*] added in darker ink   *t'haue*] underlined for deletion; preceded by high, darker ink point   *to*] added in darker ink after deleted word   2080 *dilue*] added in darker ink   *haue*] added to left of line in darker ink   *mee*] underlined for deletion   2082 *Her.*] stop high

Her   If he had seased mee within his Fist,
      By Cytheræaes grace, he shoud not reape it.
Lean. Lyke wordes distill heale drops of Balsamum
      Into my seuerd wound, Then, this once, See,
      I giue thee leaue; But therewithall, Hero ———————   2090
Her. Nay, what with all? my deare Leander (Lean) Thou
      Wouldst, from point to point, be circumspect now.
Her. Come, what needed these Deprecations?
      I will perfourme it, Man. Thy self anone,
      [*When [she's to] takes leaue, present ˄ \thou/ mee, onelye,*]
      \When she's to take leaue present thou mee but/
      Fore Cytheræa, in open Hall (Lean) But
      Shall I find you Trew in what you say? (Her) Trewe.
Lean. Now thou persuadst, Not the whole world before.
Her. Come on thy wayes and follow mee (Leand) I doe.   2100
dilue [First sing, I prithy. * Come,] first sing you whoore.

Leander sitting, Hero singing to the gentlemen

The Fourth Song

[FOL. 142aᵛ]

1.

Deare be not, o dismayd,
Be not affeard of Venus mayde,
She will well doe it,
What ere ensewe it,
Be not affearde of Venus Mayde.

2086 *within*] otiose ink mark below *n*   2087 *it.*] otiose ink point follows stop   2088 *Lean.*] SP high; stop high   *distill*] ²*l* possibly retraced   2090 *leaue;*] point on semi-colon possibly otiose or intended as stop   2091 *Lean)*] bracket descends into next line, touches *now*   2094 *it,*] comma merged with ascender of altered *l* in *leaue* on following line   *anone,*] *e* and comma smudged by blotting   2095 *she's to*] underlined for deletion; preceded by high ink point   *takes leaue*] *s* added in darker ink, closing gap between words; *l* altered in darker ink   ˄ *thou mee*] caret under first letter of *mee*   *onelye*] added in darker ink   **When ... onelye,*] line marked for replacement by asterisks after previous changes   2096] added in as four lines of text in left margin beginning at line 2095 to replace line 2095   *but*] blotted   2101 *First sing, I prithy. * Come,*] underlined for deletion   *first ... whoore.*] written in slightly different italic script; *f* retraced   2105] otiose ink marks precede line

       2
    Venus is one alone,   2110
  She will not refuse any one
    What they do moue
    In case of Loue,
  She will not refuse any one.
       3
dilue Come [th] along thou with mee
  Hence many howres it will not be
    That I shall fit thee
    Through her sweet pitie,
  Hence many howres it will not be.   2120

Leand Figge for old Foole now.
Her. Come.

     Act 4 Scen 3.
The mett *Aglaia Humida Arida.
Agl. Cosens Arida and Humida, I pray you, haue you seene
   My sweet Hearte Vulcan, any tyme this after noone, I
dilue haue saught him and saught [him], all about Court, nor yet
   can tell what is become.
Hum. Belyke he is buisye about his Forge, Madame, where your
   Ladiship, being of so deinty and so actable cares, as you 2130
   be, you will hardly endure the beating of the Hammers,
   I am sure, For possible, such tender ones, as you be too,
   may not so well abide the Crush of the Hammer neither,
   as well I may conceiue, Lady.
Ar. Neither the Smoake of the chimney sure, least that it
   should so commaculate the grace of that so liuely a
   Paragon of face, as your's is, Cosen Aglaia.

  2116 *th*] underlined for deletion; preceded by high ink point that merges with *3* on previous line; false start for *thou* 2117 *many*] *a* retraced 2119 *pitie,*] comma merges with *be* in following line 2120 *be*] heavy inking on *b* 2121] SP high 2122 *Her.*] stop high 2124 SD *mett*] otiose ink mark below ²*t* 2125 *Agl.*] stop high 2127 *him*] underlined for deletion; preceded by high ink point 2130 *being*] faint point on *i* ²*so*] written over *to* 2131 *of*] *f* missing cross-stroke *Hammers*] *H* imperfect; cross stroke short and does not join mainstrokes 2132 *as*] *a* altered or retraced 2134 *conceiue*] ¹*e* imperfect *Lady*] *a* imperfect, looks like *o* 2135 *Ar.*] stop high

Agl. Nay nay, come on yfaith, and tell mee, where I shall find
       him, Cosens.
Hum. What will you giue vs in recompense? if wee shall shewe   2140
       you trewe.
Ar. All the Gold she has, I am sure, Sister Humida.
Agl. The Gold I haue is conteyned vnder lock of my haires, Cosens,
       And that is a greater Portion, by the Roode, I haue bestow=
       ed on him ∧\then/ for lamenes of his Legs but.
Ar. What then? For that the squint of his eye? I beseech you.
Agl. Nay nay, my beauty is not to be much betterd by that, Lady
       Arida.
Hum. Yet so it had neede, if that so you had but beene made one
       of Cytheræa her Graces, but for cause of your beauty,   2150
       onely, Cosen.
Agl. Nay but tell mee, where he is, I beseech you, now.
Ar. She will not sell her stone horse, for twenty old Nobles,

[FOL. 142b^r]

       I dare be thy warrant, Humida.
Agl. But saye, I pray you.
Hum. He is gone but to some water Nymphe of the Court he Knowes,t
       But to wash that sweate from ∧\of/ his browe, before he may tast
       that delicate and white Breade of yours, which he hath purcha=
       sed, by Price, of his hammer so.
Agl. Nay then, wee shall neuer haue done yfaith.   2160
Ar. And to some boane setter too belyke, to pluck his leg a little
       straiter, then he is, I wisse.
Agl. O mee most miserable woman that I am. where shall I find
dilue. the Perfidious villaine? [say]. Ha.

2140 *Hum.*] stop high   2141 *you*] *o* imperfect, looks like point   2142 *Ar.*] stop high
2143 *Cosens*] ²*s* possibly added   2144 *I haue*] no gap between words   2145 ∧ *then*] added in
different ink   2146 *you.*] stop high   2150 *beauty*] *y* possibly altered   2151 *Cosen.*] stop
blotted   2153 *stone*] *to* imperfect   *Nobles*] *s* possibly retraced   2154 *Humida.*] *H* retraced;
stop high   2155] SP high   2156] SP high   *Knowes,t*] *s* possibly altered from *t*; heavily inked
t added after comma   2158 *that*] gap between *t* and *h*   *white*] otiose ink mark precedes word; *t*
short   *Breade*] *B* heavily inked   *of*] cross-stroke of *f* extends over first letter of following word   *hath*]
ink blot follows word   2159 *by*] otiose ink mark above *y*   2160] SP high   2161 *Ar.*] SP
high, stop high   '*to*] otiose ink mark above imperfect *t*, which lacks a headstroke   *some*] gap between *o*
and *m*   2162 *then he*] no gap between words   2163 *miserable*] point on *i* very faint   *where*]
w imperfect, possibly altered; gap between *w* and *h*; *h* partially retraced   2164 *say*] underlined for
deletion; preceded by high ink point that merges with top of *?* that precedes word   *Ha*] *a* possibly
altered

76

Hum. Be you then so Ieleous of him, Cosen, as you seeme to be? Ha
Agl. I no case, verily.
Hum. Why then.
Agl. For so possible, the Ioint setter may pluck his Leg furth the
   Ioint, And an organ without Ioint is not for any vse, they
   say.   2170
Ar. Then I will tell you trewly of him sweet cosent.
Agl. Come, I pray you now.
Ar. Not too fast yet, I pray you.
Agl. I want patience, till I do heare newes of him, certes.
Ar. Why then he is going buy him a face better then any he hath at
   home, for to present therwith together with \some other/ Cyclops
     in com=
   panye, a Daunce of Smiths, to Cytheræa, before she part from
   Court.
Hum I, and with eury each of them but one eye a Peice, in their heds,
   Cosen   2180
Agl. O the vnmercifull wagge that it is by my Troth. But will
   the Mask hold? be you persuade?
Hum Yes, in sadnes, will it, if I haue any Iudgment in cause
   of his Plot, Cousen Aglaia.
Agl. Why, what's the plot? saye.
Hum. Thereby, he would but gaine Cytheræa her fauour, But
   for the vp building him a Forge, neare her Grandfather
   King Saturnus his Court, where he may haue yron work
   enough, for his vse, to liue on, this deare \[golden]/ Iron tyme, sweet
   cosen Aglaia.   2190
Agl. The Plot is goode, mary, For he hath but little yron work

2165] SP low *Ieleous*] gap between *e* and *o* 2167 *Why*] *y* formed from *e* 2168 *Ioint*] point on *i* faint 2169 ¹*Ioint*, ²*Ioint*] gap between *o* and *i* 2171 *Then*] *n* altered or retraced *trewly*] *e* possibly altered from another letter 2173 *Ar.*] cross-stroke on *A* faint; stop high 2174 *heare*] *a* imperfect *him,*] gap between *h* and *i*; comma low *certes*] ink spot above *te* 2175 *is*] point on *i* very faint *going*] gap between *o* and *i* 2176 *home*] otiose point above *e* *present*] otiose ink mark follows *r* *some*] otiose ink stroke on *s*; *o* imperfect *in*] *n* possibly altered 2177 *Daunce*] *e* possibly altered *before*] gap between *o* and *r* 2179 *with*] *wi* written in darker ink over *ea*; *t* written over *r*; possibly false start for *each* later in line *a*] possibly altered or retraced *Peice*] *P* altered in darker ink; part of ¹*e* possibly retraced in darker ink 2181 *vnmercifull*] *u* formed from *i* *that it*] headstroke of ²*t* touches *i* 2183 *it*] *i* altered 2184 *Cousen*] *o* imperfect, looks like dash 2185 *Agl.*] stop high *plot?*] indistinct point on ? 2186 *Thereby*] otiose point between *he* 2187 *Grandfather*] ²*r* retraced 2188 *Saturnus*] *S* possibly retraced 2189 *golden*] underlined for deletion; preceded by ink point *Iron*] added in left margin to replace [*golden*] 2190 *cosen*] *c* retraced 2191 *goode,*] comma low

| | now, in this pure and golden Age \o/ff Saturnus, but for
| | the gain by him a farthing, thereby, certes.
| Ar. | Yet rusty yron is a good Comodity, if it be well furbisht,
| | they say, cosen Aglaia.
| Agl. | Yes, by my Troth, is it, sweet Arida, though it be drye, as is the
| | Eath it self, Sirrha.
| Ar. | Nay, good Madame, make such a Ieast on mee, for all my

[FOL. 142b^v]

| | drynes, I pray you, For possible, I might so, well haue
| | cosend you, in the Furbishing of it, I know.   2200
| Hum. | I and some of an humble Maydes water might haue made
| | your yron somewhat more stiff then it is, I am trewly
| | persuaded, Madame.
| Agl. | Verily verily, you misse your Aimes both, my sweet cosens
| | both. But what' the newes, I pray you, is come from
| | aboue?
| Hum | Lord Hermes is come, with an Expresse, from King Sa=
| | turnus himself, to hie Cytherӕa vp to Court, they say.
| Agl. | You mock, in faith, cosen Humida, saye.
| Hum. | No in sadnes, do I, Madame, For now Cytherӕa is ready   2210
| | to depart straite.
| Agl. | Nay then, for \that/ stock of gold I haue, I may not be missing, For
| | so shee may well beate mee, about the face, For my la=
| | bour, I am sure. Therefore lets all away, Come.
| Ar. | Yes, by my Troth, let vs, For I long to see how handsomelye
| | your sweet Hearte will treade furth a measure before

2192 *this*] elongated point on *i* merges with descender of *g* in *good* on previous line   *and*] *d* faint   *Age*] blotted ink marks precede word   *for*] gap between *o* and imperfect *r*   2193 *by*] *b* imperfect, with indistinct lobe   2194] SP high   2196 *drye*] *dr* partially obscured by otiose ink stroke   2197 *self,*] comma retraced *Sirrha*] *h* partially obscured by otiose ink stroke that makes the letter resemble a *k*; blotted ink smudge in far-right margin follows word   2198] blotted ink marks beneath beginning and end of line *Madame*] indistinct lobe on imperfect *d* *make*] *ke* retraced   2199 *drynes,*] ascender of *d* retraced; comma faint *haue*] *a* imperfect, possibly retraced   2200 *Furbishing*] *b* imperfect, possibly altered; '*i* imperfect, looks like point   2201–7] SPs high   2201 *might*] *t* possibly retraced *haue*] otiose ink mark on ascender of *h* *made*] indistinct lobe on *d*   2203] dark ink stain shows through in left margin from other side of folio *Madame*] dark ink stain shows through below *d* from other side of folio   2205 *newes*] extra set of minims on *w* *is*] possibly retraced   2207 *come*] gap between *o* and *m* *Expresse*] '*e* altered, possibly from another letter *from*] otiose ink stroke below *fr*   2208 *himself*] *e* possibly altered *they*] otiose stroke at top of *t* *say.*] stop imperfect, looks like short dash   2209 *saye.*] stop high   2210 *Hum.*] otiose point above *um* *ready*] *y* possibly retraced   2211 *straite.*] gap between word and stop   2212 *Agl.*] ink spot between *A* and *g*   2215] SP low *Troth,*] comma low and heavily inked   2216 *will treade*] no gap between words

     Cytheræa, Same by my trewe Maydenhed I do sweare
     to you, Couz.
Hum. I, And by that of myne, I protest vnto you, as also by th=
     at of my trewe Sister Aridaes too.   2220
Agl. So, and shall lyke you.
Ar. then hie wee in[<.>]all, I beseech you, and let vs quicklye
     be Iogging too. Nay come away, I beseech you both.
Hum. Agl. Wee come.

     Act 4 Scen 4.
    Proteus Harpax Rudens Pontcus
       Gripus.
Prot. Wa'st not wondrous, I with my wisdome might
     not get him furth his hole? Rudens.
Rud No, for I neuer thought, thou hadst any, Proteus.   2230
Prot A scruple yet, by your leaue.
Rud. Yes, for saying, Thetis should bring furth a Man grea=
     ter then be the Gods of Olympus, verily.
Prot. Mark but the end, Rudens.
Harp. I haue hearde, Fish to haue beene frighted with the
     voice of a man, But neuer yet the voice of a Man
     to haue been choakt [with] by a Fish, Proteus.
Grip. I [haue] was in good hope, of your Treacle, Mr Proteus.
dilue Harp Sirrha, what course, herein is to be taken now?
Prot. stant rigidæ horrore comæ et vox faucibus hæsit.   2240
Harp. ˆ\Gape,/ Gorelin, shalt haue a worme.

2217 *Cytheræa*] *r* heavily inked; otiose horizontal stroke on comma *trewe*] ²*e* altered from another letter; long horizonal stroke visible underneath letter 2219 *Hum.*] stop low *myne*] gap between *y* and *n* *vnto you*] otiose point below *n*; *o* of *vnto* extends into *y* 2220 *Sister*] *e* possibly altered *too.*] gap between word and stop; stop merges with descender of *y* in *you* on preceding line 2222 *then*] *t* might be imperfectly formed *T* *in*[<.>]*all*] illegible letter marked for deletion with vertical stroke *beseech*] limb on *h* extends through next word *and let*] no gap between words 2223 *be*] *b* possibly altered or retraced *away, I*] imperfect *y* touches *I*; otiose stroke between *y* and *I* *both*] otiose stroke under *b* 2224] SP low 2225 '4] ink spot on character 2226 *Pontcus*] *c* formed from *i* 2228 *Prot.*] stop high 2229 *get*] *g* poorly formed, looks like *y* *hole?*] point on ? looks like comma 2231 *scruple*] *u* possibly altered 2232 *Rud.*] otiose ink mark above stop 2234 *Mark*] otiose ink stroke precedes word *Rudens.*] stop high 2235 *Harp.*] *P* retraced 2237 *with*] underlined for deletion; dark ink point above *w* *by*] added in left margin to replace [*with*] *Proteus*] *P* altered 2238 *haue*] underlined for deletion; preceded by high ink point *was*] otiose ink mark below *w* 2240] otiose downward stroke precedes SP and descends to SP in next line 2241 ˆ*Gape,*/] interlineation begins just before start of line; caret above stop in SP on line below

79

Prot. Pop.

Popt his finger into his mouth and he potted.

Rud) Will you he\a/re, what I, that haue not one letter on the Booke, haue reade

Pont. Reade on.

[FOL. 143ʳ]

Rud. You know, Masters, certaine Hillocks stand, su suwest of his den, euen Iust on the Mouth of him.

Harp. So.

Rud. Vpon these ˄\hillocks/, wee will reare sundry Bancks of Sand. Doe you heare mee? 2250

Grip. Wee vnderstand you well.

Rud. In as much as, when the wind sitteth in that corner, It will driue the sand into his eyes, he shall not be able once to endure it.

Harp. So, Sir.

Rud. Then with a Pursnet shall be layd furth for him, wee will so, First, entangle him, so present him, this now Aphrodysiall, to Cythe=ræa, for a Prodigie.

Harp. O most excellent Rudens.

Rud. Giue the Diuill his dewe I beseech you ˄\all/. It was Sertorious 2260 his own deuice, And he was a nimbe Kerne, [I] you. knowe.

Grip. But why might not this, farr better, haue beene done, by that the fume of the sodden Fish, then by this ˄\the/ cumber of dust, For Sertorius his stratageme was perfourmed by Smoake, not by dust, you all so know.

Prot. Sic visum superis, ˄\goodman/ Gripus, Nec licet omnibus ire Corith=um, Goodman Gripus.

Grip. Oh ho, oh ho, Best of all, best of all, Then be it so, be it so. But why was not this done before then?

2245 *Pont.*] *P* possibly retraced; stop high   *on*] otiose stroke through *o*   2246 *Rud.*] limb on *R* faint; ink blot shows through from other side of folio   2247 *him.*] otiose ink mark follows *h*; stop looks like vertical dash   2248] SP high   2249 ˄*hillocks*/] gap between first point and caret; caret written over comma   *Doe*] *oe* possibly altered; otiose ink mark below *o*   2252 *sitteth*] indistinct limb on *h*   *It*] cross-stroke in *I* touches *t*   *will*] otiose stroke follows word   2253 *once*] otiose stroke above *c*   *endure*] *u* possibly altered from another letter; otiose points over *re*   2255] SP high   *So*] otiose stroke above word   *Sir*] *r* possibly retraced   2256] SP high   *First,*] comma below *t*   2257 *entangle*] 'e possibly altered   2260 *Diuill*] *ui* possibly altered   *dewe*] otiose ink mark precedes word   *was*] high otiose ink mark precedes *was*; *w* possibly altered   *Sertorious*] ²*r* possibly retraced; otiose extra point on *i*   2261 *was*] *w* possibly altered   *I*] underlined for deletion; preceded by high dark ink point   *you.*] added in left margin to replace [*I*]; stop probably otiose   *knowe*] *kn* altered in darker ink   2262 *not*] headstroke on *t* retraced   2266 ˄*goodman*/] caret low, touches *r* in *Gripus* on following line   2269 *before*] *b* possibly written over *p* or *f*

Rud. Because it was not thought on before then. 2270
Harp. Come, Proteus, come, Let vs about this First, If fayle, then
      after some other too, till that the supreame Gods of O=
      lympus shall haue determined hereupon.
Prot. First heare, then Iudge whither I be wise (Rud) Come on
Prot. A Hoarde of Mice held, one day, Parliament,
      How they might the Cat, of his Posture, stent,
      When one, among the rest, from off his sell,
      Deuisd to tye, abowt the Cat, a Bell;
      Each lykt it well, when among the Best,
      With face all wan, and hed, with yeares, inuest, 2280
      Stood vp, and sayd, I lyke the Counsell well,
      But who will tye, about the Cat, a Bell?
      So I, to you, I lyke to lay a Pursnet,
      But who, about the den, will lay this Pursnet?
Rud. That will Rudens doe.
Prot. I will not be so rude, mary.
Rud. You be too wise. But what's that Paper in thy hand? Pon=
      ticus.
Pont. It is a Catalogue of the Fish, hath beene taken toward the
      Feast, And hath beene serued in, to day, to dinner. 2290
Prot. Reade but.
Pont. First and Imprimis Oysters. What say[d]st thou to them?
      Proteus.
Prot Too too whot, too too whot they be, a good Philtrum, Mary.
Pont Playce.
                                   [FOL. 143ᵛ]
Prot. I am persuaded, the Sea Ape and he be[g]one, he so
      still maketh the Mowe at a Man.
Harp. Neuer he comes to boarde, But \am/ ready to stab the vil=
      laine, Proteus.

2270 on] o heavily inked   2271 Harp.] stop high   2273 hereupon] ²e blotted   2274 Prot.] stop high on] heavily inked; n cropped by the edge of the page   2275 Prot.] SP high; stop high   2276 Posture] headstroke on t merges with imperfect u   2279 lykt] yk smudged well, when] first letter of each word smudged   2280 wan] w possibly altered inuest,] ink spot follows comma   2285 Rud.] SP high; gap precedes low stop Rudens] s possibly retraced   2287 Rud.] stop high   2289–92] blotted ink stain in right margin   2292 Pont.] stop high Imprimis] blotted ink spot under ²i Oysters.] stop high say[d]st] d marked for deletion with vertical strokes them] m possibly altered   2294 whot,] o altered or retraced   2296 be[g]one] g marked for deletion with vertical stroke

Pont. Thorneback. 2300
Prot. The Iewes affirmed, when the red and the white str=
akes were seene on anything, And they being low=
er then the rest of the Peice, that then the Thing
was infect with Leprosye, so lykwise may be sayd of
the sousd Thorneback I suppose, as you may well
perceiue, But wee be no Iewes, Therefore they haue
beene eaten by vs.
Pont. Lobster.
Prot. A shame he is to the whole Kingdome of Fishes, Gentle
men. 2310
Rud. Why so? I pray you.
Prot. Prick him forward, He will be sure to goe backward
Pont. Shrympes.
Prot. I neuer lykt shrimpe.
Harp. Thou neuer sawest, in thy life, Little fellow looke so
grim yet, Proteus.
Pont I tooke him for a Spaniard, Mr Proteus. Gurnet.
Prot. Gurnet, quasi Gernet, he so lifteth the Mustachio,
and gerneth on a Man.
Pont. [<C>od] Cod 2320
Prot A good Iudiciall Fellow by my Fa, right lineally des
cended he is from the stoiks, I wisse.
Rud. Directly, he is descended from the Stocks, our Nets.
Pont. Tench.
Prot. Too too Ieleous, too too Ieleous he is.
Harp Of vs you meene, wee ⸢\but/⸣ catch so fewe of them.
Pont Herring
Grip. I mary, Sir, this is a good hearing now.
Pont Conger.
Prot. For because he and a Cup of wyne make congruity. 2330
Rud. So do any of the rest, Asse.

2300 *Pont.*] stop high   2302–3 *low=/er*] hyphen faint   2304 *be*] *e* imperfect, formed from a single short vertical stroke   2305 *well*] *e* altered, possibly from *i*   2306 *perceiue*] *c* altered or formed from another letter; *i* has short mainstroke and an otiose extra point   2309 *Prot.*] *r* blotted   2310 *men.*] stop high   2312 *Prick*] *r* formed from *i*   2315 *Harp.*] high otiose ink point follows SP   2318 *he*] formed from *so* in darker ink   *lifteth*] *t* possibly formed from *e*   2320 <*C*>*od*] underlined for deletion; *C* altered and blotted in darker ink, with otiose stroke above letter resembling an inverted comma; high point in darker ink precedes word   *Cod*] added in left margin to replace [<*C*>*od*]   2321 *right*] otiose point above *t*   2323–37 SPs low   2324 *Pont.*] stop high

Prot   Vincor ab Aenea.
Pont. Soles.
Rud.   Of all the Fishes of the Sea they be Sole the sweetest
Prot. Fye vpon them, I do neuer sent them, but am ready
         rise from Boarde, Sirs.
Grip. If but a whiting, am ready pisse my hose, by the lyke
         Antipathy, Gentlemen.
Pont. Smelts.
Prot. For they be not good, vnles they be smelt to.   2340
Pont   Eeles.
Prot   It is, expresly, against the saying, Thou shalt not take
         an Eeele by the Tayle.
                                                              [FOL. 144ʳ]
Rud.   A wet Eeele, And these haue beene Roasted, to<o> well you do
         know all, my Masters
Prot. I confesse it.
Pont. Salmon.
Harp. A Parson he is, Bids vs to begin the [Psmalme] Psalme on.
Pont. Trout.
dilue   Prot. Gentlemen, looke and behold * For loe you here, this is his [right] 2350
He blurted as   Character right. *
one angerd or had   \P./ Base.
the wind cholick   Rud) All begot<te>n in Fornication they be.
with eye and with
mouth both to   Pont   Item one Dolphin.
weet.   Prot. The villaine thinks that the Musitian Arion is on his back
                         For euer he supposes he heares him singing to his Dol
                         fine. (Pont) Turbot
                 Prot. Turbot, quasi Turne-boate, For if there be enowe of them
                         they will ouerturne[,] a boate, sure.

2335 ²*them*] *e* possibly altered   *but*] lobe of *b* does not join mainstroke   *ready*] *d* retraced   2337 *hose*] *o* imperfect, looks like short vertical stroke   2338 *Antipathy,*] ¹*t* faint; comma formed from stop; otiose ink mark above comma   2340 *to*] *o* merges with stop   2342 *against*] *i* missing point   *not take*] stroke joins *t* and *t*, possibly otiose; ²*t* imperfect, with mainstroke curving to the right   2343 *Tayle.*] stop high; otiose ink mark to right of line   2344 *to<o>*] ²*o* altered in darker ink and blotted   2345 *all,*] comma formed from stop   *Masters*] *a* possibly retraced; otiose stroke between *s* and *t*   2346 *it.*] stop high   2347 *Salmon.*] stop high, looks like dash   2348 *to*] *o* imperfect, looks like dash   *Psmalme*] underlined for deletion; preceded by high ink points that look like short dashes   *Psalme*] added in left margin to replace [*Psmalme*]   2350 *right*] underlined for deletion; preceded by high ink point   2352 *P.*] abbreviated SP is interlined above beginning of line; mainstroke short; stop high   2353 *begot<te>n*] *b* altered from another letter in darker ink; otiose strokes in darker ink obscure *te*   2354 *Item*] headstroke on *I* disjointed, written over *t*   2355 *Prot.*] stop high   *back*] otiose stroke over *c*   2358 *Prot.*] *ro* written over *on*; stop high and faint   *Turbot*] *T* retraced   2359 *ouerturne[,]*] *ne* smudged; faint trace of scraped comma follows word

Pont. Breame. 2360
Prot. I think they do, perpetually, breame the one the other, as
 do Hogs, they be so full of Spawn.
Pont. Carpe.
Grip. I lyke not these carping Iacks, I.
Harp. Eury each of them haue, at dinner, beene thourough\ly/, carpt,
 for it, [to peices], to fetters Goodman Gripus.
Pont. Crabs.
Prot. Mitto tibi metulas cancros Imitare legendo.
Rud. Wee vnderstand you.
Prot. But Scarce, I beleeue. 2370
Rud. Beene layd but by, For our Ladyes be crabbed sufficient, M^r
 Proteus. (Pont) Flounder (Prot) Flounder quasi floe vnder for
Pont. Mussells. (that they floe vnder ˄ \the/ water.
Grip. They haue mouselled, many and oft, these Thumbes of [myne] ours.
Pont. Sturgeon.
Prot. Stur Iohn, qu<a>si stur Iack, He is such a sturring Iack
 in ones Belly.
Pont. Anchoues.
Harp. I mary, Sir, that's the sturring Iack now.
Prot. The one stirreth before, the other sirreth behind, as righ= 2380
 tly I do conceiue them both, by their cooperations with in
 mee now.
Pont. Pearch.
dilue Rud. If but once he pearch aboue water, he is [sure] myne. sure
Prot. I am persuaded he be the right Thorneback, Gentlemen.
Harp. A Burr in thy Mawe, Proteus.
Prot. One of a fortnight old, in thyne, Harpax.
Pont. Iack.

2360–89] stops high after SPs   2363 *Carpe*.] lobe of *p* slight and separate from mainstroke; otiose point follows stop   2365 *thourough\ly/,*] *ly*/ interlined above *h*; comma low, possibly in false start for end of line or false start for a caret   2366 *to peices*] underlined for deletion; preceded by high, dark ink point   *to fetters*] added in left margin to replace [*to peices*]; *t* of *to* short   *Goodman*] G formed from P, in possible false start for *Proteus*   2369 *Wee*] W blotted   2370 *But*] B blotted   2371 *but*] *b* possibly retraced   *M^r*] *r* written above M   2372 *(Prot*] *(* written over *)*   *floe*] otiose ink mark follows *o*   2373 *(that*] *hat* altered in darker ink from other letters; otiose ink marks under bracket; bracket separates from Ponticus's speech on this line words that are implicitly a continuation of Proteus's speech on previous line   2374 *myne*] underlined for deletion   *ours*] added in left margin to replace [*myne*]   2376 *qu<a>si*] *a* obscured by dark ink blot   2380 *behind*] *e* altered   2382 *mee*] ²*e* altered   2384 ¹*sure*] underlined for deletion; dash above *s*   ²*sure*] added; *s* merges with preceding stop   2385 *Gentlemen*.] stop high   2386 *Harp*.] stop high

Prot. Adde but sauce vnto him, then right [he is] is he Iack sauce, Sirs.
Pont Finally Cockles. 2390
Prot They neuer sing, but whiles they be heated so will wee now
doe too, after the heate of our labour.

[FOL. 144ᵛ]

Harp. Come on ˄\saye./ So all wee, after, vpon this Master Fish,
Come.   **The Fifth Song.**
\1./
wee Fishermen, if any thing wee get,
     Wee sup well for it at night,
If not any thing fall to our Net,
     Too wee blowe our nayles for it.

2. 2400
Neither wind nor Tyde will bring vs in handsell,
     Except wee be loade with Fraught,
Nor [Spark] Sprat nor Minowe will forde vs one Morsell,
     For that they be good for naught.

3
Many Iohn, for Fault of Sea-water Fish,
     [With] Will Trigge them with Mylk and Butter,
Who if they but gaine one Salt-water dish
     Then they will feede on no other.

4. 2410
Greate Lord of Waters, a Sea do but send vs,
     Not troubled with wind [a] \or/ rayne.
Good store of Pilcher and Herring to mend vs,
     All wee may to Sea againe.

2389 *he is*] underlined with a blotted line for deletion; high ink blot precedes word   *is he*] added in left margin to replace [*he is*]   2392 *doe*] d possibly altered   2399 *our nayles*] no gap between words   2401 *bring*] r retraced   2403 *Spark*] underlined for deletion; preceded by high ink point   *Sprat*] added in left margin to replace [*Spark*]; preceded by low ink point, probably otiose   2404 *naught.*] otiose point follows stop   2407 *With*] underlined for deletion; preceded by high ink point   *Will*] added in left margin to replace [*With*]   *Trigge*] otiose ink point below r   2412 *a*] crossed out; possibly false start for *and*

Act 4 Scen 5.
Glauce Hero.

Glau. By my Troth, Lady Hero, Albeit your Husband,
this morning, pluckt you, vnder water, to him, yet
you shall not so engrosse him wholely, from mee, to
your self, by all that Art and meane, thou shalt, in 2420
the case, be able to perfourme, Lady Hero.

Her. Goe to, Lady Glauce, goe to, stretch furth your hearte till
it burst its strings in Twayne, Leander is myne, and
Leander shall lye with mee, this night, in spite of
that hauty hearte of yours, my Glauce fine, I vowe.

Glau. A God Leander he is now, thou but a mortall wretch, He=
ro, as thou beest, Therefore lyke a God as he is now,
he shall marry with mee a Goddesse, as both lawe of
these Seas, as also of Oceanus our King haue decreed.
Thou lyke a Paltry and peeuish gerle, shalt waite at my 2430
doore, my Page and Handmayd, the whiles, as rightly I
conceiue thee fit for to be.

Her. Nay then, I do adiure you, Madame, by graund Cyth
eræa her self, whoe's Preist I am, By Iuno Pro=
\<nu\>ba, who whylom, the first, composed that nuptial
Band betweene Leander and my self, And by all those
Gods and Goddesses, that were at our wedding daunce,
that night, you yeild Leander vp to mee his first spouse
and Make, as both Lawe and Reason require it at
your hands, Lady Glauce. 2440

[FOL. 145ʳ]

Glau. But when? can you tell, Sweet Mowse. I seasd him this mor=
ning ˰ \myne own/ before he seased you, And as myne own first I will
keepe him myne own, surely. For neuer yet has been known
conquerour such a Beast, As for to deliuer that Hold, he has

2415 *Act*] otiose ink mark precedes word   2417 *Glau.*] stop high   2418 *him*] point on *i* faint
2419 *you*] *o* and *u* look like dashes   2423 *it*] point on *i* merges with descender of *G* in *Goe* on previous
line   *Twayne*] ink shows through from overleaf around *Tw*   2425   *hauty*] *u* poorly formed, looks
like *r*   *I vowe*] cross stroke of *I* touches *v*   2426 *thou*] *h* possibly altered   *He=*] bottom stroke on
hyphen faint   2428 *both*] *o* looks like short dash   2430 *peeuish gerle*] no gap between words
2431 *whiles*] *i* imperfect, looks like stop   2434 *whoe's*] apostrophe over *e*   *I*] retraced
2434–5 *Pro=/\<nu\>ba*] *nu* imperfect and heavily inked   2435 *whylom*] *w* possibly altered   *composed*]
d possibly retraced   *nuptial*] faint point on *i*   2439 *Make,*] comma high, looks like mainstroke of a
letter   2442 *myne*] short descender on *y*   2443 *For*] otiose stroke above *r*

> possessed once, to the conquered his Foe. Shall I then, that
> am not onely a Goddesse, but also daughter to Lord Nereus,
> Prince of all narrow Seas, shewe mee such a dasse for to
> be, so to deliuer that Prize, I haue wun to myself, and that
> with the full labour and strengh of these armes of myne also,
> to a Mortall and wretched Princocks, such as thy self [art?] art   2450
> Hero. Faith, Sir, No.

Her.   Doe your worst, Madame, and spare not, For I haue, And as but
> now but, Fabricated such a holding Platforme, within the
> Intricate Laborinth of my Brayne, that in Spite of that [prou'd] prowd
heart   of yours, and that also, with such full and a flushing ˄ \blood/ of your
> shame besyde, you shall leaue the Prize to its owner, And
> get you to your Tritons, with whom, whylom, you haue
> beene but too too familiar, I suppose, if that those Reports
> be trewe, that haue ˄ \gone/ on you, Sweet Madame myne.

Glau.   A crott, in thy Teeth, sweet Lady Hero, For the Gods of Olym   2460
> pus haue wooed Thetis and myself, being but water Nym=
> phes, vnto their beds, whom I notwithstanding haue with
> Scorne reiected, And haue rauished a mortall wight ˄ \but/ this
> morning, such as Leander is, vnto my vse, And such as he is,
> In spite of that pretie Mouth of thyne, I will keepe him from
> thee, And that onely for that his more Ardent and more
> Firme affection, he hath borne mee since his Rape,
> my Hero deare.

Her.   If you get him from mee, then say I haue no brayne in
> this nolle of myne. For I will so bind you[r] to confesse,   2470
> your self ˄ \to be/ so trewly vanquished herein, that Cytheræa
> And the whole companie of those Gods, that now be descen
> ded all to this the now Aphrodysiall, shall both hoote,
> and whistle you for your labour, Lady Glauce. And if so
> I do not, then call mee Hauback, Madame.

2445 *Foe*] pencil dot below *e*   *then*] *h* faint; *e* retraced   2446 *onely*] ink spot on *y*   2447 *a dasse*] *a* touches *d*   2448 *be*] heavily inked   *deliuer*] 'e formed from *i*   2450 *Princocks, such*] comma merges with *s* of *such*   *art?*] underlined for deletion; ink point above *a*; otiose stroke like an apostrophe follows *t*   *art*] added in left margin to replace [*art?*]   2451 *Hero.*] stop high   2452 SP low   2454 *prou'd*] underlined for deletion; preceded by high ink point   *prowd*] added in left margin to replace [*prou'd*]   2455 *heart*] added to left of line   ˄ *blood/ of*] caret under *of*   2459 ˄ *gone/ on*] caret under *o* of *on*   2460 *Glau.*] stop high   2465 *spite*] *e* imperfect, looks like *o*   2466 *that onely*] no gap between words   2469 *Her.*] gap precedes stop   2470 *you[r]*] *r* marked for deletion with a vertical stroke   2474 *your*] *y* possibly altered   2475 *Madame.*] stop preceded by otiose stroke, possibly in pencil

Glau. Nay Nay, do thy worst, my Iaunting Hero, thou.
Hero. And you do your worst you.
Glau. And be hangd to boote Lady Hero you.
Her. Eia Eia.
Glau. And Eia vnto you.   2480
Her. And be berayd too, Madame Glauce you.
Glau. Goe to.
Her. And goe to you.
Glau. Adieu
Her. And Adieu you.

   Act 4 Scen 6.
    The Direction
Talus Arion, Each of them with an Oare on his shoulder, And a veluet Scrip by his syde.

                 [FOL. 145ᵛ]
   Talus Arion.   2490
Tal. Freind Arion, well met, hast sped, Man? say.
Ar. Rather hast thou sped? Coriual, Talus.
Tal. I will make thee, with thy Lute, dance attendance,
     At my Ladyes doore, while I haue wrought her.
Ar. I will aduaunce her, degree by degree,
     So on the Scale, aboue thy reach, Talus,
     Possible, thou mayst, vnioint thy neck with.
Tal. The one wrench of my little finger, Sirrha,
     Shall lay thy labour in the dust (Ar) My self
     Will scale her first, then batter thou and spare not.   2500
Tal. Musitians, I'haue hearde t'haue builded Towns,
     But neuer yet t'haue pulld one down (Ar) Lysander
     Batterd the walles of Sparte with harmony.
Tal. I. I, with engin Harmony (Ar) I haue
     A Iin will beare the Fortresse lowe (Tal) Thy Iins
     Be made of wyres (Ar) Thyne be such dough ware, They
     Will hardly force the Breach (Tal) I haue a charme

2486] otiose ink spot in left margin   2488–9 *shou-/lder*] dash short, like a stop   2492 *hast thou*] headstroke on *t* of *hast* touches *t* of *thou*   2497 *Possible*] P possibly retraced   2498 *Tal.*] SP high; stop high and looks like dash   2500 *not.*] otiose ink marks around word   2501 *Towns*] otiose ink mark follows *n*   2502 *Lysander*] *e* imperfect   2503 *of*] *o* tight, looks like point   *harmony*] *a* tight and heavily inked   2506 *ware,*] comma faint   *They*] *T* retraced or written over another character; otiose stroke on *h*; *e* possibly retraced

		Hath mou'd and queld the desead Ocean	
	dilue	Since ˄\that/ my [late] being with thee (Ar) Thou talkst but	
	Tal.	But I do say that thou (Ar) What wilt say? Man	2510
		I do cast it in thy Teeth (Tal) Hast, Knaue, say,	
		Rifeld my Knap-sack? Ha (Ar) Hast thou it, Sirrha	
	Tal.	Haue I the vse of my eyes? pray \y/ou (Ar) la *	
Here they turnd vp their sleeues both.		Sirrha, knowst thou this? (Tal) And you this? say you	
	Ar.	Myne will thunder (Tal) Sir, so will myne (Ar) goe	
	Tal.	And goe to you. (to	

The Direction.

It thunderd and Lightend, being each their [wrest rol=]
[les] Bracelets and armes stretched furth on hie, their whole
lengh to weet. Arion first, after touch of \t/he[<s>]   2520
\thombe . threon./

Tal. O wonderous. Now myne
Ar. Wondrous. Talus, I can not sure but wonder
     At strangenes of the Accident, They both
     Thunderd alyke, so lykwise was the Lighting,
     The continuance, the measure and the Crack.
Tal. Sirrha, If but well thou dost obserue them,
     They haue same gyres, same weight, same workmanship
     That th'one graine of Mais is not more lyke to th'other
Ar. I deeme the Gods do floute our Miserye.   2530
Tal. I think, rather, that they ˄\do/ enuie vs.
Ar. Wilt heare my counsell? (Tal) say on (Ar) By
     This Cytheræa is ready take Sea,
     Vnto her Arbitriment put wee it.
Tal. Sirrha, with willingnes, Come on thy ways.

2509 ˄\that/ my] caret under m   late] underlined for deletion; ink blot above l   2511 thy] h partially retraced   2512 Knap-sack] smudged ink blot below sa, stretches down through next line   Ha] a tight   2513] otiose ink mark in left margin   \y/ou] y added above o   2515 Ar.] otiose ink mark above stop   2516   (to] implicitly a continuation of Arion's speech on previous line   2518–19 wrest roll=/les] underlined for deletion; preceded by high ink point and otiose stroke   2519 Bracelets] added in darker ink on a pasted slip in left margin to replace [wrest rol=/les]   2520 first] ruddy spot behind word   2520-1 after ... thereon.] added   2520 touch] uch faint   \t/he[<s>]] interlined t added in smaller hand; e altered from i; <s> marked for deletion with a vertical stroke   2521 thombe.] th possibly retraced   2523] SP low   Talus,] comma low   2526 ¹the] he faint; h retraced   2528 workmanship] ip retraced   2529 not more] no gap between words   2530 deeme] ²e written over what appears to be a scraped i   Miserye] otiose point over s   2533 Cytheræa] æa imperfect; possibly altered   2535] SP high

Ar.	Now will I swim, in pleasures, all my dayes.	
Tal.	To Cupid I will build a gallant shryne	
Ar.	I for the same will set songs diuine (Tal) But	
	Come (Ar) stay Fellow Cupedinaire, First here	

[FOL. 146ʳ]
2540

Let mee take your oath you will be trewe,
Not to forestall before the doome be giuen.
Tal. Truth I do sweare on handle of this chaire
Ar. I, vpon the other (Both) so help vs trewe *
No kisse   Bountifull and good Lady Cytheræa.
            Here they knockt vp the Consort.

                Act 5 Scen 1.
                 The Direction
Vsherd in by   * Cytheræa Oceanus Thetis Humida
Mercurye alias Arida Nereus, The Three Graces, Glauce
Hermes.   Attendaunts, Cytheræa with an Arrowe in   2550
                her hand held, And in her Sea attyre onely, to
                behold. Enterd [w]\t/hereupon a Sea Nymphe with
                crown white and blewe of sea weedes, And stood
                Aloofe. Then Cytheræa spake as followes.

Cyth. My Lords, so royally, you haue, this day,
Celebrated my Aphrodysiall,
With such coast, cheare and such Magnificence,
That, while I liue, I shall be mindfull of it,
In my plenary thanks, vnto you, for it.
But now I must to heauen, Hermes hath brought   2560
Speciall letters, to hie mee vp to Court,
Then, good my Lord, if any thing there be,
Wherein, I may steede you, from King Saturnus,
Firmely do you expect it soone as may,
And till the tyme receiue our thanks in paye.
Oce. Madame, if so you please, to staye all night,
E[r]arely, with Phosphorus, you may be stirring.

2539 *here*] ink blot above imperfect ¹*e*; ²*e* imperfect, possibly altered   2541 *giuen*] *e* imperfect
2547 *Direction*] ink spot over *ec*   2552 [*w*]\t/*hereupon*] *w* blotted; *t* added above blotted *w*
2553 *of*] *o* tight, looks like a point   *weedes*,] comma overlaps *s*   2555] SP high   2558 *it*,] comma
low   2561 *hie*] *e* possibly altered   *Court*,] comma merges with ascender of *b* in *be* on following line
2562 *Then*,] comma below *n*   *Lord*,] comma faint   *any thing*] otiose point above *i*   *be*,] comma low
2567 E[r]*arely*] *r* marked for deletion with a vertical stroke

Cyth. No, good my Lord, I must away, this Night
　　　The strangers come, and soone the Bal will be.
Thet. So bad hath beene your cheare, that to our mights　　　　　2570
　　　Wee would amend it, with out Pastyme, Madame,
　　　Then breifly know, wee haue bespoake a shewe
　　　To present you with, humbly requiring you
　　　To take the benefite in any sort.
Ar.　Trewly, Madame, it will be worth the obseruing.
Cyth. What's the Tyme of day (Hum) Sun's but now in West.
Cyth. But earely dayes, Come, each elect his seate,
　　　Cytheræa, vnto sport, neuer cometh late. *

Here they place them on the bank Cytheræa in the chaire of state.

　　　　　　　*Act 5 Scen 2.
dilue　　　　　The Direction.　　　　　　　　　　　　　　　　2580
　　　[Here Cupid, once Harpax, in his godlyke habit] Here Harpax
　　　alias Cupid in his Fisher=mans sute wafted etcæt wafted in Vulcan
　　　with a wanton Fiddle, in womans attyre of scales or woman
　　　Monster inclining to some strange Fish, with whip, Bitt and
　　　Bridle in hand held lyke Lady Reuenge of the Sea Ioculus waf=
　　　ting him lykwise with Cytheræas Fan of feathers, white and dun
　　　Doues and Swans, Venus chariot Birds. Finny wings, hands and feet
　　　too. Tuskye Teeth withall.
　　　　　　　　　　　　　　　　　　　　　　　　　　　　[FOL. 146ᵛ]
　　　　[Cupid] Harpax Cytheræa Oceanus Nereus
sic de cæteris　Ioc<o>\u/lus Thetis Humida Arida Aglaia Vulcan　　　2590
　　Cup. Along, Along, I beseech you, Along.
　Harp.

2572 *know*] mainstroke of *k* obscured by crease; extra set of minims on *w*, possibly an imperfect *e*　　2573 *present*] ′*e* possibly altered　　2577 *Come*] *o* tight, looks like stop　　2580–8] written in darker ink on a pasted slip, lines of text cramped; edges of another pasted slip underneath visible after 2588, with visible parts of text showing through　　2580 *dilue*] blotted; smudged ink blotting below word, extends through two lines of marginal text below word　　2581 *Here … habit**] underlined for deletion; asterisk above first letter of following word (i.e. *wafted*)　　2581–2 *Here … etcæt*] added in darker ink as five lines of text in left margin of pasted slip to replace [*Here … habit*] and probably intended to be one line of text, shown here as two because of length　　2582 *wafted*] *f* partially retraced　　2586 *feathers,*] comma blotted　　2587 *wings, hands*] *ing* imperfect; comma low, added below *h*　　2589 SD] added in darker ink in left margin (referring to the correction of *Cup.* to *Harp.* in this scene)　　*Cupid*] underlined for deletion; preceded by high smudged high ink point　　*Harpax*] added in darker ink in left margin to replace [*Cupid*]; faint otiose ink stroke follows word　　2590 *Ioc*[<*o*>]*u*/ *lus*] added in darker ink; <*o*> blotted; *u* written above blotted letter　　2591 *Harp. Cup.*] *u* retraced or altered; *Cup* presumably intended for deletion and replacement with *Harp.*, which has been added in different ink　　³*Along*] *g* has indistinct bowl, obscured by crease

91

    Cyth. Is this the shewe, you told mee, Ladyes myne?
       His foote sure certifieth mee he halts.
       Ioc<o>\u/lus, flush the woodcock, prithy, Boy.
    Ioc. See you looke steddy, on our Mother, Come.

The Direction.

       Here Ioc[o]\u/lus hauing blown him ouer hed, Vulcan
       appeared all and whole in his own lyknes and in his
       gold lact sute, Hammer and Aprone. Iocolus with
       his Mothers Fan in hand held. The whip Bitt <and>   2600
       and bridle in Vulcans hand still held Lykwise:
    Cyth Out you most egregious foole, out out.
    Hum. My Lord's going t'our Sea-horse market sure
    Ner. A propper leg, Masse, for him go <o> a wooing.
Harp. [Cup.]Can he haue a better to wife, then one
       The fairest of my Mothers maydens? Ha
    Thet. Was going to Prigge some Sea-[Iade] Mare rather.
    Arid. Dreads Triton his Trumpe lyke the stop-Theife call.
    Oce. Madame, I haue obserued long yond Nymphe
       That holds a Crown, seemeth some thing she hath 2610
       To say to you, Madame, And all the while
       To haue expected your leisure onely.
    Cyth. How lyke a Theife he louches, on mee, loe.

2592 *Ladyes*] L retraced; *a* faint   2594–5] written in darker ink on pasted slip, edges of which come down to 2600 and which bears a smaller paper slip on top, containing 2596–600.   2594 *Ioc[<o>]\u/lus*] <o> scraped and blotted; *u* added above blotted letter *prithy*] *h* possibly retraced 2596–600] written in darker ink on pasted slip which has been pasted onto a larger slip, top of which begins at 2594 2596 *The Direction.*] stop faint; *se*= from slip underneath visible to right of line 2597 *n* from slip underneath visible to right of line *Ioc[o]\u/lus*] *o* marked for deletion with vertical stroke; *u* written above blotted letter 2598] *th* from slip underneath visible to right of line 2599 *lact*] blotted ink spot above *ac* 2600 *Mothers*] otiose stroke follows word, possibly an ascender from line below, which has been obscured by pasted slip bearing 2601–4 *The*] written over *and* and blotted *Bitt <and>*] retraced, blotted; text straddles edges of pasted slip 2601–9] written on a pasted slip, with 2605–8 added on a smaller pasted slip; 2601 cramped and in darker ink; 2602–4 and 2609 in lighter ink except for *foole, out out*; 2605–8 added on a smaller pasted slip in light ink 2601 *and*] added to left of line *hand*] descender of *h* partially obscures ²*e* in *egregious* on following line *still*] otiose ink mark under *i* *Lykwise*] *Lykw* blotted; otiose point over stop 2604 <o>] blotted *o* written over illegible letters; otiose point above *wooing*] ²*o* imperfect, looks like imperfect *v* or *u* 2605–8] written on separate slip, pasted onto larger slip bearing 2601–4 and 2609 2605 *Cup.*] underlined for deletion; otiose horizontal stroke above *C* *Harp.*] added in left margin of pasted slip to replace [*Cup.*] 2607 *Iade*] underlined for deletion; preceded by high ink point *Mare*] added in left margin of pasted slip to replace [*Iade*] 2608 *Dreads*] *ds* imperfect 2609] written on same slip that bears lines 2601–4 and smaller slip bearing lines 2605–8; partial text visible above line, mostly obscured by smaller slip bearing lines 2605–8 2609 *Oce.*] stop faint; an *O* partially visible under bottom left edge of slip 2611 *Madame*] ¹*a* tight, obscured by crease *the*] otiose stroke on *e* 2612 *leisure*] *l* possibly formed from another letter 2613 *louches*] *l* possibly retraced or altered

     Aglaia, take him to thy self, I prithy,
dilue   And some [one] looke ◌\vn/to him I do beseech you..
  Agl. Cheare you, my Lord, and giue t'old things their passe.
  Vul. Deare, I ask thee forgiu\<e\>nes from my hearte:
     Better had, seldome comes a worse, they saye.

        Nulla Desunt.

  Cyth. Aproach, good Nymphe, hast any thing deliuer   2620
     Vnto the Queene of Gnide.

     Act 5 Scen 3.
    Nymphe Cytheræa Chorus of Gods
  Nymp. Madame, I haue.
  Cyth. What is it? Troe. (Nymph) Some doubtfull Paramours
     Stout contending about their Mistrisses,
     Appeale to your Ladiship to accord them
     By your Iust verdict (Cyth) Nymphe, be it but that
     I am contented with my whole heartes boote.
  Nymph. First commaunded I am, vse our wordes on you   2630
     Of Consecration, so the whiles t'enstall,
     And inuest you ◌\the/ Empresse of our Sea.
The Imperiall Cyth. Sweet honest Nymphe, begin, I prithy, thou:
crown white and
blew, seaweede

2615–19] written on pasted slip; partially visible word above top edge of slip   2615 *some*] otiose ink points over *om* *one*] underlined for deletion and preceded by a high point, both in different ink ◌*vn*/*to*] caret and *vn* added in different ink; otiose stroke follows *to* *you..*] second stop probably otiose 2616 *Agl.*] tear in slip renders *A* imperfect and shows partial text underneath slip; otiose stroke under high stop *Lord*] otiose ink points above *o* *things*] *h* formed from *i*; otiose point visible above limb of letter 2617 *thee*] otiose stroke below *t* *forgiu\<e\>nes*] tear in slip around \<e\> shows illegible letters underneath pasted slip *hearte*] ink spot below *h*; colon might be otiose point above stop 2618 *Better*] '*e* faint *had*] possibly retraced *saye.*] stop retraced 2619 *Nulla Desunt.*] stop high; large gap between line and bottom edge of slip; edges of another slip visible underneath; partial letters visible under bottom edge of bottom-most slip 2620 *Cyth.*] otiose strokes follow *h* 2621 *Gnide.*] *n* imperfect; stop high 2622] blotted otiose strokes in left margin *3.*] stop looks like hyphen 2623 *Gods*] ink blot below *G*; otiose blotted point above and below *s* 2628 *Cyth*] *C* retraced or altered from another letter; *y* formed from *i* 2629 *whole*] otiose point follows word 2630 *vse*] *v* partially obscured by crease 2631 *the*] *h* retraced 2632 ◌*the*/] *e* obscured by comma on line above 2633 *Cyth.*] SP high; *C* blotted, possibly altered *thou*] otiose stroke below *u*

The Apologie.

Nymph   [FOL. 147ʳ]

  Lady, you about to marrie the Roome,
  If good you be, may it, with Cressies, bloome,
  But if you do rule our People Amisse,
  Turne may his Sea-weede to Adders that hisse,
  God keepe you fro Ruth, God keepe you fro teene,
  So for the while liue you our Water Queene,   2640
  Whiles I, with this song, shall conclude my Theame. *

Here the Nymphe crowned Cytheræa with the sea-wee=de crown.

Nymphe) The Sixth Song.

    1
  All Hayle vnto our Water Queene
  Doe she off, with her mo\r/tall Habit,
  Each corruption may be seene
  Her heauenly good soule to inhabite.
    2
  Doome she the cause with Sooth and Right,
  Let her not decline from the Truth,   2650
  Doe she decide that that is meet,
  With full-fed Equitie and Couth.
    3
  Farr be remoued from her syde
  All hate and Partiallitye,
  All Auarice, Rancour and Pride,
  While she is in Autoritye.
    4
  The cause is but winning of Fewe,
  Then be not your Ladiship seene   2660
  The loosing of these coupples nowe,
  But be you|their good Lady Queene.

2634 *Apologie.*] *e* retraced, with otiose point underneath letter; stop imperfect; ink spot follows stop   2635 *Roome*] otiose point above ¹*o*; two otiose points over ²*o*   2635–6] ink transfer from fol. 146ᵛ in right margins   2637 *Amisse,*] otiose point follows comma   2639 ²*God*] dark ink spot obscures top of *G*   2643 1] numeral merges with second mainstroke of *H* in *Hayle* on following line   2647 *good*] otiose strokes below word   *inhabite.*] *in* imperfect, otiose stroke below letters; gap precedes high stop   2649 *cause*] otiose strokes above *se*   *with*] otiose strokes below *i* and above   *Sooth*] otiose stroke above *t*   2652 *Equitie*] *t* retraced or altered   *Couth.*] stop faint and high   2662 *you|their*] vertical rule separates cramped words and runs through *u*

Corollarium
Hayle, Lady, off our Water-Greene

Nulla Desunt.

Cyth. Bring them now in, our eares be ope to heare them.
dilue But what's the noise? [I suppose] of Saylours, [I] I suppose

  Act 5 Scen 4.
  Rudens Proteus Ponticus Gripus, Arida
  Humida Cytheræa Oceanus Nereus   2670
  Coüs Cupid Glauce Thetis.
Rud. Hey yeu, hey yeu.
Prot. Well sayd, Rudens, tugge him thou in, Sirrha lustilye.
Rud. Shalt see, that I haue eaten Brawn and Mussels too, Seig=
  neur Proteus. Hey yeu, Hey yeu.
Prot Well sayd, Ponticus, pulle thou in as liuely.
Pont. I haue eaten with him for a wager I warrant him.
  Hey yeu, Hey yeu.
               [FOL. 147ᵛ]
Rud. Yet, will not come vp the Knaue, Hey yeu.
Pont. Pull, Hey yeu, Hey yeu.   2680
Grip. Lustily, my Mates, Hey yeu.
Pont Well sayd, Bald Father Gripus, Hey yeu.
Grip. Hey yeu, Hey yeu.

2663–5] written in different ink on pasted slip; ascenders from *ll* and point from *i* visible above top edge of slip; a small square slip added to top right corner of larger slip, presumably to cover show-through of text 2664 *off*] *ff* written over *ur*, false start for *our* 2665 *Nulla Desunt.*] otiose points and ink spots surround words; empty space between line and bottom edge of slip; partial text visible under bottom edge 2666 *Cyth*] otiose ink point precedes SP; otiose point above *C* *heare*] ²*e* possibly altered 2667 *noise?*] ? altered from comma *I suppose*] underlined for deletion *Saylours, [I]*] comma formed from stop, followed by faint *I* marked for deletion with strokes *I suppose*] added following [*I*], with terminal letter smudged 2672] SP high 2673 *Prot.*] SP high; stop faint 2674] SP high 2674–5 *Seig=/neur*] *r* possibly altered or retraced 2675 *Proteus.*] stop possibly retraced ¹*Hey*] otiose point above *y* *yeu, Hey*] blotted ink stain around *u, H*. 2676 *Well*] *w* possibly altered *Ponticus,*] comma smudged 2677 *Pont.*] high faint stop *eaten*] ²*e* retraced *with*] blotted ink stain on word 2678 ²*yeu*] *e* imperfect, looks like *o* 2679] ink spot in left margin 2682] SP low *Bald*] dark ink spot on *d* 2683 *yeu.*] otiose ink mark above high stop

Prot Yet one pluck more, I prithy.
Grip. Hey yeu.
Prot Nay but then I will ^\once/ trye myne old cables too. Hey yeu
      Hey yeu. Now the Lord be praysed for it, Post va=
      rios casus post tot discriminarerum Tendimus
      in Latinum, After much sweate and diuers Agonies
      wee haue brought vp but common ware, see.   2690
Rud. Fyeth vpon him, what a stirr wee haue had with the
      knaue?
Grip. I would not take the lyke paine with him againe for the
      whole Doctrine in his belly, I wusse.
Cyth. Fishermen, what haue you brought vp there?
Rud. Such a Fish, Madame, as neuer was hearde of in me=
      mory of our Fathers, Madame.
Pont. Madame, he will speake you greeke, Latin, French, Cal=
      dee, Faery, vtter Oracles, daunce the Canaryes, Quid
      non? whom now, since wee haue taken him, wee be   2700
      come present him your Ladiship for a Noueltie.
Cyth. \I thank you, sirs, your paines shall be requitt./
Cyth. Waft asyde but, wee may consydcr him.
      As huge an Ork, as ere my eyes beheld.
Arid. Myne eyes will not endure to looke vpon him.
Hum. Nor myne, I do assure thee, Arida.
Cyth. Lord Proteus, How was he taken? Say.
Prot He was dusted furth his den, Madame, Then
      Taken with a Pursnet, for him layd furth.
Ner. Certes, I haue seene, in our Seas, as bigge,   2710
      But that he vtters Toungs and Oracles,
      I can but muse.
Thet. I' haue hearde my grandame say

2685 *Grip.*] stop high   ²*yeu*.] stop high   2686 *too*] ²*o* possibly retraced   *yeu*] *eu* retraced   2687 *Hey*] no cross-stroke on *H*   *yeu*.] high stop   2687–8 *va=/rios*] *a* altered or retraced   2689 *Latinum*] ink mark under *a*   *Agonies*] *es* possibly retraced   2691 *the*] *e* possibly altered from *o*   2692 *knaue*] *a* possibly altered   2693 *Grip.*] stop high   2696] SP low   2698 *Pont.*] stop high   2698–9 *Cal=/dee*] *a* imperfect, looks like *u*   2699 *Canaryes*] ¹*a* and ²*a* tight and heavily inked   2702] interlined; additional SP high   *you,*] *o* merges with ascender of *d* in *asyde* on following line; comma merges with ascender of *b* in *but* on following line   *sirs, your*] comma merges with descender of *y* in *your* on line above; ²*r* merges with *L* in *Ladiship* on previous line   2709 *Pursnet*] *s* possibly altered; high otiose point follows word   2710] otiose ink marks in right margin   *Ner.*] stop high

	There is a Fish, that if a man but eate off	
	He shall vtter Oracles, So, I weene doth he.	
Hum.	I think Pythagoras has crept into him.	
Arid	The greisly God of Tartarus rather.	
Oce.	My Masters, rippe ope his belly and see.	
Rud.	Will you giue vs leaue, your worship, pick ope	
	your Oracle?	2720

The Direction.

An Enginers Boy with greasy pouch by his syde, gnaw
ing on a whole half cheate loafe spred with Butter,
with workmans Aprone and greasy flat cap inuested.

Rud.	Oh Iupiter (**Grip**) Pluto.	
Pont.	Neptune (**Thet**) Heauenly Gods permit mee Patience	
Prot.	By Dis, Acheron, by Cocytus streame,	
	By Styx, Cerberus, and by Phlegethon ———	
Hum.	The heauenly Gods be mercifull to vs all.	
Ner.	The wonders of our liquid Element.	2730

[FOL. 148ʳ]

Arid.	The supreame Gods auert the Augury	
Glau.	And graunt vs all their mercyes from aboue.	
Cyth.	Masters, I charge you silence, Peace, I say,	
	And say Cytheræa hath Imposd it.	
	Sirrha, say, who art thou? whence? or how	
	Camst thou, first, into this Fishes belly?	
Coüs	My name is Coüs, Seruaunt to one Talus,	
	Famous Inginer in the Isle of Creete,	
	He supprised, by the Enemye, one day,	
	Was hurld into Sea, he and his Familye,	2740
	What of the Rest became, I may not say.	
	Mee this Fish was curteous to receiue	
	Into his Mawe, so præserud he my life (**Oce**) Wondrous.	
Cyth.	How couldst liue, in so foule a den? Saye.	

2714 *There*] ²*e* imperfect   2715 *So*,] comma low   2716 *Hum*.] stop high   *Pythagoras*] otiose stroke under ²*a*; *o* tight, looks like point   2717 *of Tartarus*] no gap between *f* and *T*; *u* imperfect   *rather*.] stop high   2722 *by*] altered from illegible characters   2722–3 *gnaw/ing*] *a* retraced   2723 *loafe*] *f* written over *u*   2727 *Dis*] *D* possibly retraced   *Cocytus*] *C* written over *c*   2729 *mercifull*] *c* possibly formed from *i*, point visible above letter   2730 *Element*] otiose stroke under *l*   2738 *Creete*,] comma formed from stop   2740 *Was*] *w* possibly altered   2743 *Wondrous*.] stop high

	Coüs	Mee thought, the while, I was in Paradice,	

Coüs Mee thought, the while, I was in Paradice,
      Where I had such honour done vnto mee,
      As neuer. Prince the lyke, Moreouer spake
      Greeke, Latin, French, Nay vtrred oracles.
Rud   Wast you, in a Pox, wee did th'honour to[<o>]?
Coüs More, Madame, I had sacrifice done to mee,   2750
      Where my Mouth so waterd, Lord, after Greene Fish,
      It is not to be spoken, Deare Madame.
Grip. I told you so, If I did not mistake, Rudens.
Cyth. Sirrha Coüs, shalt better be hearde soone.
      Now matters, of Importancy, wee haue
      That must be dispatcht first, you Fishermen,
dilue Doe you get [you] in into the Buttery,
      Towe|in the Monster and call for drink, your
      Reward shall be Princely (Pont) Thank you, Madame.
Rud. Pull Harpax. ([Cup] Harp.) Rudens, take thou, this, and learne 2760
      Better to know the Gods an other Tyme. *

A boxe on the eare. Stared long on him then spake

Rud. * Then goe, and be hangd, vnto thy calling,
      What did wee know who thou wert.
Harp [Cup.] Vant, villaine. *

Gaue him the vant on his Bum

      Act 5 Scen 5.
      Arion Talus Coüs Cytheræa Nere=
      us Thetis Oceanus Arida Humida
      Glauce. Leander and Hero crowned with
      Myrtle Both, and standing aloofe. Hermes.
Ar.   Long life, vnto the heauenly Queene of Loue.   2770
Coüs Master, Master, Quomodo vales, Master.
Tal. Coüs? I thought, thou hadst beene put to sword.
Coüs I haue seene wonders, Master. (Tal) Peace, seest not?
      Who's in Presence? Sir. Shalt be heard soone. Goe.

2745] SP low   2747 *neuer.*] stop probably otiose   2749 *did*] two points above *i*   *to*[<o>]] <o> marked for deletion with a vertical stroke   2750 *More,*] comma low   2751 *Where*] otiose point precedes word   2753 *you*] *u* flat, looks like dash   *Rudens.*] otiose stroke precedes stop   2754 *shalt*] *t* imperfect, indistinct low headstroke   2755 *matters,*] comma imperfect, followed by otiose stroke   2757 *you*] underlined for deletion; preceded by high ink point   2758 *Towe|in*] vertical rule separates words   2760 *Cup*] underlined for deletion; preceded by high ink point   *Harp.*] added below *Rud* to replace [*Cup*]   2764 SP low   2769 *Hermes.*] added in different ink on a pasted slip; stop visible to the right of slip   2770] SP high   2772 *put*] ink smudge below *u*   2773 *Peace,*] comma low

Cyth. Be you of those seek Iustice at our hands?
Both. Wee be (Cyth) who's the Defendaunt (Both) Thetis.
Cyth. Thetis, stand furth, and answere to the Things
      Shall be layd against you. Now speake your minds.

[FOL. 148ᵛ]

Ar.   The Rector of the Sea, no sooner had
      Graunted vs full libertye of his Court,   2780
      When both in one made Loue vnto this Lady.
      Long were our Prayers, and many were our vowes,
      When she, quite to barr vs of these our hopes
      I had, quod she, now many years agone
      A Ceston for my wrests, which long I held
      As pretious as these eyes, with this I queld
      The waues, with this the waues I lykwise raised
      When at any tyme I crossd the Maine,
      Raisd lykwise with this th'Affections of Loue.
      The same I lent, one day, to Vlysses,   2790
      Moued with compassion on the Man,
      Whilst he in dangerous perill was of life,
      To bring him safe on shoare, which since the tyme
      Neuer my eyes could see it more, And then
      She sayd, he vowd to|marry none but him
      That brought it her, there withall Imposed
      The Taske vpon vs. (Cyth) Thetis, say they trewe?
Thet. Trew, faire Empresse (Cyth) Hath either of you? Say.
      Obteyned this [Loue-rolle] Ceston., surety of her Loue?
Ar.   I haue bright Goddesse (Tal) I haue dreaded Queene.   2800
Ar.   That myne it is th'Experience will showe.
Tal.   That myne it is th'Experience will showe.

2775 *seek*] ²*e* imperfect, possibly altered   *hands*] h possibly altered   2776 *Defendaunt*] ²*e* possibly formed from *a*   2782 *vowes*] otiose stroke between *v* and *o*   2784–8] written on pasted slip; partial letters visible above top and bottom edges of slip   2789 *Loue.*] *e* possibly altered; otiose point precedes stop   2792 *perill*] ²*l* imperfect   2793 *bring*] ink stain below *ri*   2795 *to*|*marry*] rule separates words and possibly crosses a small *o* added above *om*   2796 *brought*] larger than usual gap follows word   2797 *vpon vs. (Cyth)* no gap between *n* and *v*; stop merges with bracket   *trewe?*] ? altered; ink spot follows ?   2798 *Cyth*] *t* retraced   *Say.*] stop faint   2799 *Loue-Rolle*] underlined for deletion; preceded by blotted high ink point   *Ceston.*] added in larger script in left margin on pasted slip to replace [*Loue-Rolle*]; stop probably otiose, followed by ink marks   2800] SP low   *Queene*] ink transfer from text on pasted slip on fol. 149ʳ above and following ³*e*   2801] SP low   2802] SP low   *will*] otiose strokes above *w*

Cyth. Deliuer them, both, into my hands, you.
   My self will try th'Experience of both.
Ar. This myne (Tal) And myne, Madame (Cyth o mighty
   What doe these my Immortall eyes behold? (Gods,
   The [gyres] Rolles be one, the Figures be alyke,
   The Gold, the shape, the weight, the workmanship,
   Now if in Properties they also meet
   Cytheræa shall not tell what to weet.   2810
   Oh Iupiter. Now this. you heauenly Gods.
      The Direction.
   It thunderd and Lightend, their [Rolles] Bracelets tyed about Cy=
   theræas either wrest, Either Arme stretched
   furth on high, one after the other, [And ^\a/ Button]
dilue [let loose] after some touch of the Thumbe.
Ar. Of Cytheræa'es doome wee waite the Point.
Tal. Wee will agree to that she does appoint.
Cyth. Albeit, in Things thus hard, wee can not giue
   Such equall censure, as the Thing requireth,   2820
   Yet since wee must needes, Thus wee giue vnto you.
   The old Romanes had an vse among them,
   To put their case, furth, to the Flight of Birds,
   And he that noted most obteynd the suite.
   So you (According to the Element,
   Wherein you be,) obserue the glide of Fish,
   And he that most in number shall perceiue
   The syluer virgin, for his meede, receiue.

                   [FOL. 149ʳ]

2803] SP low 2806 *(Gods)* implicitly a continuation of Cytheræa's speech on previous line 2807 *gyres*] underlined for deletion; preceded by blotted high ink point *Rolles*] added in larger script and lighter ink in left margin on pasted slip to replace [*gyres*]; *s* retraced 2811 *Iupiter.*] otiose ink mark under stop *Gods.*] stop high 2812 *The*] *h* smudged; blotted ink stain follows end of line 2813 *Rolles*] underlined for deletion, with line extending to first letter of following word, probably unintentionally; ink point above *R* *Bracelets*] added in different ink on a pasted slip in left margin to replace [*Rolles*]; *s* possibly retraced 2814 *either*] otiose point on *i* 2815 *And* ^ \a/ *Button*] underlined for deletion; preceded by high ink point; *a* added above *B*; otiose strokes follow *Button* 2816 *let loose*] underlined for deletion; underline retraced *of*] *f* smudged *Thumbe.*] stop looks like dash 2817 *Point.*] point on *i* merges with descender of *h* in *Thumbe* on previous line; stop high 2819 *thus*] ink smudge below word, extends down through *censure* on following line 2821 *you*] *o* possibly altered 2822 *old*] *o* heavily inked and blotted 2824 *suite.*] stop high 2826 *be,)*] comma merges with bracket 2827 *perceiue*] ³*e* possibly retraced or altered

Thet.	Since needes now I am vrged vnto it,
	I'll reueale that my hearte concealed long. 2830
	Boue that I raisd and queld the Sea, by this,
	Alone, I also trewly Prophesyde,
	Expounded dreames, and vtterd oracles,
	To the wonderment of all that hearde mee,
	Raist lykwise with this th'affections of Loue
	Now, Lordings, if you haue a trewe and not a false
	In Cabin tell mee what I did last night.
Ar. Ar.	That's aboue Arions cunning, Virgin.
Tal.	And Talus too, I assure you, Mayden.
Coüs	Mistris, I can tell you. you looking last night into your Bas= 2840
	kit, First and Imprimis you tooke thence a ^\faire and/ goodly glasse
	Button, that was riueted into the hoope of a copper Ring,
	you kist it with both your eyes, then with a sorrowfull sigh
	you lapt him vp. So by vertue of the sub pæna I greete
	you, loe.

                The Direction

      He took a Third [Rolle the whole lengh of him] Bracelet furth his slop
      or Pouch (whither the better) Lyke vnto the former [Loue=]
      [Rolles] Two Bracelets. Slop the Best.

Thet.	Villaine. 2850
Oce.	Sirrha, say, how camst thou by the Loue-rolle?
Coüs	Flat and faire, Master, I found him in the Fishes belly, And
	for the same I am Canonized sure, See.
Ar.	Has done a Taske the Gods of heauen should not.
Tal.	Nor the Gods of the Sea neither. (Thet) o mee,
	Most haples (Cyth) Looke to the woman, she falls.

Hum. Cosen, cheare your [Sprights] Sprites, and looke vpon vs,
Arid. Ist any thing that I may steede you? saye.
Ner. Daughter, what ayle you? (Oce) stand by, she reuiues.
Thet Then must I be bestowed on him? Ha.   2860
Cyth. Madame, your vowe is past, And according
    Your vowe needes must awarded your doome be.
    Yet if, by any meane, alterd he may be,
    Reuerst may be the doome, One howre I giue you
    To feele his Mynd. Humida, Arida,
    Employ your Eloquence vnto the man,
    And be your cosens spoksmen in her cause,
    Meane while, I do adresse mee to these other.

        The Direction
    The Two Ladyes buisye in Talk with the clown, He talk=   2870
    ing to them with an ill fauourd motion of his mouth
    lyke a Clown as he was. Meane while Cytheræa spake
    as followes to Leander and Hero.
Cyth. He're and Leander, well am I not pleasd with you,
    You haue, this day, my Sacrifice neglect.
Lean. Dreade Queene of Paphos, that wee haue neglect
    Thy Feast wee doe confese, yet, in amends,

[FOL. 149ᵛ]

    Haue brought a nobler Sacrifice for it.
Cyth. What's your offring? say (Leand) Lord Oceanus
    Made mee promise, yet it vnweeting, I vowe,   2880
    I should reconcile, vnto his Bed, my Spouse,
    Myne oathe was past and might not be recalld
    If I should haue layne my deare hearte to gage

2857 *Hum.*] stop merges with *m*   *Sprights*] underlined for deletion; preceded by high ink point   *Sprites*] added in left margin to replace [*Sprights*]   *vs,*] comma high   2858–60] written on pasted slip in darker ink   2858 *Arid.*] darker ink blots above *id*; two points for *i* above top edge of slip   2860] partial letters *Th* visible under bottom left edge of slip   *Ha.*] ink smudge below *a*   2861] SP low   2863 *meane*] otiose stroke below *m*   2865 *To*] *o* tight and heavily inked   *Mynd*] stop blotted   2866 *your*] *o* tight and heavily inked   2867 *your*] *o* tight and heavily inked   *her*] gap between *h* and *er*   2870–1 *talk=/ing*] *k* short and imperfect   2872 *spake*] *e* possibly altered   2874] SP high and faint   *He're*] apostrophe high, above *r*   2876] SP high; stop high   *Queene*] *ee* altered   *Paphos,*] *o* tight; comma high   2877 *confese,*] *o* looks like *v*; comma low   *yet,*] comma low   *amends*] otiose point over *n*; ascender of *d* possibly retraced   2882 *was*] otiose point over *a*   *recalld*] *ec* possibly retraced or altered; *a* imperfect, looks like *u*   2883 *layne*] *e* imperfect, possibly altered   *gage*] otiose point above *a*

	(For I had sworne by the Poole of Styx, Madame)
	For the which I haue brought her to thy Shryne,
	Thou mightst, to Oceanus, hand fast myne.
Cyth.	Done it thou hast lyke my faithfull seruaunt,
	And for the same, Leander, I can tell,
	With all thy Mistrisses thoult prosper well.
	Ocean, must you be handfast to my Preist? 2890
Oce.	Trew, Madame (Cyth) Be you contented? Hero
Her	I am, so he'ele but sweare by the styx too
	To graunt my suite (Cyth) How say you? Ocean.
Oce.	By the styx, I graunt (Cyth) Now Preist your suite
Her	Ocean, I take your graunt, and this the suite.
	I haue in this Scallop of Gold conteyned
	A composition of Mortallity,
	Whence Cytheræa takes a dram, what tymes
	She listeth descend to her Mortall Louers.
	Now, Ocean, if you loue mee, as you say, 2900
	Take but a dram and be a man one day.
Oce.	Oh oh (Her) How? Man. No one dram for my loue?
Oce.	I can not brook it, Prithy, Pardon mee
Her.	Is this your Resolution? (Oce) It is.
Her.	Speake once more I pray you? (Oce) It is It is.
Her.	Then you do giue mee quit? (Oce) I doe, I doe.
Her.	Will you, Glauce, take one to be a woman
	For Leander\s/ loue? (Glau) So I may not doe.
Her.	No? (Glau) No (Her) say once againe I pray you.
Her.	Now will you, Leander, take one for me? (Glau) No 2910
Lean	Hero, the whole box, loe, too (Her) In deed la?
Lean	˄\Yes (Her)/ In deede? (Lean) yes (Her) by the styx? (Lean) by

2884 *Madame*] otiose points above and after *M*; *e* possibly altered   2886 *fast*] cross-stroke on *f* retraced   2887] SP high; stop high   2891 *Madame*] *d* possibly altered   *contented*] ascender on *d* faint and imperfect   2894 *styx*] *x* retraced or altered   2895 *suite*] *i* lacks point   2898 *Whence*] ²*e* possibly altered   *what tymes*] no gap between words   2902 *oh*] indistinct limb on *h*   2903 *Pardon mee*] no gap between words   2906 *mee*] *m* flat and imperfect   ¹*doe*] *e* possibly altered or retraced   2907] ink smudge at end of line   *Glauce*] *ce* possibly retraced or altered   2908] ink smudge at end of line   *Leander\s/*] *s* added above *r* in darker ink   2909 *No?*] otiose second point on *?*   *say*] ink blot below *s*, extends downwards into following line   *you.*] stop high   2911 *Hero,*] ink blot to top right of *o*, possibly a cancelled letter; comma obscured by bracket on line below   *loe*] *l* written over *t* in false start for *too*   *Her)*] bracket short and imperfect   *deed*] otiose ink stroke below ¹*d*   2912] otiose ink marks precede SP   *Yes (Her)*] interlined over SP and beginning of line; *Her* retraced   ²*by*] *y* retraced

Her. Thanks, Leander for this tryde Constancy.   the Styx.
      It is enough, thou needst not now take it.
      Yet thou assured be, and vaunt thou this,
      Worthily hast thou conquerd Hero twise.
      How sayst now? Haue I not trew wun him? O
      Glauce. (Glau) yes, by my Troth, Hast thou, Hero,
      At heauuens high rate, I dare boldly say too.
      So take him whole, vnto thy self, I prithy.   2920
Cyth. Ladyes, haue you compounded with the Fellow.?
Hum. By all th'entreaties wee may poure vpon him,
      Hee'l not be persuade but needes will haue her.
Arid. I, and the whole Portion, she hath, with her too.
Cyth. How? will he so? Nay then Cytheræa
                                                              [FOL. 150ʳ]
      Will doe that earst the which he did neuer.
      Sirrha, thou knowst the Lady farr vnmeet
      For men of thy descent, she must bring furth,
      By certaine Oracle of Iust Themis,
      A Sonne, a man at armes, far greater, if   2930
      She but Consent to marry with them, Then
      Be the Gods themselues, Then for a round summe
      Restore her to her freinds, goe to I say,
      Restore her to her freinds, and vaunt therwith
      Once Cytheræa to haue entreated thee *

With face gra=   Coüs) Truly, Madame, I would done any thing so I had my
cious to the   ransome, For loe you, Madame, my Father is a passing poore
clown.   Man, And I am little better my self, Now if wee should
                 haue beene but capped with such a Summe of Money,

2913 *Her.*] stop low, preceded by gap   *Constancy*] otiose ink stroke above *n*   *the Styx*] implicitly a continuation of Leander's speech on previous line   2914 *take*] *k* imperfect, limb does not join mainstroke   2915] otiose ink marks to left and right and under line, possibly ink transfer from text on pasted slip on fol. 150ʳ   2916] otiose ink marks at end of line, possibly ink transfer from pasted slip on fol.150ʳ   *conquerd*] *q* lacks bowl   *Hero twise*] *r* retraced; *o* imperfect, looks like *w*; no gap between words   2917 *not trew*] headstroke of *t* of *not* touches short, imperfect *t* of *trew*   2918 *by*] indistinct lobe on *b*   *Hero,*] otiose point precedes *H*; comma retraced   2919] otiose low point in left margin   *heauuens*] *eau* retraced in darker ink   2920 *So*] *o* blotted   *vnto*] smudge through *n*   *prithy*] ink spot below *h*   2921 *Ladyes*] *a* looks like dash   *haue*] *e* imperfect   *Fellow.?*] ? high, added above stop   2923 *Hee'l*] apostrophe above ²*e*   2924 *whole*] *l* possibly altered   *Portion*] ¹*o* possibly retraced   *her*] *h* possibly altered   2925] otiose ink marks at end of line   2926 *doe*] altered from *to*   2928 *bring*] indistinct lobe on *b*; angular strokes resembling a *c* above *i* instead of point   2929 *Oracle*] *e* possibly altered   *of*] *o* blotted   2933 ¹*her*] *e* possibly altered   2937 *poore*] ²*o* written over imperfect smaller *o* or *u*   2938 *Man*] otiose ink marks above *n*

	as is, they say, set in the Toale Booke on vs, wee should	2940
dilue	both [vs] so haue run into woodes, giuen over Beife and	
	Mustard and fed there vpon Acornes and Crabs, Therefo=	
	re what is your Ladiship aduice, I shall doe herein now.	
Cyth.	Thy Ransome is remitt, so be theirs.	
Coüs	Goe to. Then I do remitt the Lady also, protesting to you,	
	That from beginning of the world to this present howre	
	now, I haue not had any thing doe with her.	
Cyth.	I thank thee, Coüs. Now Arion and Talus,	
	I intreate you would relate, to mee, each,	
	How you came by your Cestons? (Tal) Ennameld	2950
	My Father forged myne in Illusion.	
Ar	Myne's a Fantastique dreame of Proteus	
Cyth.	Vulcan diddest not know the Penaltie	
	Instampt in our leaues of Adamant Gainst	
	Feyning holy things and wilt neuer leaue [Feyn\<ing\>] Feyning	
	By dreade styx, were it not my Birthday,	
	Thou mightst abye it, But of it be quitt,	
	And (Pa\c/khed) See, hence furth, you looke vnto it.	
	And this a Thing, I should haue told you, loe.	
	And you leaue make false contracts by your spell	2960
	[Els] Or King Saturnus will not lyke it well.	
Oce.	O mee (Cyth) What makes Ocean sigh and groane?	
Oce.	Why, in the feilds of Loue, do Louers moane.	
Cyth.	Do you put your confidence in mee? say.	

2940 *is,*] comma partially obscured by blotted ink point on line below   2941 *vs*] underlined for deletion; preceded by blotted high ink point; underlining merges with ascender of *d* in *Mustard* on line below   *Beife*] ʻ*e* formed from *r*   2944 *Cyth*.] SP high; stop high   *Thy*] high otiose point follows *y*   2945 *Coüs*.] SP high; bottom of *C* extends under *o*   *to.*] stop looks like dash   2947 *any*] *a* retraced or altered   2948 *Cyth*.] SP high; stop high   *thank*] *a* written over *n*   *Coüs.*] stop blotted   2951 *myne*] *y* possibly formed from *i*   2952–5] written in a mixture of darker and lighter inks on a pasted slip; edge of another pasted slip visible at bottom left edge   2952 *Myne's ... of*] in darker ink; ink stain extends through *Myne* and down through the beginning of the next two lines   2953 *not know the*] retraced in darker ink   2955 *Feyn\<ing\>*] underlined for deletion; preceded by high ink point   *Feyning*] added on small pasted slip in left margin of line 2956 to replace [*Feyn\<ing\>*]   2958 *Pa\c/khed*] *c* added above *a*; *k* altered from *c*   2960–3] added in darker ink on pasted slip; text underneath slip shows through   2961 *Els*] underlined for deletion; preceded by high ink point   *Or*] added in left margin to replace [*Els*]; otiose ink mark below *O*; *r* blotted   2962] SP high   2963] text partially visible below bottom edge of slip   *Oce.*] SP high; stop high   *of Loue*] cross-stroke of *f* touches *L*   2964 *Cyth.*] stop faint and high   *in*] point on *i* merges with descender of illegible letter extending down from under slip

	Oce.	I doe (Cyth) Think I may cure you? too? (Oce) you too
		Thus, [loe] thus, I touch your Hearte, Lord Ocean,
Toucht his hea=		With the Butt end and bid you recouer *
rte with Butt	Oce)	All honour and Thanks to Cytheræa.
end of her arr=	Cyth.	You of your Loues seruice I remitt too.
owe.	Iup.	Graund Queene of Loue, Loe, Iupiter giues thee 2970
		Thanks for his discharge (Nept) And yong Neptune, loe.

The Direction.

dilue	Here Arion, [first,] stuck into his Hatt a s[<a>]mall Egle of
		[FOL. 150ᵛ]
	Gold, of the Bignes of a Cognisance. Talus into his a
	little greate stone Horse, dapple graye, of Syluer, the
	Badges of their Acknowledgments, both taken furth
dilue	their Scrips or Pouches, Cytheræa at sight [of them]
<...>ue	starting [vp], from off her seate, vpon her feete the
dilue	whiles.
Cyth.	O the wonder of the Gods, my Father? 2980
	Myne vnk Neptune eake? your pardons both, For
	My default I treate, (Iup) Noble daughter, Our
	Pardons both you haue (Nept) Although wee haue
	On vs, humaine shapes, you see, to possesse tayne,
	An Impe non pareild, yet se\e/ing by crosse, now,
	The Parques haue confirmd Thetis should be spowse
	Of Mortall Bed, that she should bring furth too
	A Sonne, should be greater then Man or God,

2966 *loe*] underlined for deletion; preceded by high ink point   *thus*] added in left margin to replace [*loe*]   *Ocean,*] *e* possibly altered; comma merges with asterisk on line below   2970 *Loue*] *o* heavily inked, possibly altered   2973 *first*] underlined for deletion with double line; preceded by a high ink point that merges with mainstroke of *T* on previous line   *s[<a>]mall*] <a> marked for deletion with a vertical stroke   2974 *Cognisance.*] large vertical serif added to top of *C*; stop blotted   2975 *greate*] *t* imperfect   2976 *Acknowledgments*] otiose point follows *d*   2977–80] glue and paper transfer from fol. 151ʳ in left margin   2977 *Pouches*] *c* imperfect   *of them*] all letters except *o* underlined for deletion, but *o* presumably meant for inclusion; high ink point over *o*; blotted point follows *them*   2978 *vp*] underlined for deletion; blotted high ink point above *v*; *ue* visible in margin, presumably from *dilue* but partially obscured by glue and paper transfer from fol. 151ʳ   2979 *whiles*] otiose ink marks above *s*   2980 *Cyth.*] glue and ink transfer in left margin from fol. 151ʳ over SP   *Father*] ink spot under *a*   2981 *Myne*] *ne* imperfect, looks like *m*   *vnk*] otiose ink mark under *n*; otiose point above *k*   *both,*] comma low   2984 *possesse*] *o* retraced   *tayne,*] implicitly a continuation of line 2983, inserted below the end of the former line; *t* imperfect; comma low with ink spot below   2986 *be*] *be* possibly retraced   *spowse*] ink spot under *ws*   2987 *too*] ²*o* altered   2988 *God,*] otiose ink marks follow comma

     If she but take either to her sacred bed,
     Wee, loe, yeild thee, Neice, thanks for our Remissions,   2990
     And lowly bend Our states to this greate Seat.
Cyth. Much good do it you, noble Lords, I wish.
A Pawse. Now my discharge, This day longs to mee but *
     Now I doe see, I haue perfourmed each
     According to the equitie of each,
     Hard were the cases, and many were the suites,
     The Tumult strange, so were the Accidents,
     Mighty the wonder and Perplexitye;
     But now I find my Kingdome at an end,
     And to the owners must resigne my Roome,   3000
     As, in rightfull equitie, it is meete,
     Therefore, loe, Lords, you all, with Loue, I greet,
     Withall resigne the Kingdome where tis meet.

The Direction.

     Here she rose with the rest, The Imperiall ghirlond
     first taken ˆ \from/ off and by her self and deliuerd to some ˆ \one/ of
     the Attendaunts [and] then hurld vp the Croc, Then spake as
     followes.
Cyth. Is my shallop come? I think it be late.
Thet. Madame I come, to giue you humble thanks,   3010
     For the Speciall honour, you haue done to mee.
Cyth. Pardon mee, Lady, if rigrous I'haue beene,
     A Iudge may neuer discharge well his dewty,
     Vnles, of Affection, he do despoyle him,
     More, where Cytheræas Breast hath been euer
     Ope to Lenity, the case required her
     To inuest the marble hearte of Iuno.

2990 our] otiose point below *r* *Remissions*] no points on either *i* *2991 Our*] *O* written in darker ink over illegible letter; ink spot under *O* *Seat.*] high stop merges with headstroke on *t* *2994 doe*] *e* retraced *perfourmed*] otiose ink marks around 'r and o *each*] ink spot in right margin follows word *2996 'the*] ink blot on *h* *2997*] ink spot in far left margin *2999*] ink mark in left margin *end*] *e* possibly altered or retraced *3000 resigne*] high otiose point follows word *3001 equitie,*] comma low *meete,*] comma low *3002 all,*] comma low *Loue,*] comma low *3005–10*] written in darker ink on pasted slip *3007 and*] underlined for deletion; preceded by high ink point *then*] added in left margin of pasted slip to replace [*and*] *3011 honour*] *hon* written over *Fau* in darker ink *3012*] otiose point follows SP *if*] point on *i* merges with descender on *h* in *honour* on line above *beene,*] otiose ink mark above comma *3014*] ink smudge to left of line *3015*] otiose spot in right margin *3016–17*] otiose ink spot between lines in left margin *3017 inuest*] otiose ink spot on *n* *hearte*] ink spot above *te*

    But now I must to Heauen, the day growes old,
    Besyde, from hence, it is a good way vp.
    My noble Lords, I bid you all farewell,   3020
    The Bounteous Gods rewarde your meritts well.
                    [FOL. 151ʳ]
Oce. On Dolphins wee'l conduct you on your way
Cyth. I thank you, Lords, tis late, make hast I pray.
Herm. To Court, Madame, to Court (**Cyth**) Lo Hermes with
    The best speede I may (**Herm**) Come, come on, I pray.
     The Direction.
    Here went furth the whole chorus in a shuffle
    as after a Play in a Lords howse, Hermes wafting
    them furth with his winged wand. Vulcan and
    Proteus after them. Or went furth in state all,   3030
    as riding vpon Dolphins, Hermes wafting them
    about the stage with his wand. Whither the bet=
    ter you may chuse the better, all singing the 7ᵗʰ
Dilue Song following. [Vide vacants the last vt infra]
     The Seauenth Song
       1
    Horse and away, my Masters all,
     My Lady is now on Post,
    Trusse the whole baggage, vp, in Hall,
     She will away by the Coast.   3040
       2
    Bridle Dolphin, eury each one,
     On her wee attend, as is meete,
    She shall not feare, Bridle once on.
     Of Orkes, an hundreth, the Fleete.

3021 *meritts*] *i* lacks point 3024 *Lo*] *o* imperfect, looks like point 3025 *Come,*] otiose ink mark on comma 3034 *Dilue*] added in different ink and larger script in left margin *Vide … infra*] underlined in different ink for deletion; preceded by blotted high ink point 3040 *She*] *S* altered *will*] otiose second point on *i* 3042 *one,*] comma blotted 3043 *attend,*] comma merges with ascender of *d* in *Bridle* on following line

     3
 But why should she feare by Dan Cupid?
  The fellst Beastes, that in Sea moue,
At th'encounter of any * send-Tyde,
 Will [vayle] Bend to the Queene of Loue.   3050
     4.
 Hoa, why should wee longer now staye?
  Loe Phæbus hastens his way.
Before it be the shutt of day,
 To Horse away, t' horse away.

    Exeunt Omnes

    The Apologue
    The Direction
Here Harpax after their song and goings furth
came in againe their Apologue, with his Mothers   3060
Fan in his hand held.
   Harpax their Apologue, Solus,
     Verte Folium.

            [FOL. 151ᵛ]

Harp. Gallants, I that haue wings to ouertake
 Am left their Apologue, and thus they spake.
 A Curr passing a Foorde with boane in mouth
 Caught at a shaddowe and forwent them both.
 Wee who, your Peace obteynd, your Prayse [ex\<ac>t] exact
 If wee should but reape according our Fact,
 Your Peace, your Prayse, wee loose, in one, I wote,   3070
 Yet, as you euer done, your Prayse allot,
 The which, if deseurd, wee'l count to our gaine,
 Els take, for a mylde cordiall, for our paine *
 And now our now farewell, vnto you all, Sirs *

   Finis 1602.

Margin note (left, opposite lines 3047–3050): Any vast and extraordinary Billowe comes against ship or other ves=sell the say=lours call it a send of the Sea

Margin note (left, opposite lines 3073–3075): A Pawse Here he wafted them furth with his Mothers Fan all.

3050 *vayle*] underlined for deletion; high ink point above *v*   *Bend*] added in left margin of line 3048 to replace [*vayle*]   3064 *Harp.*] stop faint and high   3065 *spake*] *e* possibly altered   3068 *ex\<ac>t*] underlined for deletion; high ink mark like dash above *e*; \<ac\> altered   *exact*] added in left margin to replace [*ex\<ac>t*]   3074 *farewell,*] comma faint   3075 *1602.*] stop high

APPENDIX 1

PENCIL ANNOTATIONS AND MARKS IN HUNTINGTON MS HM4 COPY OF *THE APHRODYSIAL*

A number of pencil annotations in grey pencil appear in *The Aphrodysial*. These annotations mostly take the form of crosses (*x*) of varying size, although there are also some instances of straight vertical and horizontal lines that run in the margins of the text, in the text itself, or partially box off marginal text (for a discussion of their possible purpose, see Introduction). The location and nature of the pencil annotations is described here:

58–67] cross to left of text

69 SD.1–.3] faint line to left of text; faint line below text; cross to right of text

82–91] transfer from opposite page; narrow cross on text, beginning at *cause*, ending on *mee in*

94–6] transfer from opposite page; cross on text, beginning at *Scruples*, ending on *you* ˰ *would*\\ *but*; vertical line in right margin

96] transfer from opposite page; diagonal horizontal line through *obteyne* and under *your*

325–7] transfer from opposite page; vertical line in left margin

327] transfer from opposite page; horizontal line through *gainst my will pluckt*

344] transfer from opposite page; vertical line under *I come* and partially through *(Lean)*

369–73] cross in right margin

372] line under *Iron Milles*

390] line under *Properties*

519–22] transfer from opposite page; cross on text, beginning at *For I*, ending on *this*

563–6] cross to left of text

1190–1] transfer from opposite page; cross through text, beginning at *your*, ending on *you*

1238–40] cross between SPs and text; line under *stithye*

1548–50] transfer from opposite page; cross through text, beginning at *est*, ending at *grownd*

1555–7] transfer from opposite page; cross through text and blank space, beginning at *more stiff*

1596–7] cross to left of text
1602–3] cross to left of text
1937–8] possibly transfer from opposite page; small cross in left margin
1937–43] large cross in left margin
1987] small cross in right margin
1987–92] possibly transfer from opposite page; large cross in right margin

APPENDIX 2

VARIANTS BETWEEN HUNTINGTON MS HM4 AND ALNWICK MS 509 COPIES OF *THE APHRODYSIAL*

The following notes identify variants in spelling, capitalization, punctuation, and material that is lacking in one of the copies. While the notes sometimes necessitate the inclusion of information about deletions, alterations, or placement, the list of variants does not attempt to provide an exhaustive record of emendations (and their positions) in each of the manuscripts. The following conventions are used in the notes: a tilde (~) is used to indicate that the spelling of a given word is identical in MS 509, and a lowered circumflex (ˌ) is used to indicate where a punctuation point is missing in one of the copies. Where the spelling of a given word (or words) is different in MS 509, the words are written out in full.

4 *1602.*] ~ˌ
5 *Marinall.*] ~ˌ
11 *monstra*] Monstra   *Pontus.*] ~ˌ   *Virg*] ~.
12 *6*] 6 \o/
14 *Apologus,*] ~ˌ   *A*] a
16–18 *A graue old man with crown of gold and / brayded haire, crown white and blew enameld / And long white Bearde also.*] a graue old man, with crown of Gold, long white /Bearde and braided Haire. Crown white and / blew ennameld.
24 *Marinall,*] ~.
29 *Lusty*] lusty
30 *Taller*] taller   *Hero.*] ~,
31 *Lady*] Ladye
32 *virgin.*] ~ˌ
33 SD 1–.2 *cloth of syl= / uer blewe. / or clowd cull= / our, the Best.*] cloth of syluer   SD 2 *the one*] th'one
34 *Nymphe*] Nimphe
36 *days**] dayesˌ   *Bearded*] marked for deletion in 509
37 *dayes,**] daysˌ also   *Bearded*] marked for deletion in 509
38–9 *Leander ... / Elbowes.*] follows *Arida ... Land* in 509
46 *Sea.*] ~ˌ
47 *Tritonˌ*] ~.
49 *for*] For

50 Me\r/cury] Mercurye
52 Midde] midde   Pallace] Court
55 Iumpe and euen] Iumpe / euen
56 Bank] Banck
58 Pallace] Court
59 The Aphrodysial] the Title The Aphrodysial
61 Den] Denne   hung] hong   if] If
62 clowd cullour] clowd-cullour
63 Arras˄] ~,
64 befitting.] ~,
66 Sand-cullour] Sand cullour
68 Aphrodysial.] Marinal˄
69 SD.3 called˄] ~.   Luporum˄] ~,
71 1602˄] ~.
75 Sea-Feast˄] ~.   1602.] ~˄
76 sounding.] ~˄
78 from] From
82–3 comm= / ing from] coming to you from
88 new bedded] new-bedded
90 Feast.] ~,
96 your] you
97 Long-wisht] long-wisht   each] eury each
98 fragrant] Fragrant
99 sitt] sit
104 Third˄] ~.
108 Glauce.] ~;
109 blewe] blew   weedes,] ~˄
110 Bound] bound
111 Proteus.] ~;   and] And
112 thigh,] Thigh.
114 Pompe] pompe
115 way] waye   rest] Rest
117 worde,] ~˄   fifth] Fifth
119 Talus.] ~,
120 Paire] paire
123 relate] Relate
124 Lucks] lucks
126 gold] Gold   honour] Honour
128 Coue'tous] Cou'teous

131 *And*] and
135 *Treason*] treason
138 *Treasure*] treasure
141 *water.*] ~;
143 *Raging*] raging
144 *Moyst*] moyst   *Drye*] drye
145 *not*₋] ~,
146 *gold*] Gold
147 *Threasure*] Treasure
149 *Pelf*] pelf
151 *Armes*] armes
152 *armes.*] ~,
154 *Mouthes*] Mouths
158 *Face*] face
159 *funrall*] fun'rall
160 *vocall*] vocal
161 *dietyes*] dieties
168 *Twynd*] twynd   *harmonius*] harmonious   *foure*] Fowre
171 *Lampreys*] Lampreyes
172 *Naturall*] naturall
177 *Better,*] ~₋
179 *flowing*] Flowing   *flowe*] [Pace] Flowe
180 *Back*] back
183 *thrice*] Thrice
186 *swim,*] ~₋   *vowe,*] ~₋
192 *Pickt*] pickt   *my my*] my
196 *Tyme*] tyme
198 *horse*] Horse
199 *Guide*] guide
200 *Wind*] Wynd
204 *rage*] Rage
205 *Heauens*] Heauen   *Browe*] Brow
208 *(Seemeth intend)*]₋~ ~₋,
209 *Harmonye*] Harmony
210 *mile of*] myle off
212 *sweet*] sweete
215 *strange*] straung
216 *satisfactory*] satisfactorye
217 *anone*] Anone

218 *turne.*] ~,
220 *Aduersity*] *Aduersitye*
222 *famous*] *Famous*   *Enginer*] *enginer*
223 *name*] *Name*
224 *fifteene*] *fifteenth*   *when,*] ~ˌ
226 *profitt*] *profit*
228 *sawe*] *Sawe*   *compasses*] *Compasses*
230 *now borne*] *new borne*
237 *Sea.*] ~;
238 *rest*] *Rest*
240 *dwell.*] ~ˌ
243 *remit*] *remitt*
249 *please*ˌ] ~,
255 *please.*] ~;
256 *haire,*] ~ˌ
259 *our*] *Our*
264 *Lets*] *Let's*   *Toale.*] ~?
265 *Pen*] *pen*
267 *ioy*] *ioye*
268 *1.* ~ˌ]   *2.*] ~ˌ
269 *fyrie*] *Fyrie*
275 *tymes*] *Tymes*
277 *Tymes*] *tymes*
278 *Returnd*] *returnd*   *Then*] *Thẽ*
280 *Poure*] *poure*
286 *number*] *Number*
289 *hearte*] *Hearte*   *blood,*] ~ˌ
291 *Sea,*] ~ˌ
292 *hero*] *Hero*
297 *Boanes*] *boanes*   *share.*] ~,
299 *waues*ˌ] ~,
302 *Oh*] *oh*
306 *beautye*] *beauty*
311 *caru'd*] *carud*   *Iuourye*] *Iuorye*
312 *Two*] *two*
314 *him.*] ~,
315 *Fault*] *fault*
318 *3.*] ~ˌ
320 *appeared*] *appeard*

321 *weedes,*] ~ ₐ
324 *lookes*] *looks*
325 *is.*] ~,
329 *Lean.*] ~ ₐ
331 *while* ₐ] ~,   *Light*] *light*
332 *sau'd* ₐ] ~.   *sillie*] *silly*
335 *deepe*] *Deepe*   *mee.*] ~ ₐ
336 *spelles*] *spells*
339 *Lean.*] ~ ₐ
341 *Blisse.*] ~ ₐ
342 *Flye*] *flye*
350 *Rage*] *rage*
351 *two*] *Two*   *Thumbes* ₐ] ~,
356 *before*] *Before*
358 *Pont.*] ~ ₐ   *More,*] ~ ₐ   *Hebrew*] *Hebrewe*
360 *Grip.*] ~ ₐ   *Aphrodysial*] *Aphrodysiall*   *belly*] *Belly*
361 *Prot.*] ~ ₐ   *Horrendum*] *horrendum*
363 *while.*] ~,
364 *Fowle*] *Fou= / le*   *Sir* ₐ] ~.
367 *Pont* ₐ] ~.   *set*] *sett*
368 *Harp* ₐ] ~.   *set*] *sett*
369 *come,*] ~ ₐ   *Asyle* ₐ] ~.
372 *Ho[a].*] *Hoa* ₐ
375 *Tinkerlye*] *Tinkerly*
376 *Harp* ₐ] ~.   *pisseth.*] ~ ₐ
378 *Harp.*] ~ ₐ
380 *Grater*] *grater*
382–3] two lines in HM4; shared line in 509
382 *Baskit*] *baskit*
386 *Harp.*] ~ ₐ
387 *Prot.*] ~ ₐ   *And*] *and*   *Foure*] *Fowre*
388 *All*] *all*
390 *Prot)*] ~ ₐ   *say*] *saye*
391 no SP] *Rud.*
396 *foame*] *Foame*
401 *shoemakers*] *shoomakers*   *benefit*] *benefite*
402 *thousand,*] ~   *hundreth,*] ~ ₐ   *foure*] *fowre*
403 *quintal*] *quintall*
404 *half* ₐ] ~.

406 *Rud*ˏ] ~.   *nose*] Nose
407 *Prot*ˏ] ~.
408 *Fourthlye*] Fourthly
410 *Propertie,*] ~ˏ
411 *dances*] daunces   *or droane*] or to droane
413 *Sixthly*ˏ] ~,
417 *An*] And
421 *repast?*] Repast?   *Say*] Saye
426 *Rud.*] ~ˏ   *for high*] for you high
427 *how.?*] ~?
429 *Harping-yron*] Harping-Iron
430 *Parts*] parts
431 *int,*] ~.
433 *verily,*] ~ˏ   *deed*] deede
435 *Mee*ˏ] ~,   *Roapes*] roapes
436 *nose*] Nose
437 *Boothe*] Booth   *wee here again*] here againe
438 *soone.*] ~,
439 *Pithyly*] Pithylye
440 *Prot*ˏ] ~.   *Part*] part
446 *buye*] buy   *buye*] buy
450–1] between these lines 509 has an additional line: *Or other of the same Prizing?*
452 *Rewarding,*] ~ˏ
455 *buye*] buy   *buye?*] buyˏ
462 *Regarding*] regarding
463 *Fine*] fine
465 *buye*] buy   *buye,*] buyˏ
466 *flight*] Flight   *mee*ˏ] ~?
467 *boane*] Boane
468 *protest,*] ~.
469 *Thick*] thick   *Arrest*] arrest
472 *Retarding,*] ~ˏ
473 *Fine*] fine
474 SD.3 *stalking.*] ~ˏ   *mee* *] ~.
480 *Harp.*] ~ˏ
481 *ways*] wayes
482 *Boy*] boye
483 *my*] My   *Lord*ˏ] ~.

484 *seruant*] Seruaunt   *do*] doe
485 *Buisines*] buisinesse   *say*] saye
487 *sort*] sorts
489 *Letters*] letters   *one.*] ~?
490 *To*] to
491 *newe*] new
493 *I˾*] ~.
494 *soritically*] Soritically
497 *Drye Land*] Land
498 *Loue*] loue
499 *other,*] ~˾
500 *Net-work to*] Networck vnto   *Packstaff?*] Pack-staff,
502 *Mistresses*] Mistrisses
505 *chosen*] chosen sure
506 *Sanctuaries*] Sanctuaryes   *Practising*] practising
512 *mee?*] ~.
513 *blesse*] blisse
514 *Bayes˾*] ~,
515 *honours hornes the koaks*] honours both Hornes, the / (Coakes   *hood.*] Hood˾
516 *Farewell,*] Farwell˾
517 *calf*] Calf
518 *Two*] two
519 *tyme*] Tyme   *I;*] ~,
520 *humaine*] Humane   *Body*] body
522 *Gally pot*] Gally-pot
523 *Humida,*] ~˾   *as Moyst as*] moyst as is
524 *as drye as is a chich*] drye as \is/ a kicks
525 *thunder thump*] thunder-thumpe
526 *his,*] ~˾   *against*] Aga= / inst
528 *Fast*] fast   *Hearte*] hearte
530 *loue,*] Loue?   *Vulcan?*] ~.   *thing*] Thing
533 *bacon*] Bacon
535 *that the*] the
538 *them˾*] ~,
539 *Osanna˾*] ~,   *come,*] ~˾
542 *Madame,*] ~.
545 *thou˾*] ~,   *Nemesis˾*] ~,
546 *Bit*] Bitt
547 *heark*] hearke   *conciue˾*] con / ceiue,

550 [or] noise supposd For] or noise supposed for
551 Also] \also/   Rose-water] Rose water   confits,] comfits   was] was once
552 church,] ~‸   Oxford,] ~‸
554 woork] work   chaunce‸] ~,   dinner‸] ~,
555 shells,] ~‸
557 moreouer] Moreouer   besyde] Besyde
558 Cyclops‸] ~.   Lord.*] ~.‸
559 ²come;] ~,   ⁴come‸] ~.
561 Scen‸] ~.
562 Direction‸] ~.
563 Bagge] Bag
564 Baggage,] ~‸
566 stood] stoode
567 her.] ~‸
569 deepe] Deepe
570 Ar.] ~‸
571 doe] do
572 greater] greate   Poseys?] Posyes‸
574 bound] Bound   Mistrissis] Mistrisses
579 lockes] loo\c/kes   Plight] plight
580 Feete] feete
581 Tal.] ~‸   ioyes] Ioyes   Earth,] ~‸   before.] ~‸
582 forlore.] ~‸
583 here.] ~,
585 Tal.] ~‸
586 gather.] ~‸
587 loue] Loue   bright.] ~‸
588 Ar.] Arion   loue] Loue   syluer] Syluer   feet] feete
589 long,] ~‸
590 woo\r/des] words   ardent,] ~.
591 oft] of
592 loue] Loue
594 bidds] bids
595 The‸] Thet.
596 Begin.] ~;
601 loue;] ~‸
603 Man] man
606 my] myne
611 Deare] Deere

612 *(The)*] *(Thet)*
614 *This,*] ~ˬ   *do*] *doe*   *yet.*] ~,
615 *do*] *doe*
616 SD.2 *eare:*] ~.   *Flint-heartest*] *flint-heartest*
617 *Thet.*] ~ˬ
618 *you*ˬ*] ~. *
619 ˬ*Thet)*] *(*~*)*   *too,*] ~ˬ
620 *tyde*] *Tyde*   *pray,*] ~ˬ
621 *flowe*] *flow*
622 *meet*] *meete*
623 *woodcoaks*] *woodcocks*
626 *one*ˬ] ~,
627 *Loynes*] *loynes*
641 *Florish*] *florish*
645 SD.1 *In*] *in*
646 *Euph.*] ~ˬ
651 *Aphrodysial*] *Aphrodysiall*
652 *raysd*] *raisd*
654 *Three;*] ~,
657 *Ribbes*] *ribbes*
660 *Masterye*] *Masterie*
661 *raisd*] *raised*
662 *Euph.*] ~ˬ
669 *Bucklers,*] ~ˬ   *day,*] ~ˬ
675 *Gold*] *gold*
681 *But what*] *Yet what*   ˬ [*good/*] *sister*ˬ] *sister,*   *say.*] *saye.*
682 *Loue*ˬ] *loue*<,>
684 *Hammer*] *hammer*
687 *watery*] *watry*
692 *he*] *He*
693 *should*ˬ] ~,   *Trice*] *trice*
694 *Vnto*] *vnTo*
699 *Matter*] *matter*
701 *that:*] ~.
702 *Hee'rs*] *Here's*   *now.*] ~?
713 * *Glauce*] ~,
714 SD] not in 509
721 *Den*] *den*
722 *Prot.*] ~ˬ

724 *Harping-yron*] harping yron
730 *Twayne*] Twayn
731 *I,*] ~ ˷
734 *Aliam*] aliam
735 *postulat*] Postulat
739 *Prot ˷*] ~.   *So.*] so,   *Can*] can
740 *Powt*] powt   *simul?*] simul.
741 *Rud ˷*] ~.
743 *priuie*] priuy   *knows*] knowes
745 *you.*] ~,   *Making*] making
749 *Pont.*] ~ ˷
750 *Rud.*] ~ ˷
750–1] separate lines in HM4; shared line in 509
751 *gloating.*] ~ ˷
752 *all [of them] them*] all of them
754 *I,*] ~ ˷   *Toungs.*] ~ ˷
755 *Grip.*] ~ ˷   *rem\ẽ/ber*] remember
757 *Set,*] Sett.
763 *capacity*] capacitye
763–4 *To= / ken*] token
765 *This*] this
767 *Rud.*] ~ ˷
768 SD.2 *the faces.*] faces but.   *Lastly ˷*] ~ ,   *Sir ˷*] ~ ,   *This?*] ~.
772 *pray,*] ~ ˷   *The*] the
777 *God.*] ~ ˷
780 *Pont ˷*] ~.
782 *was ˷*] ~.
786 *Grapsato*] Grasato   ¹*para,* ³*para*] par
787 *Proteus ˷*] ~.
789 *damned*] damb\ned/[d]
790 *For*] for
790–1 *damna= / ble*] damned
792–3 *Sy= / prisse*] Sypris
796 *Bi,*] Be ˷   *Bo,*] ~ ˷   *B[o]\u/mb.*] Bumb ˷
797 *scuruy*] scuruie   *you,*] ~.
798 *Pont.*] ~ ˷
799 *my*] deare
806 *straite.**] ~ ˷*
807 SD *squinted ˷*] sq<.>inted.

808 *Ie*] I
811 SD.2 *French*.] ~ ⌄
812 *Prot*.] ~)
815 *Harp*.] ~ ⌄
816 *Antick\s/*] anticks
817–18 *Ac= / count*] account
821 *Thou'lt*] Thoult   *Fist*] fist
823 *Be*] be
828–9 *whis= / tle*.] whistle,
829 *Past*] past   *Things*] things
830 *Kitchin* ⌄] ~ .
831 *bidding*] Bidding
832 *Rud* ⌄] ~ .
833 *to pick*] pick   *Say* ⌄] saye,
834 *befell*.] ~ ?
835 *thee,*] ~ ⌄
837 *Pont*.] ~ ⌄
838 *Cods*] Codds
839 *verily* ⌄] ~ .
840 *Two*] two
841 *sexe*] Sexe
845 *daughters?*] ~ .   *say*] Saye
846 *Two*] two
848 *you*.] ~ ⌄
849 *Accounts*] accounts
850 *Rud* ⌄] ~ .
851 *foure*] Fowre
852 *Full*] full   *Gentlemen*] gentlemen
852–3 *my= / ne*.] myne ⌄
854 *token* ⌄ *] ~ ,*
854–5 *what to day / shall*] what \shall/ to day
855 SD *hornes*] horns   *shall be*] be
856 *suppose*.] ~ ⌄
857 *heartily*] hartily
858 *Prot*.] ~ ⌄   *Apes,*] ~ ⌄   *as I sayd before,*] (~ ~ ~ ~)
863 *as*] As
864 *Full*] full
865 *beleeue*.] ~ ⌄
866 *ie*] Ie   *qu'eau*] qu eau

873 *hind*] hinde[<.>]   *Man*] man
874 *Lustily*] lustily   *Ha.*] ~;
875 *Galbanon.,*] Galbamon,
877 *Two*] two
878 *Diaphenicon.*] ~ ˄
881 *Prot ˄*] ~.
882 *first.*] ~ ˄
887 *And*] and
893 *you.*] ~;
895 *According*] acc= / ording
901 ²*crookt*] crook   *Inuention*] Inuension
902 *wherefore,*] ~ ˄   *breife*] Breif
904 *he hath done*] he done
905 *letters*] Letters
906 *then*] Then   *fellows*] fellowes
907 *Paugeaunt*] Pageant
908 *But,*] ~ ˄   *loe,*] ~ ˄
909 *come.*] come, see.
910 *2.*] ~ ˄   *6.*] ~ ˄
913 *Perukes*] with Perukes
913–14 *The one / cloth of Syluer blewe,*] the one cloth of syluer blew or clowd cullour.
914 *yelow*] yelowe
914–16 *for expres= / sions of the sheene – blewe water Sea and the yelowe dry= / land shoare*] for their better expressions of the [blewe sea] sheene water blewe. and of / the drye Land shoare coullours.
918–19 *this morning / at our rising˄ so Pregnaunt*] [this morning,] / at our Rising, \this morning,/ so pregnaunt
921 *thing*] Thing   *moyst*] Moyst   *præfer\e/d*] præferred
922 *Man*] man
924 *And*] and   *sits*] sitts
925 *Sister.*] ~ ˄
928 *Honestye*] Honesty
931 *whoore.*] ~ ˄
934 *Thing*] thing
935 *Harp.*] ~ ˄
939 *Harp.*] ~ ˄
941 *Harp.*] ~ ˄
942 *Answere*] answere

943 *Harp.*] ~ ₐ
944 *Hum.*] ~ ₐ
945 *Harp.*] ~ ₐ   *honours?*] ~.
949 SD.1–.2 *they reade / their*] *thy red / ouer their*   SD.3–.4 *fir= / st.*] ~ ₐ
951 *hearte,*] ~ ₐ   *Humida* ₐ] ~.
957 *concubine* ₐ] ~.
958 *thee* ₐ] ~,
959 *breifly*] *brei= / flye*   *deuice*] *Deuice*
961 *by*] *By*
963 *aerye*] *aery*
966 *one*/ ₐ] *one,*   *do*] *doe*
974 *Spung*] *Spunge*
975 *heauye*] *heauy*
980 *deuice.*] ~ ;
981 *Drye*] *drye*
982 *say,*] ~ ₐ   *Agree*] *agree*
987 *night* ₐ] ~.
990 *fopperye*] *fopperie*
995 *Metamorphe*] *Metamorphose*   *vs,*] ~ ;   *land*] *Land*
996 *drye*] *Drye*
997 *Ridiculous* ₐ] *ridiculous,*
998 *you;*] ~,
1000 *dinner.*] ~ ?
1002 *too.*] ~,   *on,*] ~ ₐ
1003 *letters*] *Letters*
1005 *Hum* ₐ] ~.
1006 *you* ₐ] ~.
1008 *Song* ₐ] ~.
1009 *contrary*] *contrarye*
1013 *about,*] ~ ₐ
1015 *agree* ₐ] ~.
1019 *Lye,*] ~ ₐ
1021 *3* ₐ] ~.
1022 *know*] *knowe*
1023 *Neuer* ₐ] ~,   *say* ₐ] ~,
1024 *wisse* ₐ] ~,
1026 *4.*] ~ ₐ
1027 *Moyst*] *Moyste*
1028 *earne* ₐ] ~.

1029 *againe*˰] ~,
1030 *paine*˰] ~.
1038 *Poope*] poope   *coneye.*] coney˰
1041 *7*˰] ~.
1043 *out*˰] ~,
1044 *Drye*˰] ~,
1045 *Be,*] ~˰   *you,*] ~˰   *fee*] Fee
1046 *Hum*˰] ~.   *ydressed,*] ~˰
1046–7 *cul= / lours,*] cullours˰
1047 *Court*˰] ~,
1048 *dinner.*] dinner; Come.
1050 *7*˰] ~.
1051 *Godlyke*] godlyke
1053 *dietyes*] Dieties
1057 *Immortallity*] Immortallitye
1060 *vnmeet*] vnmeete   *Dignitye*] dignitye
1061 *loue*] Loue
1062 *Then,*] ~˰
1063 *Say*] Saye
1065 *Breif*] Breife
1066 *Lean.*] ~˰
1067 *you.*] ~,
1068 *Bounties*] bounties
1072 *will,*] ~˰
1073 *Oce.*] ~˰
1075 *ere'*] ~˰
1077 *Oc.*] Oce.
1078 *Lean*˰] ~.
1079 *Oce.*] ~˰   *other.*] ~?
1080 *Freind*] freind
1087 *place*] Place
1088 *mee.*] ~?
1089 *seye.*] ~˰
1093 *Lean.*] ~˰   *willingly*] willinglye   *now.**] ~˰*/
1094 SD.2 *Fish*˰] ~.   SD.3 *with Posye about him*] not in 509   *Leand)*] Lean˰
1095 *Oce)*] ~˰
1102 *losse*] Losse
1103 *Immortallity*] Immortallitye
1104 *that*˰] ~,   *Longer*] longer   *Tardation,*] ~.

126

1105 *bed*] Bed
1116 *Onely,*] ~₍ Fact,*] ~₍
1121 *Attendaunts,*] ~₍
1123 *Oce.*] ~₍
1124 *say*] saye
1132 *but streighten*] streightens
1135 *from the Beginning*] From beginning
1136 *bounden*] bownden
1142 *Thanks*] thanks
1145 *indewd*] endewd   *sapience*] Sapience
1146 *conteynd;*] ~,
1147 *first*] First
1153 *helpe*] Helpe
1154 *is,*] ~₍
1166 *Lusty*] lusty
1173 *sure₍*] ~)
1178 *am.*] ~₍
1179 *you₍*] ~,
1185 *Aphrodysial*] Aphrodysiall
1188 *vs.*] ~₍
1191 *way,*] ~₍
1195 *Els Iron-work*] els yron work
1196 *Hammers for*] ham/mers For   *Armes*] armes
1197 *stithie*] stithy   *Also*] also
1198 ¹*their*] theire   *by mouing*] by the mouing   *Armes*] armes
1203 *Present*] present   *By*] by
1205 *Tymely*] tymely   *it.*] ~₍
1206 *Pythagæran*] Pythagorean   *wisse₍*] ~.
1207 SD.2 *been*] beene   *Sett,*] ~₍
1211 *Lady*] Ladye
1215 *Rauenous*] rauenous
1218 *Mouth?*] ~.
1220 *Lord?*] ~.
1223 *heade*] hed
1224 *rusty*] rustie
1225] separate line in HM4; continues previous line in 509   *how?*] How₍   *you.*] (~
1226 *Venus,*] ~₍
1227 *waxes*] waxeth   *cold.*] ~₍

1228 Lord.] ~ˏ
1232] separate line in HM4; continues previous line in 509
1234 butˏ] ~.
1239 stithye] stithy
1240 Force] force
1243 for] For
1244 Pocket] pocket
1245 Brontˏ] ~.   good] Good   Repairer] repairer
1246 oft,] ~ˏ   yeare,] ~ˏ
1253 She,] ~ˏ   tricks] Tricks
1254 Carrian] carrian
1256 Hed] hed
1260 Round] round   foure] Fower
1261 Come.] ~ˏ
1264 SD.1-.2 hamm / ers] Ham / mers
1266 ¹stithye] stithy   soone,] ~ˏ
1267 hand.] ~,
1270 patˏ] ~,   sound,] ~ˏ
1271 patˏ] ~,
1272 2.] ~ˏ
1273 Metall] mettall   brittle] Brittle
1276 Bane] bane   polld.] ~ˏ
1277 ¹patˏ] ~,
1278 patˏ] ~,   ²Pit] pit
1282 Hallˏ] ~,
1284 ¹patˏ] ~,   ²Pit] pit   ²patˏ] ~,
1285 ¹patˏ] ~,   pit] Pit   ²patˏ] ~,
1291 ¹patˏ] ~,   ²patˏ] ~,
1292 ¹patˏ]~,   ²Pit] pit   ²patˏ] ~,
1297 Goe,] ~ˏ   againe,] ~ˏ
1298 work;] ~ˏ
1300 3.] ~ˏ
1304 succour] succor
1305 Man,] ~.
1308 wee'le] wee'll
1309 I,] ~ˏ   it were] t'were
1313 Erebusˏ] ~,
1316 say.] sayeˏ
1319 graunt?] ~ˏ

1321 point.] ~⌄
1322 agone⌄] ~,
1326 Tyme] tyme   Maine] Mayne
1328 lent⌄] ~,   day⌄] ~,
1329 Man] man
1330 Perill] perill
1335 Task] task   So,] ~⌄
1339 say,] ~.
1342 Same] same
1344 Enameld⌄] ~,   sight⌄] ~,
1346 all⌄] ~?
1347 Blisse?] ~⌄
1348 thee.] ~?
1352 leg] Leg
1354 Trick] trick
1355 then⌄ \be/ the] then the
1358 buisinesse] buisines
1364 Prot.] ~⌄   Mates] mates
1366 Pont.] ~⌄
1368 Rudens] Ruden
1369 Roapes] roapes   thy] the   leauer] Leauer
1370 Grapple,] grapple.
1371 all?] ~.
1375 I,] ~⌄   circle] Circle
1377 scarff] Scarfe   list] List
1378 floore] Floore   Book] Booke
1380 strange] straung
1381 list] List
1382 Pont.] ~⌄   plact himself] plact him \himself/
1382–3 Pole= / tick] Poletyck   warie] warye   Captaine⌄] Cap= / taine,
1384 trew] trewe
1385 Harp.] Har
1386 loe.] ~⌄
1388 Harp.] ~⌄   Oxe-sumner] oxe summoner   rather] Rather
1389 I will] I'll   him⌄] ~,
1391 Sir⌄] ~.
1392 Harp.] ~⌄
1393 sel[f]ues.] selues⌄
1394 With] Wee   Sir.] ~⌄

1396 *Pont.*] ~‸
1397 *Prot*‸] ~.   *Call,*] ~‸
1404 *Scene*‸] ~,
1406 *Prot.)*] ~.‸   *Oysters*] *Oyster*
1412 *Do*] *Doe*
1414 *sett*‸] *set,*
1415 *Meate*] *meate*
1416 *Seruaunts*] *seruaunts*
1417 *you,*] ~‸   *boate*] *whole boate*
1424 *measurd*] *mea= / surde*
1431 *Remedy*] *Rem= / edye*   *Sir,*] ~‸
1434 *Prot)*] ~.
1435 *dish*] *Dish*
1437 *Sunshine*] *Sun-shine*
1438 *State,*] ~‸
1446 *chu*‸*re*/*lously*] *chulerously*
1448 *Letcherye*] *Letcherie*
1449 *Belly,*] ~‸
1450 *Pont*‸] ~.
1452 *him*‸] ~,   *suffiently*] *sufficiently*
1454 *Sir.*] ~‸
1455 *Baite*] *baite*
1457 *Prot.*] ~‸   *him,*] ~.
1458 *Prot)*] ~.
1463 *Poule,*] ~;
1468 *A*] *a*
1471 *Pont.*] ~‸
1472 *Belly*] *belly*   *you*‸] ~.
1479 *boarde*] *Boarde*
1480 *Prot*‸] ~.
1481 *Prot)*] ~.
1487 *Fright*] *fright*
1491 *Harp*‸] ~.   *my*] *My*
1492 *loe.*] [*loe.*] *Foth*
1495 *Marine;*] ~‸   *Foh*] *loe*
1496 *saye*] *say*
1499 *meates,*] ~‸
1502 *Salt-Fish*] *Salt Fish*
1504 *saye*] *say*

1508 *Prot‸] * ~.
1512 yeare‸] ~,
1519 furth,] ~‸
1520 lyking,] pleasure‸
1523 Powtins] Powtings
1526 satisfyd] satisfyde
1528 for] For   vitium‸] ~,
1529 say] saye
1530 Pont.] ~‸   Goodman] goodman
1531 fruite] Fruite
1533 toasted.] ~‸
1535 thereof] there / off
1536 Prot)] ~‸
1537 Prank] prank
1545 boarde] Boarde
1549 lib.] ~‸   Cap.] ~‸
1552 Roapes‸] Ropes,
1554 Pont.] ~‸
1555 Hold] hold   Grapple] grapple
1564 Tyme] tyme
1564–5 Fel= / lowe] Fellow
1568 Prot‸] ~.
1571 Pont.] ~‸   Come Come] [Then] come, come
1575 Troth.] ~,
1576] separate line in HM4; continues previous line in 509   Pont.] (~)
        Proteus,] ~.   Hoa.] ~‸
1579 From] from
1579–81 *Then enterd an Antick lyke an ill fauourd Herm= / ite of the Sea: A
        Bason and Towell before him, with capouch, / Long Bearde, Finnye feet*]
        *Then a Bason and Towell before. Thẽ enterd an Antick / lyke an ill fau-
        ourd Hermite of the Sea, with capouch, long Beard / Finnye feete*
1585 Prot)] ~.   Hearte] hearte
1590 farr] far
1595 Direction.] ~‸
1598 but] But
1601 night‸] ~,
1602 Cutt] Cut
1605–6 *in an Aire-cullour, [Light] syluer dead Ash-cullour, or shep= / pards
        Graye cullour suite,*] *in an Aire cullour, Light Ash-cullour, or Shep= /*

ards Gray cullour Suite, (underlined for deletion in 509, but deletion presumably cancelled, as three lines of marginal text initially intended for insertion have been struck out: [*In cloth / of Gold / <...>.*])

1607 *farr.*] ~ ͜   [*Light*] *syluer Dead sheppard-Graye I deeme*] [*Light shepard-graye I deeme*] *In a dead / Ash cullour / suite.*
1608 *extraordinarye*] *Extraordinary*
1609 *3.*] ~ ͜   *followes* ͜] ~.
1614 *Loue,*] ~ ͜   *From*] *from*
1615 *Alacrity*] *Alacritie*
1616 *Refuse*] *refuse*
1618 *thick*] *Thick*   *now*] *nowe*
1620 *est, If*] *est* [*<...>*] */ now*   *any.*] ~,
1621 *But*] *but*
1622 *hot*] *whot*
1626 *Thing* ͜] *thing,*   *mee.*] ~,
1628–9 *Therefo= / re*] *therefore*
1629 *Pardoned,*] *pardond.*
1630 *say*] *saye*
1631 *Peremptory*] *Peremptorie*   *trew*] *trewe*
1633 *Amisse*] *amisse*
1634 *the stiffer*] [*the*] *stiffer*
1638 *perfecter*] *Perfecter*   *Resolued*] *resolued*   *deuice,*] ~ ͜
1639 *Theorike*] *Theorick*   *know*] *knowe*
1640 *Iupiter* ͜] ~,
1641 *that* ͜   *same/*] *that* [*same*]/
1643 *againe* ͜] ~,
1645 *earthly*] *earthlye*   *Paragons* ͜] ~,
1648 *loue*] *Loue*
1649–50 *so= / one,*] *soone* ͜
1650 *Matter*] *matter*
1650–1 *Mat / ter*] *matter*
1652 *7.*] ~ ͜
1654 *Ruff,*] ~ ͜
1654–5 *of gold / sand*] *of sand*
1657–8] line not duplicated in 509
1659 *lured*] *Lured*
1661 *kid*] *Kid*   *doue*] *Doue*   *honey*] *Honey*
1662 SD *Here he started / back*] *He starteh back*
1664 *starting*] *start*[*ing*]*ed*   *far*] *farr*

1665 *leapt*] *lept*   *not*ˏ] ~,
1666 *reade*] *Reade*   *worde*] *word*
1668 *Humida*ˏ] ~,
1668–70 *(if … / … / … shooe)*] no parentheses in 509
1669 *Foote*] *foote*   *As*] *as*
1671 ˏ*Liuely*] (~   *Fifth*] *fifth*
1674 *Sir.*] ~;
1676 *drye*] *Drye*   *gerle.*] ~,
1677 SD.1 *back*ˏ] ~,
1678 *Aire t'haue*] *Aire [so Lumpish]. B. t'haue*
1679 *Hum.*] ~ˏ
1680 *further*ˏ] ~,   *For*] *for*   *Gods*] *gods*   *sake,*] ~.
1681 *Hum)*] ~ˏ   *thyne*] *thy*
1682 SD *stopt*ˏ] ~.
1683 *Hum.*] ~ˏ
1685 *Hum*ˏ] ~.
1686 *No;*] *no,*   *Heigh*ˏ] ~ *
1688 *Lord*ˏ] ~. *
1689–90] speeches appear on separate lines in HM4; speeches continue previous line in 509
1689 *Hum.*] *(~)*
1690 *Ho.*] ~ *
1694 SD.2 *flowd.*] ~,   *not. X*] ~ *
1695 *Busse.*] ~ˏ
1696 *Hum)*] ~.
1698 *say*] *saye*
1700 *Hum*ˏ] ~.   *hence*] *Hence*
1706 *say,*] ~.
1709 *sayes that*] *sayes*
1710 *Gods*] *gods*   *all?*] ~.
1714 *hor*] *her*   *thee.*] ~ ——
1715 *Mottley*ˏ] *motley,*   *I*] *I do*   *Lady*ˏ] *Ladye.*
1716 *Fact,*] ~.
1718 *Foulest*] *foulest*   *(Harp)*] *Harp.* (in regular SP position on next line in 509)
1722 *bleed*] *bleede*
1723 *Reede.*] ~?
1724 *Loue;*] *loue,*
1730 *Boy*] *Boye*

1731 fælle] felle   fæcundissimus] Fæcundissi= / mus
1733 License] license   same.] ~‸
1735 Ioy] Ioye
1744 do] doe
1747 [a] little as] little as   May] may   notwithstanding,] ~‸
1748 Flame-] flame-
1749 Habitude,] ~‸
1753 Troth.] ~,
1755 .8.] ‸~.
1756 orpharian.] ~,
1758 fixe] fix
1760 As] as
1762 Harmeles] harmeles   seekes.] ~,
1766 Bloods] bloods   'of] off
1767 seuen-string] seauen-string
1768 days‸] dayes,
1772 rimes] rymes
1775 Seas‸] ~,   Heighth] Height
1777 bed] Bed
1779 shells] shelles
1780 Long-desired] long-desired
1781 weene‸] ~,
1783 Pray‸] praye,
1787 dwelles] dwells
1791 As] as
1794 Direction‸] ~.
1795 Daunce] daunce
1798 Ash] \a/sh   cullou\r/] cullor
1799 Threds] threds
1800 bigge] as bigge
1801 The] the
1802 omitted,] ~‸   daunce] Daunce
1802–3 Por= / pusses] Porpusies
1806 blessing] Blessing
1811 Prot.] ~‸   Arion‸] ~,   diuide] deuide
1814 Catt] Cat   Tabour?] ~,
1815 The] This
1817 Turne] turne
1820 Bracelet] bracelet   gold,] ~‸

1820–1 *enter= / changeablye*] Enterchangbly
1825 *Nulla Desunt.*] not in 509
1826 *So,*] ~ˬ   *Thanks*] thanks   *leaue,*] ~ˬ
1827 *Benefite*] Benefit
1832 *soule,*] ~ˬ   *thee.*] ~,
1833 *muse,*] ~[,]
1834 *rest*] Rest
1835 ˬ*I*] * ~
1837 *knewe*] knew
1839 *Properties*ˬ] ~,   *him*ˬ] ~,   *knows*] knowes
1840 *any.*] anye)   *Fellowe*] fellow
1842 *fare*] Fare
1844 *Troth.*] ~,
1845 *Arions*] arions
1847 *house*ˬ] ho= / wse,
1851 *Direction.*] ~ˬ
1853 *Flame-cullour*] Flame / cullour
1853–4 *Red / gold coullour*] red / cullour gold cloth
1856 *behold,*] Beholdˬ
1857 *again*] ag= / aine
1859 *First*] first
1861 *bunch*] Bunch
1863 *Totall*] totall   *my*] my\ne/
1864 *for*] For
1866 *dry*] drye
1867 *According*] according   *complexion,*] ~ˬ
1868 *letter,*] ~ˬ
1871 *My*] my
1871–2 *which / to say*] which is to say
1872 *mee*ˬ] ~,
1873 *stay*] staye   *fearest* [*thou*]] fear\e/stˬ \thou/
1875 *mee*ˬ] ~,
1877 *thanke*] thank
1878 *same,*] ~ˬ   *Perpetuall*] perpetuall
1880–1 *ro= / sted*] roasted
1881 *not*ˬ] ~,   *hither*ˬ] ~,
1883 *coales,*] ~ˬ
1886 *Direction*ˬ] ~.
1887 *Peruke*ˬ] ~,   *All*] all

1888 *Syluer-Sea-blewe*] Syluer sea blew   *The Best.*] the best. Harpax Squiring
       her
1890 SD.3 *him.*] ~ ⌄
1891 *mee.**] ~.
1892 *Vul.*] ~ ⌄   *thee.**] ~. ⌄
1893 *Followe* ⌄] ~.
1894 *Harp.*] ~ ⌄   *follow*] Followe   *Plump*] plumpe   *Lord* ⌄] ~.
1896 SD.1 *from*] frõ   *say*] saye
1897 *beest*] art
1898 *Bucket*] bucket
1898–9 *wa= / ter* ⌄] ~,
1900 SD.1 *flowes*] flows   *mee,*] ~ ⌄
1901 SD.1–.2 *He sings and / followes.*] He sings ⌄   *Vul)*] ~.   *Tarry*] tarry
1902 *Ar)*] ~.   *face,*] ~ ⌄   *say* ⌄ ***] ~.*
1903 *Vul)*] ~.   *of*] off   *Face*] face   *first.*] ~ ⌄
1906 *Ar)*] ~.   *you* ⌄ ***] ~.*
1907 *Vul)*] ~.
1908 ²*Follow,*] follow ⌄   *Followe*] followe
1911 SD *stopt.*] ~ ⌄   *But**] ~ ⌄
1912] separate line in HM4; added as two lines of text in right margin of
       line 1910 and boxed off in 509   *Ar)*] (~)   on, Sir, I] on ⌄ / I   say ⌄] ~.
1913] separate line in HM4; added in right margin of space between lines
       1911–12 in 509   *Vul.*] ~)   *Oa.*] ~ ⌄
1914 *say*] saye
1916 *say*] saye
1917 *Beaten*] beaten
1924 *Harp*] HArp
1925 *Ar.*] ~ ⌄   *mixe,*] ~ ⌄   *armes,*] ~ ⌄
1927 *Fye,*] ~ ⌄
1928 ²*againe,*] ~ ⌄
1930 SD *back.*] ~ ⌄
1934 *Troth?*] ~,   *Vulcan.*] ~?
1941 *of* ⌄ \that/ *my*] [of my] \that/ of my   *turned,*] ~ ⌄
1945 *Feathe\r/s*] feathers
1951 *Admissi*] admissi
1954 *what* ⌄] ~,
1955 *how* ⌄] ~,
1958 *Harp.*] ~ ⌄
1959 *Aduice*] aduice   *Sirrha.*] ~ ⌄

1960 *famous*] Famous
1964 *Playster*] playster   broken] broaken   heade] hed
1966 *Harp.*] ~⌃
1967 *lane*] Lane
1968 *you,*] ~⌃
1969 *Whip,*] ~⌃   Bitt,] ~⌃
1970 *and*] And   thither,] ~⌃
1971 *forme,*] ~⌃
1972 *Transformation*] transformation   reueng\d/] reuenged
1973 *Harlots?*] ~,   Sirrha] Boye
1975 *Manner*] manner   thither⌃] ~.
1977 *persuaded*] perswaded
1978 *Follow*] Followe
1981–2] 509 inserts between these lines an extra line: *The Direction*.
1983 *Thalia⌃*] ~,   *Aglaia.*] ~,
1984 *Angle Rods*] Angle-Rods   Angle-rod] Angle / Rod
1986 *take.*] ~⌃
1989 *numbers*] Numbers
1990 *not,*] ~⌃
1994 *Try*] Trye   th'experience] th'Experience
1996 *loue*] Loue
1999 *gracious*] gratious
2000 *attempt⌃)*] ~,)
2001 *Lot*] lot   th old] th'old
2013 *greet*] greete
2014 *Ner.*] ~⌃
2015 *Mackrell*] Mackrill
2016 *Mackrell*] Mackrill
2018 *flowre*] Flowre
2019 *virginity*] virginitye
2023 *Mouth⌃*] ~,
2026 *manners*] Manners
2027 *sooner,*] ~⌃
2033 *Maydenhed*] Maydenheade
2037 *Foole⌃*] ~.
2039 *but,*] ~.
2040 *Antonye*] Anthony
2041 *mary.*] ~;   wayes] ways
2046 *Heartes*] heartes   Then] (~

2047 *(Come]*˷*come*
2048 SD.2 *Poesye] Posye   4*˷*] 4.*
2049 *Hero Leander.]* not in 509
2053 *thee] the*
2056 *head] heade*
2058 *inuent*˷*]* ~,
2059 *Heartes] heartes   Lust?] lust,*
2060 *trust] Trust*
2062 *done it] doont*
2063 *that*˷*]* ~,   *night*˷*] Night,*
2069 *Although*˷*]* ~,   *dew] dewe   Profession*˷*]* ~,
2071 *Loues] loues   Petition*˷*]* ~,
2072 *wee'nst] weenst*
2074 *maintained] maintayned*
2075 *Then,]* ~˷
2078 *lou'd] loud*
2080 *haue] Haue   Half] half*
2086 *Her*˷*]* ~.
2090 *Hero*˷*————]* ~, ————
2093 *Her.]* ~˷
2097 *Cytheræa,]* ~˷
2098 *Trew] trewe   say] saye*
2099 *Not] not*
2100 *follow] followe*
2101 SD.3 *gentlemen*˷*]* ~.   *whoore.]* ~˷
2102 *Song*˷*]* ~.
2104 *dismayd] dismayde*
2105 *affeard] affearde   mayde] Mayde*
2106 *it,]* ~˷
2107 *it,]* ~.
2111 *one*˷*]* ~,
2118 *thee*˷*]* ~,
2121 *Leand*˷*]* ~.   *now] nowe*
2124 SD] part of main text in 509   SD *The] they   * Aglaia]* ˷~   *Arida.]* ~,
2130 *so actable] tractable*
2136 *commaculate] Commaculate*
2138 *come] Come*
2140 *recompense] Recompense*
2142 *Ar.]* ~˷

2143 *Agl.*] ~ˌ
2145 *lamenes*] *lamenesse*   *Legs*] *legs*   *but*] *But*
2146 *For*] *for*
2150 *beauty,*] ~ˌ
2153 *horse*] *Horse*
2154 *thy*] *her*
2155 *saye*] *say*
2156 *Knowes,t*] *Knowes,*
2157 *of*/] *off*
2158 *Breade*] *breade*
2159 *Price*] *price*   *hammer*ˌ] ~,
2160 *done*ˌ] ~,
2161 *boane setter*] *Boane-setter*
2165 *Ha*ˌ] ~.
2166 *I*] *In*   *case,*] ~ˌ
2168 *the Ioint setter*] *The Ioint-setter*   *Leg*] *leg*
2171 *cosent*] *Cosen*
2174 *patience*] *Patience*
2175 *buy*] *buye*
2176 *therewith*ˌ] ~,
2176–7 *com= / panye*] *companie*
2179 *Hum*ˌ] ~.   *Peice*] *peice*   *their heds*] *his hed*
2180 *Cosen*ˌ] ~.
2182 *persuade*] *persuaded*
2183 *Hum*ˌ] ~.
2184 *Cousen*] *Cosen*
2185 *saye*] *say*
2191 *goode*] *good*   *work*] *worke*
2192 *o*/*ff*] *of*
2193 *gain by*] *gaining*
2194 *yron*] *Iron*   *Comodity*] *Commoditye*
2195 *say*] *saye*   *cosen*] *Cosen*
2197 *Eath*] *Earth*
2198 *make*] *make not*
2199 *drynes*] *drynesse*
2200 *Furbishing*] *furbishing*
2202 *then*] *that*
2204 *Aimes*] *aymes*   *cosens*] *Cosens*
2205 *what'*] *what's*

139

2207 Hum‸] ~.   from] From
2210 do] doe
2212 for \that/] for that the
2214 sure.] ~,
2215 handsomelye] handsomely
2217 Maydenhed] Maydenheade
2219 vnto] to
2222 then] Then
2224 Hum.] ~‸   come] Come
2226 Pontcus] Ponticus
2229 hole?] ~.
2230 Rud‸] ~.   for] For
2231 Prot‸] ~.
2233 Olympus,] ~‸
2234 Prot.] ~‸
2239 Harp‸] ~.
2240 faucibus] Faucibus
2241 Gorelin] gorelin
2242 Pop.] ~.*
2243 SD.1 Popt his] Popt in his   SD.3 potted.] ~‸   letter] Letter
2244 reade‸] ~.
2249 Rud.] ~‸   \hillocks/] Hillocks   Bancks] banks
2252 In as] In so
2258 for] For   Prodigie] Prodegie
2259 most] Most
2260 Diuill] Diuell   you‸\all/] you   Sertorious] Sertorius
2261 knowe] know
2263 cumber] Cumber
2266 goodman] Goodman
2266–7 Corith̃= / um] Corin= / thum
2268 Best] best   Then] then
2271 Harp.] ~‸   Let] let   First] first
2274 wise‸] ~.
2275 Prot.] not in 509
2276 Cat] Catt   Posture] Pasture
2277 rest] Rest   sell] Selle
2278 Cat] Catt   Bell;] ~,
2279 when among] when one among
2280 hed] heade

2282 Cat] Catt
2283 I,] ~₍
2284 lay] laye
2286 mary] Mary
2292 Pont.] ~₍   them?] ~₍
2293 Proteus.] ~?
2297 Man] man
2298 boarde] Boarde   ₍\am/] *am
2301 red] Red
2301–2 str= / akes] streakes
2302 And] and
2311 Rud.] ~₍
2312 backward] Backward
2313 Shrympes] Shrimpes
2317 Pont₍] ~.
2320 Cod₍] ~.
2321 Prot₍] ~.
2324 Pont.] ~₍
2326 Harp₍] ~.
2327 Pont₍] ~.   Herring₍] ~.
2328 hearing] Hearing
2329 Pont₍] ~.
2330 congruity] congruitye
2331 rest] Rest
2333 Pont.] ~₍
2334 sweetest₍] ~.
2338 Antipathy] Antipathye
2341 Pont₍] ~.
2342 Prot₍] ~.   expresly] expreslye
2344 Roasted] roasted
2345 all,] ~.   Masters₍] ~.
2348 Bids] bidds
2349 Pont.] ~₍   Trout] Trowt
2351 SD.3 cholick] colick   SD.6 weet] weete   right] Right
2352 \P./] Pont)
2354 Dolphin.] ~₍
2355 back₍] ~,
2357] shared line in HM4; two lines in 509   (Pont)] ~.   Turbot₍] Turbote.
2358 Turbot] Turbote   Turne-boate] Turne boate

141

2359 *boate*] Boate
2365 *Harp.*] ~₋
2370 *Prot.*] ~₋
2372 *(Pont)*]₋~.   *floe*] Floe
2373 *Pont.*] ~₋   *(that they*]₋they
2374 *mouselled*] mouseled   [*myne*] *ours*] myne
2375 *Pont.*] ~₋
2376 *He*] he
2377 *Belly*] Bellye
2383 *Pont.*] ~₋
2384 *once*₋] ~,   *myne.*] ~,   *sure*₋] ~.
2385 *persuaded*₋] ~,
2386 *Harp.*] ~₋
2387 *Prot.*] ~₋
2388 *Pont.*] ~₋
2389 ¹*sauce,* ²*sauce*] sawce
2390 *Finally*₋] ~,
2391 *heated*₋] ~,
2392 *the heate*] heate
2393 *Harp.*] ~₋   *saye*/] say   *wee,*] ~₋
2396 *Fishermen,*] ~₋
2398 *fall*] do fall   *Net*] net
2402 *Fraught*] fraught
2403 *Morsell*] morsell
2404 *naught.*] ~₋
2405 *3*₋] ~.
2406 *Fault*] fault   *Sea-water*] sea water   *Fish,*] ~₋
2407 *Mylk*] mylk   *Butter*] butter
2408 *but gaine*] gaine but   *dish*₋] ~,
2412 *rayne.*] Rayne,
2413 *vs,*] ~₋
2417 *Husband*] husband
2420 *Art and*] art or
2425 *hauty*] haug / hty
2429 *decreed.*] decreede,
2431 *Handmayd,*] ~₋
2434 *whoe's*] who's   *By*] by
2437 *Goddesses*] goddesses   *daunce,*] ~₋
2438 *to mee*] to mee, to mee

142

2439 *Make*] make   *Reason*˰] ~,
2441 *can*] call   *tell,*] ~?
2442 ˰ *myne own*/] (~ ~ (as hanging line in 509)
2443 *surely.*] ~,   *been*] beene
2444 *As for*] as For
2445 *Foe*] foe
2448 *deliuer*] deliuer up
2450 *Mortall*] mortall   [*art?*] art] art?
2452 *Her.*] ~˰
2453 *Fabricated*] fabricated
2454 *Laborinth*] Laborynth   *Brayne*] brayne   *Spite*] spite   *prowd*] prowde
2455 *heart*] hearte
2456 *And*] and
2457 *whylom*] whilom
2460 *Glau.*] ~˰   *crott*] Crott
2462 *their*] theire   *beds*] Beds
2463 *Scorne*] Schorne
2464 *And*] and
2465 *In*] in   *Mouth*] mouth
2466 *Ardent*] ardent
2467 *Firme*] firme
2470 *to confesse,*] confesse˰
2471 *Cytheræa*˰] ~,
2472 *And*] and
2473 *hoote,*] ~˰
2475 *do*] doe
2476 *do*] doe   *Hero,*] ~˰
2481 *you.*] ~˰
2484 *Glau.*] ~˰   *Adieu*˰] ~.
2485 *Her.*] ~˰
2487 *The Direction*] not in 509
2488 *Arion,*] ~˰
2490 *Talus Arion*] not in 509
2491 *met*] mett   *sped,*] ~?   *Man?*] ~.   *say*] Saye
2492 *Rather*˰] ~,   *Coriual,*] Coriuall˰
2493 *dance*] daunce   *attendance*] attendaunce
2497 *mayst,*] ~˰
2501 *hearde*˰] ~,   *Towns*] Townes
2503 *harmony*] harmonye

143

2504 I.] ~˷
2505 Fortresse] fortresse
2506 They] they
2507 Breach] breach
2508 queld] quelld   desead] deseasd
2509 but˷] ~.
2510 Man˷] ~,
2512 it,] ~?
2513 SD Here they] They   \y/ou˷] you.   la˷*] La, *
2515 Ar.] ~˷   thunder] Thunder   goe] Goe
2516 (to] ˷~.
2518 Lightend] lightend
2520 weet] weete
2521 . threon] ˷thereon
2522 Tal.] ~˷   myne˷] ~.
2524 strangenes] strangenesse
2525 lykwise] lykewise
2531 think,] ~˷   enuie] enuy
2533 This˷] ~,
2535 ways] wayes
2537 shryne˷] ~.
2538 Ar.] ~˷   I˷] ~,   same˷] ~,
2539 Fellow] fellow
2540 oath] oathe   trewe,] ~˷
2542 chaire˷] ~.
2543 trewe *] ~,
2544 SD] not in 509   good] Good
2546 Act 5 Scen 1.] follows *behold* on line 2552 in 509
2548 SD.2 Mercurye] Mercury   SD.3 Hermes.] ~˷
2549 Graces,] ~˷   Glauce˷] ~,
2550 Attendaunts,] Attendants.   Arrowe] arrow
2552 behold. Enterd [w]\t/herevpon] behold, [Here] enterd with the rest
2553 weedes,] weede˷   And] and
2554 Aloofe.] aloofe˷   Then ... followes.] not in 509
2555 Cyth.] ~˷   day] daye
2557 coast] Co[a]st   cheare˷] ~,
2558 That,] ~˷
2560 heauen] Heauen
2562 Lord] Lords

2563 Wherein,] ~ ⌄
2565 tyme] Tyme   þaye.] ~ ⌄
2566 staye] stay
2569 strangers] straungers
2571 it,] ~ ⌄   Madame,] ~.
2572 shewe] showe
2574 benefite ⌄] ~,
2575 Ar.] Arid.   Madame,] ~ ⌄   the obseruing] th'obseruing
2576 day ⌄] daye?   Sun's] Suns
2577 each] Each
2578 SD.2 bank] banks
2579 2.] ~.*
2582 Fisher=mans sute wafted etcæt wafted in Vulcan] wafted in / Vulcã
2583 wanton] watton   Fiddle,] fiddle ⌄
2583–7 attyre of scales or woman / Monster inclining to some strange Fish, with whip, Bitt and / Bridle in hand held lyke Lady Reuenge of the Sea Ioculus waf= / ting him lykwise with Cytheræas Fan of feathers, white and dun / Doues and Swans, Venus chariot Birds.] habit, / ⌄ \of scales/ / lyke to Madame Reuenge ⌄ \of the Sea/ with / whip Bridle and / [<b..>] Snaffle in hand, / Iocolus lykwise / wafting him with / Venus Fan, Swans / and Doues [<gray>] dun / and white [featherd] / couloured fether / Fan. (in 509 an insertion also appears to the right of the Act and Scene division, with no indication of where it is to be inserted: * A woman Monster / Inclining to some / strange fish.)
2587 feet ⌄] feete.
2588 too. Tuskye Teeth] Tusk teeth
2589 SD] not in 509
2590 Ioc<o>\u/lus] not in 509   Vulcan ⌄] Vul= / can.
2591 Harp.] not in 509
2592 shewe,] ~ ⌄   mee,] ~ ⌄
2593 certifieth] certifyeth
2594 Ioc<o>\u/lus,] Iocolus ⌄
2595 steddy,] ~ ⌄   Mother,] ~.
2598 lyknes] lyknesse
2599 gold lact sute, Hammer and Aprone] gold-lact suite ⌄ and Apron
2600 his Mothers Fan in hand held. The whip, Bitt <and> / and bridle in Vulcans hand still held Lykwise.] Venus / (Fan.
2602 Cyth ⌄] ~.   Out ⌄] ~,   foole,] Foole ⌄
2603 Hum.] ~ ⌄   sure ⌄] ~.

2604 *propper*] Propper   *wooing.*] ~ˏ
2605 *Harp. [Cup.]] Cup.   a better*ˏ] one better,   *then*] The
2606 *maydens*] Maydens
2607 *Thet.*] Thetis)   *rather.*] ~ˏ
2608 *Arid.*] Ar)   *Trumpe*] Trump   *stop-Theife*] stop-theif[<.>]s
2609 *Oce.*] ~)
2610 *holds*] Holds
2613 *louches,*] ~ˏ   *loe*] Loe
2615 *looke*ˏ] ~,   *him*ˏ] ~,   *you..*] ~.
2617 *ask*] aske   *hearte:*] ~, *
2618 *worse,*] ~ˏ   *saye.*] sayˏ
2619] not in 509
2620 *good*] Good
2624 *Nymp*] Nymph
2625 *Cyth.*] ~ˏ
2626 *Mistrisses,*] ~ˏ
2629 *heartes*] Heartes
2630 *Nymph*] Nymp   *First*ˏ] ~,
2631 *t'enstall,*] ~ˏ
2632 *you* ˏ \the/ *Empresse*] you Empresse
2633 SD.3 *blew,*] ~ˏ
2634 ˏ*The*] * ~   *Apologie.*] ~ˏ
2635 *Roome,*] ~ˏ
2640 *Queene,*] ~.
2641 SD.3–.4 *sea-wee= / de*] sea weed   *I, with this song, shall*] with this song
    I [do] shall   *Theame.**] Thea= / (meˏ
2642 *Nymphe)*] Nymph) (precedes line 2644 in 509)
2643 *I*ˏ] ~.
2644 *Hayle*] ˏ\hayle/   *Queene*ˏ] ~,
2645 *mo\r/tall*] motall   *Habit*] habit
2647 *inhabite.*] ~ˏ
2648 *2*ˏ] ~.
2651 *meet,*] meeteˏ
2652 *Equitie*] equitie
2653 *3*ˏ] ~.
2657 *Autoritye*] Autoritie
2658 *4*ˏ] ~.
2664 ˏ*Hayle,*] * [chorus.] Hayle.   *Water-Greene*ˏ] Water Greene.
2665] not in 509 (at the equivalent point is a line reading * [*The Direction*]

  followed by three lines of illegible text marked for deletion by crossing out)
2667 *noise*] noyse *Saylours,*] ~.
2669 *Gripus,*] ~ˌ
2671 *Glauce Thetis.*] Glauce.
2672 *Rud.*] ~ˌ
2673 *Sirrha*ˌ] ~, *lustilye.*] lustilyˌ
2674 *see,*] ~ˌ
2676 *Prot*ˌ] ~.
2677 *wager*ˌ] ~,
2680 *Pont.*] ~ˌ *Pull,*] ~.
2681 *Mates*] mates
2682 *Bald*] bald
2683] separate line in HM4; added as two lines of text to the right of line 2682 in 509 *Grip.*] (~.)
2684 *more,*] ~.
2686 *Prot*ˌ] ~. *cables*] Cables
2687 *praysed*] praised
2689 *Agonies*ˌ] ~,
2692 *knaue?*] ~.
2694 *belly*] Belly
2695 *vp*ˌ] ~,
2696 *of*] off
2696–7 *me= / mory*] me= / morye
2698 *he*] He *greeke*] Greeke
2699 *Faery*] Faerye *Canaryes*] Canaries
2701 *Noueltie*] Noueltye
2703] SP not duplicated in 509
2704 *Ork*] Orke
2706 *myne,*] ~ˌ
2708 *Prot*ˌ] ~. *Then*] then
2709 *Pursnet*] Purse-net
2711 *Oracles,*] ~ˌ
2712 *muse.*] ~ˌ
2713 *say*] saye
2715 *So,*] ~ˌ
2717 *Arid*ˌ] ~,
2719 *Rud.*] ~ˌ
2721 *Direction.*] ~ˌ

2722 *greasy*] *greasye*   *pouch*] *Pouch*
2724 *inuested*] *Inuested*
2726 *Patience*ˏ] ~.
2727 *Prot.*] ~ˏ
2729 *Hum.*] ~ˏ   *heauenly*] *Heauenly*
2731 *Arid.*] ~ˏ   *Augury*ˏ] *Augurie.*
2732 *Glau.*] ~ˏ
2734 *say*ˏ] *saye,*
2735 *Sirrha,*] ~ˏ
2736 *belly*] *bellye*
2737 ¹*Cöus*] *Cous*
2738 *Inginer*] *enginer*   *Creete,*] ~.
2741 *Rest*] *rest*   *say.*] ~,
2744 *Saye*] *say*
2745 *Cöus*] *Cous*
2747 *neuer.*] ~ˏ
2748 *Nay*] *nay*
2749 *Rud*ˏ] ~.   *you,*] ~ˏ   *Pox,*] *pox*ˏ
2750 *Cöus*ˏ] *Cous.*
2752 *to be spoken, Deare*] *to spoken, deare*
2754 *Cöus*] *C|ous*   *hearde*] *heard*   *soone.*] ~,
2755 *matters*] *Matters*
2758 *Towe|in*] *Towe in*
2760 [*Cup*] *Harp.*)] *Cup*)   *Rudens,*] ~ˏ   *thou,*] ~ˏ   *this,*] ~ˏ
2761 SD.1 *boxe*] *box*
2762 *calling,*ˏ] ~, *
2763 SD.1 *Stared*] *starde*   *wert.*ˏ] ~. *
2764 *Harp* [*Cup.*]] *Cup.*   *villaine.**] ~.ˏ
2765 SD.1 *Gaue*] *ga*[<.>]*u/e*   SD.2 *Bum*ˏ] ~.
2766 *Coüs*] *Cous*
2768 *Glauce.*] ~ˏ
2769 *Both*] *both*
2770 *life,*] ~ˏ   *Loue*] *loue*
2771 ²*Master,*] ~ˏ   *Quomodo*] *quomodo*   *Master.*] ~ˏ
2772 *sword.*] ~ˏ
2773 *Master.*] ~ˏ
2774 *Sir.*] ~ˏ   *heard*] *hearde*
2775 *Cyth.*] ~ˏ   *seek*] *seeke*
2776 *be*ˏ] ~.   *Defendaunt*ˏ] ~?

148

2777 *Thetis*,] ~ˌ
2780 *libertye*] *Libertie*   *Court*,] ~ˌ
2781 *Lady*.] ~,
2783 *hopes*ˌ] ~.
2784 *agone*ˌ] ~,
2786 *queld*] *quelld*
2787 *raised*ˌ] ~,
2789 *th'Affections*] *th'affections*
2790 *day*] *daye*
2793 *tyme*] *Tyme*
2795 *he vowd*] *she vowd*
2797 *Taske*] *Task*   *vs*.] ~ˌ
2798 *Trew*] *Trewe*   *Say*.] ~ˌ
2799 *Ceston*.,] ~ˌ
2800 *Ar*.] ~ˌ   ¹*haue*ˌ] ~,   *Queene*.] *Queen*ˌ
2801 *th'Experience*] *th'Eperiment*
2802 *th'Experience*] *th'Experiment*
2803 *them*,] ~ˌ
2804 *th'Experience*] *th'experience*
2805 *myne*,] ~ˌ   (*Cyth*ˌ] (~)   *o*] *O*
2806 (*Gods*] *O / mighty gods*
2807 *be alike*] *are alyke*
2810 *weet*] *weete*
2812 *Direction*.] ~ˌ
2813 *Lightend*] *lightend*
2814 *Either*] *either*   *Arme*] *arme*
2815 *one after the other*] *interchange = / (ably*
2816 *Thumbe*] *thumbe*
2817 *Ar*.] ~ˌ   *Cytheræa'es*] *Cytheræas*   *Point*] *point*
2819 *Things*] *things*
2822 *them*,] ~ˌ
2823 *Flight*] *flight*
2824 *most*] *Most*   *suite*] *Suite*
2826 *be*,)] ~ˌ)
2827 *number*] *numbers*
2828 *virgin*,] ~ˌ   *meede*,] ~ˌ
2831 *queld*] *quelld*
2835 *th'affections*] *th'Affections*   *Loue*ˌ] [*Men*] *loue*,
2838 *Ar. Ar.*] SP not duplicated in 509

2842 *Button*] *but= / ton*
2843 *sorrowfull*] *sorofull*
2847 *Bracelet*] *bracelet*
2848 *Pouch*] *Pouch or Codpeice   better*] *Better*
2849 *Two Bracelets*] *Bracelets   Best*] *best*
2850 *Thet.*] ~ ˏ   *Villaine.*] ~ ˏ
2851 *say*] *saye*
2852 *faire,*] ~ ˏ   *belly*] *bellye*
2854 *Taske*] *Task   heauen*] *Heauen*
2855 *mee,*] ~ ˏ
2858 *thing*] *Thing   saye*] *say*
2859 *Daughter, what ayle you?*] *What ayle you daughter* ˏ
2860 *Ha.*] ~ ˏ
2861 *And*] *and*
2862 *be.*] ~ *,*
2864 *Reuerst*] *Rewerst*
2865 *Mynd.*] *mind;   Arida,*] ~ ˏ
2867 *your cosens*] *your your cosens*
2868 *while,*] ~ ˏ   *adresse*] *Adresse*
2869 *Direction* ˏ] ~ *.*
2870 *Two*] *two   Talk*] *talk   clown*] *Clown*
2871 *fauourd*] *fourd   mouth* ˏ] *Mouth,*
2872 *was.*] ~ *,*
2873 *followes*] *fol= / lows*
2876 *Lean.*] *Leand.*
2877 *doe*] *do   confese,*] *confesse,   yet,*] ~ ˏ   *amends,*] ~ ˏ
2879 *say* ˏ] ~ *.   (Leand)*] *(Lean)*
2880 *vnweeting,*] ~ ˏ
2881 *Bed*] *bed*
2883 *hearte*] *Hearte*
2884 *Madame* ˏ *)*] ~ *,)*
2885 *Shryne,*] ~ *.*
2889 *thoult*] *thou'lt*
2891 *Trew*] *Trewe   contented?*] ~ ˏ   *Hero* ˏ] ~ *?*
2892 *he'ele*] *he'el*
2894 *suite* ˏ] ~ *.*
2895 *Her* ˏ] ~ *.*
2896 *Gold*] *gold*
2899 *Mortall*] *mortall*

2900 *say,*] ~.
2901 *dram*ˏ] ~,   *man*] Man
2903 *brook*] brooke   *Prithy*] prithy   *mee*ˏ] ~.
2905 *more*ˏ] ~,   *you?*] ~ˏ
2906 *doe,*] ~ˏ
2908 *loue*] Loue
2910 *No*] no
2911 *Lean*ˏ] ~.
2912 *deede*] deed   *by*] By
2913 *Her.*] ~ˏ   *Leander*ˏ] ~,   *Constancy*] Constancye
2914 *it.*] ~,
2916 *Worthily*] Worthilye
2917 *Haue*] haue   *trew*] trewe
2918 *Glauce.*] ~ˏ
2919 *heauuens*] Heauens   *too.*] ~,
2920 *prithy*] prithye
2921 *Fellow.?*] Fellowe?
2923 *Hee'l*] Hee'll   *persuade*ˏ] perswade,   *but*] But
2924 *and*] And   *her*ˏ] ~,
2925 *Nay*] nay
2926 *he*] she
2930 *far*] farr
2931 *Then*] then
2934 *therwith*ˏ] \t/herewith,
2936 SD.1 *With face*] With a face   SD.1–.2] *gra=* / *cious*] gra / tious   *Truly*] Trewly
2938 *Man*] man   *little*] but little
2939 *Money*] money
2941 *both* [*vs so*] both vs so
2942 *Mustard*ˏ] ~,
2944 *theirs*] theirs too
2945 *Coüs*] Cous   *protesting*] Protesting
2946 *That from*] that from the
2950 *Ennameld*] Enameld
2952 *Ar*ˏ] ~.   *Fantastique*] fantastique   *dreame*] Dreame   *Proteus*ˏ] ~.
2953 *Penaltie*ˏ] ~?
2954 *Instampt*ˏ] \In/stampt,
2955 *Feyning holy things*] [Feyning holy] Forging [\sacred/ holy]things   *neuer*] nere'   *Feyning*ˏ] feyning?

151

2958 it.] ~,
2963 moane.] ~?
2964 Do] Doe
2965 you?] ~ˬ
2966 SD.1–.4] not in 509   Thus,] ~ˬ   Hearte] hearte
2967 recouer *] ~.
2968 Oce)] ~.   Thanks] thanks
2971 yong] young
2974 Congnisance.] ~,
2975 graye] Gray
2976 Acknowledgments] acknowledgments
2977 Pouches,] pouchesˬ
2978 [vp] from] vp from   off] of   seate,] ~ˬ   vpon] on   feete] feet
2981 eake?] ~,
2982 treate,] ~ˬ
2984 humaine] humane   tayne] taine
2985 se\e/ing] seing
2986 spowse] spouse
2989 bed] Bed
2991 Seat] Seate
2992] 509 adds an SD in the left margin: *A Pawse*. (in addition to *A Pawse*.
       that appears in the left margin of 2993)   do] doe
2993 This] this   butˬ*] ~.*
2994 doe] do
2998 Perplexitye;] Perplexitie,
3001 As,] ~ˬ   equitie,] ~ˬ
3002 greet] greete
3003 meet] meete
3006 from] frõ   deliuerd] de= / giuen
3007 the Attendaunts] the ser / uaunts or atten= / daunts
3007–8 Then spake as / followes.] not in 509
3009 shallop] shalop
3010 Madameˬ] ~,   thanks,] ~ˬ
3011 to mee] mee
3016 Lenity] Lenitye
3017 hearte] Hearte   Iuno.] ~,
3018 Heauen] heauen
3021 Bounteous] bounteous   rewarde] reward
3022 Dolphinsˬ] ~,   wayˬ] ~.*

3023 *pray.*] ~ : *
3025 *The*] the   *speede*] speed
3026–34 *The Direction. / Here went furth the whole chorus in a shuffle / as after a Play in a Lords howse, Hermes wafting / them furth with his winged wand. Vulcan and / Proteus after them. Or went furth in state all, / as riding vpon Dolphins, Hermes wafting them / about the stage with his wand. Whither the bet= / ter you may chuse the better, all singing the 7th / Song following.* [*Vide vacants the last vt infra*]] 509 has illegible text marked for deletion by heavy crossing out in equivalent place; an additional page (fol. 157ᵛ) in 509 has corrected text intended for insertion here: *For the* [*Marinal*] *Aphrodysial. / in fine. / For Actors Thus. / Act 5 Scen 5. / The Direction. / Aboue in its place be the Song Following (Horse and / away) sung, the chorus walking about the stage / in state as riding on Dolphins, In lieu of that the fore / sayd Propertie of shuffling furth* ⁁ *vide et infra*/, *It being but a Court / Propertie, and not so conuenient abroade. vide va= / caunts and Song last vacant vt infra being now the / Seauenth Song of this Marinall Pastorall, whithers / the wither you may chuse the Fitter.** [marginal text: *on the other syde of / the leafe is the Di = rection for Powles*] *The First best / for Powles, Not this that Followes here. Mercury / wafts them about the stage All singing the song / Following.*
3035–56 *The Seauenth ... Omnes*] a different version of the seventh song intended for the Children of Paul's appears on fol. 221ᵛ in 509 and is marked for deletion with a large cross (traces of this song are visible on the torn stub of fol. 194ᵛ in HM4)
3035 *Song*⁁] ~.
3039 *baggage*] Baggage
3041 *2*⁁] ~.
3044 *on.*] ~,
3046 *3*⁁] ~.
3047 *Dan*] dan
3048 *Beastes,*] ~⁁
3049 *send-Tyde,*] ~⁁
3050 *Bend*] crouch   *Loue*] loue
3051 *4.*] ~⁁
3052 *staye*] stay
3053 *way.*] ~,
3054 *shutt*] shut   *day,*] ~⁁

3056 *Exeunt Omnes*] in 509 an additional page with the seventh song (fol. 157ᵛ) contains a section of text marked for deletion by crossing out, headed by visible text: * *Or thus for Poules aboue m*

3057–63 *The Apologue / The Direction / Here Harpax after their song and goings furth / came in againe their Apologue, with his Mothers / Fan in his hand held. / Harpax their Apologue, Souls, / Verte Folium.*] The Apologue. Cupid came in againe with his mothers Fan of feathers / in his hand held Cupid The Apologue. solus.

3064 *Harp.*] Cup.

3065 *Apologue,*] ~ ˬ

3067 *shaddowe*] shadowe   *both.*] ~,

3068 *who,*] ~ ˬ   *obteynd,*] ~ ˬ   *exact* ˬ] ~,

3071 *Yet,*] ~ ˬ   *done,*] ~ ˬ   *allot*] alott

3072 *which,*] ~ ˬ

3073 SD *A Pawse*] A ˬ \long/ Pawse   *mylde*] myld   *paine* ˬ *] ~ . *

3074 SD.1–.3 *Here he wafted*] He waft   SD.3 *Mothers*] mothers   *farewell*] Farewell   *Sirs* ˬ *] ~ . *